HONORING THE SELF

OTHER BOOKS BY NATHANIEL BRANDEN

Who Is Ayn Rand?

The Psychology of Self-Esteem

Breaking Free

The Disowned Self

A Nathaniel Branden Anthology
(includes *The Psychology of Self-Esteem,*
Breaking Free, and *The Disowned Self*)

The Psychology of Romantic Love

The Romantic Love Question & Answer Book
(with E. Devers Branden)

If You Could Hear What I Cannot Say

HONORING THE SELF

Personal Integrity and the
Heroic Potentials of Human Nature

Nathaniel Branden

JEREMY P. TARCHER, INC.
Los Angeles
Distributed by Houghton Mifflin Company
Boston

Library of Congress Cataloging in Publication Data

Branden, Nathaniel.
  Honoring the self.

  Bibliography: p. 257
  Includes index.
  1. Self-respect—Psychological aspects. 2. Autonomy (Psychol-
ogy) 3. Egoism. I. Title.
BF697.B687   1983   158'.1   83-18001
ISBN 0-87477-270-2

Jeremy P. Tarcher, Inc.
9110 Sunset Blvd.
Los Angeles, CA 90069

Design by Tanya Maiboroda

Manufactured in the United States of America
S 10 9 8 7 6 5 4 3 2

First Edition

To Devers Branden

Contents

Acknowledgments

My thanks to my publisher, Jeremy Tarcher, for his enthusiasm for this project since its inception, as well as for our discussions concerning the personal meaning, to him, of "honoring the self," which always sent me back to my desk inspired.

My appreciation and deeply felt regard for the skill of my superb editor, Janice Gallagher, whose suggestions, feedback, and ruthless willingness to drive me past exasperation, always in the best interests of the book, contributed so much to the ultimate outcome.

My thanks to Ken Wilber for our illuminating discussions concerning the perspective of transpersonal psychology.

And finally, my deepest gratitude to my wife, Devers, to whom this book is dedicated—because of her unfailing emotional support during the writing, because of the many valuable psychological and literary suggestions she offered, and most of all because she embodies that attitude toward life I have loved, admired, and wanted to celebrate in my work, as long as I can remember.

Introduction

Of all the judgments that we pass in life, none is as important as the one we pass on ourselves, for that judgment touches the very center of our existence.

We stand in the midst of an almost infinite network of relationships: to other people, to things, to the universe. And yet, at three o'clock in the morning, when we are alone with ourselves, we are aware that the most intimate and powerful of all relationships and the one we can never escape is the relationship to ourselves. No significant aspect of our thinking, motivation, feelings, or behavior is unaffected by our self-evaluation. We are organisms who are not only conscious but self-conscious. That is our glory and, at times, our burden.

We monitor, assess, and question ourselves in a way possible to no other species. We ask, Who am I? What do I want? Where am I going? What is my purpose in life? Is my behavior appropriate to this purpose? Am I proud or ashamed of my choices and actions? Am I happy or unhappy to be who I am?

We have the ability to ask such questions, and we have the ability to run from them. But the questions are always there, waiting for our response, even if we choose to pretend they do not exist or do not concern us. They are there when we come home after a day of frenetic activity at work, when we come home from a party, the arms of a lover, a political rally, a charitable function, a religious encounter.

This book will be concerned, then, with the ultimate human encounter: the relationship of the "I" to the "me," of the ego to the self. The issues entailed by this encounter reach into and affect virtually every significant human experience—from the level of our self-esteem, to the kind of person we are likely to fall in love with, to the ambitions and life goals we are likely to set ourselves, to our most intimately personal sense of what it means to be a human being.

1

At each step of the way, we shall confront some form of the question, Shall I honor or shall I betray the self? Not that we necessarily identify the issue in these terms; in fact, we rarely do, often preferring not to know the nature of the choice we are making. But in the natural course of our development, we inevitably face a variety of questions that bear on the same ultimate alternatives: Do I belong to myself or to others? Is the primary purpose of my self the pursuit of my own happiness and the fulfillment of my own positive potentialities, or is it compliance with the wants and expectations of others? Do I live by my own vision of things or by the vision of others? Is my basic concern with my own approval or with the approval of others? Am I to rely chiefly on my own mind or on the minds of my parents or teachers, leaders or guru?

Such questions are not only psychological, they are also philosophical and, more specifically, ethical. Psychology and ethics are intimately interrelated fields, although neither psychologists nor moralists have always been eager to acknowledge the connection. This book is written at the interface of the two disciplines.

How we relate to our selves affects how we relate to others, to the world around us, to the visible and invisible universe that constitutes our ultimate context—just as how we relate to others and to the world affects how we relate to our selves. But we begin with the self and we shall conclude with the self, and why this is so should be clear by the time we arrive at the end of our road.

In a world in which selflessness is commonly regarded as a synonym of virtue and selfishness a synonym of evil—and in which the presumed goal of spiritual evolution is self-transcendence—a book entitled *Honoring the Self* may sound strange, even a bit disorienting.

This volume is grounded in the recognition that self-esteem and personal autonomy are indispensable conditions of human well-being. Its focus is the exploration and illumination of the meaning of these states and of the conditions of their realization; that goal is the guiding principle of all the chapters that follow.

In the course of our analysis, we shall need to examine the meaning not only of *self*, *self-esteem*, and *autonomy*, but also of such ideas as self-concept, self-actualization, selfishness, self-alienation, self-sacrifice, self-transcendence, ego, identity, individualism, and individuation. Our discussion will be set against a consideration of the various forces in our culture—familial, educational, religious, ethical, social—that subvert the evolution of self and self-esteem and foster self-disowning, self-alienation, and destructiveness of life. I propose to demonstrate that not selfishness but absence of self is the root of most of our evils, that selflessness is our greatest personal, interpersonal, and social danger and has been so throughout most of our history.

In short, I shall invite the reader to reexamine some of our most prevalent beliefs about ego, selfishness, goodness—and human survival.

While I will need the entire book to develop fully what I mean by "honoring the self," I offer a brief statement of its essence here.

The first act of honoring the self is the assertion of consciousness: the choice to think, to be aware, to send the searchlight of consciousness outward toward the world and inward toward our own being. To default on this effort is to default on the self at the most basic level.

To honor the self is to be willing to think independently, to live by our own mind, and to have the courage of our own perceptions and judgments.

To honor the self is to be willing to know not only what we think but also what we feel, what we want, need, desire, suffer over, are frightened or angered by—and to accept our right to experience such feelings. The opposite of this attitude is denial, disowning, repression—self-repudiation.

To honor the self is to preserve an attitude of self-acceptance—which means to accept what we are, without self-oppression or self-castigation, without any pretense about the truth of our own being, pretense aimed at deceiving either ourselves or anyone else.

To honor the self is to live authentically, to speak and act from our innermost convictions and feelings.

To honor the self is to refuse to accept unearned guilt and to do our best to correct such guilt as we may have earned.

To honor the self is to be committed to our right to exist,

3

which proceeds from the knowledge that our life does not belong to others and that we are not here on earth to live up to someone else's expectations. To many people, this is a terrifying responsibility.

To honor the self is to be in love with our own life, in love with our possibilities for growth and for experiencing joy, in love with the process of discovering and exploring our distinctively human potentialities.

Thus we can begin to see that to honor the self is to practice *selfishness* in the highest, noblest, and least understood sense of that word. And this, I shall argue, requires enormous independence, courage, and integrity.

In contrast to the state of being I have just described, the two most striking characteristics of men and women who seek psychotherapy are a deficiency of self-esteem and a condition of self-alienation. In some crucial ways they do not feel appropriate to life and to its requirements, and they lack adequate contact with the world within, with their needs, wants, feelings, thoughts, values and potentialities. Thus diminished in consciousness, they are estranged from their proper human estate. Large areas of the self lie undiscovered, unexpressed, unlived. They are sleepwalkers through their own existence.

But this group is hardly a breed distinct from the rest of humanity. They are, in fact, a mirror reflecting the predicament of most individuals, to varying degrees. No study has ever suggested that people in therapy are, on the average, more troubled or demoralized than people who are not in therapy. Rather, they tend to be distinguished by the fact that they have chosen to confront the problems of poor self-esteem and inadequate contact with the self, and they thereby offer us an opportunity to learn a great deal about the psychological condition of the general population.

I am a psychotherapist, and the context in which I write is that intimate arena where it is *always* three o'clock in the morning, where the practical effects of theories, ideologies, family and social environments, educational systems and political structures are ultimately felt: the private experience of the individual human being struggling to create a meaningful and fulfilling existence.

In contrast to the conventional perspective of psychotherapy, however, which tends to view aspects of this struggle in terms of illness or disease and to see human beings as more or less helpless pawns manipulated by forces outside their control, I see the endeavor as potentially heroic. It contains all the elements of great myth or great drama, from the start along the path to self-actualization, which entails breaking free of the gravitational pull of mother, father, and family, to the adventures, crises, anxieties, rites of passage, victories, and defeats that are all part of the growth process, and on to the heights to be climbed, the depths to be explored, the adversaries to be confronted in the world and in the psyche itself—and, intrinsic to the drama from the beginning, the terrible and exhilarating uncertainty concerning the ultimate outcome of the story.

We shall have many occasions to see the ways in which the challenge to honor the self calls on the heroic possibilities of our nature—on the will to think, to understand, to remain true to our understanding, to struggle, to endure, to persevere, and to remain open and responsive to life, sometimes in the face of dread, despair, confusion, and loneliness.

That the concepts of honoring the self and self-esteem are intimately related is obvious almost from the words themselves. The nature of this relationship is explored in part one. Here I address myself to the role of self-esteem in human life, to the conditions on which positive self-esteem depends, and to the many ways in which our life is affected by the nature of our self-appraisal.

Virtually all psychologists recognize that there is some connection between the degree of a person's self-esteem and the degree of his or her overall mental well-being, just as there is some connection between the condition of a person's self-esteem and his or her behavior in work and human relationships. And yet there has been surprisingly little exploration into this area. It has been a relatively neglected field of study. I cannot help but feel that the discussion that follows is long overdue, and one of my hopes is that it will serve as a springboard for the further explorations of others.

I first wrote about this subject in *The Psychology of Self-Esteem*, and I developed some of the themes in *The Disowned Self*.

But it is now more than a decade since these books were published. The present work, based on my studies of the past thirteen years, represents a new examination of the role of self-esteem in human development, as well as a fresh treatment of the issues of self and the world, self and society, self in the cosmos. Inevitably I have had to retrace some of the steps covered in the previous books. I have allowed myself to borrow from or paraphrase material from these books, without burdening the present work with unnecessary references or quotation marks.

I approach the twin themes of honoring the self and self-esteem from another angle in part two, where I address myself to the process by which an individual evolves, or fails to evolve, toward increasing autonomy and individuation. Here, I focus on the process of self-actualization from a perspective that is predominantly developmental—as contrasted with part one, in which the focus is predominantly the here and now. In this section I also move into the problem of self-alienation. I discuss how the less than autonomous individual—the self-alienated man or woman—can move toward increasing wholeness, rediscovering and bringing into harmony previously dissociated aspects of the self.

In part three I shift to the ethical perspective—the role of values in human life and the ways in which the moral precepts we accept can contribute to or diminish self-esteem and personal evolution. In this section I deal with the morality of honoring the self. I conclude this discussion by addressing myself to the spiritual, or transpersonal, perspective; examining the view that holds self-transcendence to be the ultimate goal of human evolution. Should we strive to go "beyond ego"? Is the self merely a scaffolding to be discarded at a higher stage of our development? Is the disappearance of self the final triumph of maturity?

Throughout the book, in a variety of ways and contexts, I shall be concerned with the process of change and with what we ourselves can do to facilitate rising to higher levels of self-esteem, autonomy, and an integrated sense of self.

My goals in this work, then, are as follows: to demonstrate, specifically and concretely, what honoring the self means and to show the overwhelming importance of this issue to human life and well-being; to examine the kinds of behaviors by which self is honored or betrayed; to develop a deeper understanding of the meaning of self-esteem and its potency as a force in determining the course of our existence; to show on what the attainment of positive self-esteem depends; to explore the meanings of autonomy and individuation and the path to their realization; to point the way out of the widespread problem of self-alienation; to illuminate the morality of honoring the self and to integrate the psychology of self-esteem with an ethics of rational or enlightened self-interest; and, finally, to show that ego, properly understood, is not an obstacle to spiritual fulfillment but rather that without which no fulfillment is possible.

PART ONE

THE DYNAMICS OF
SELF-ESTEEM

1
Self-Esteem in Human Life

"The greatest evil that can befall man is that he should come to think ill of himself," wrote Goethe. While he may have been defying certain religious beliefs, he was acknowledging a profound truth about human nature.

The greatest barrier to achievement and success is not lack of talent or ability but, rather, the fact that achievement and success, above a certain level, are outside our self-concept, our image of who we are and what is appropriate to us. The greatest barrier to love is the secret fear that we are unlovable. The greatest barrier to happiness is the wordless sense that happiness is not our proper destiny. This, in simplest statement, is the importance of self-esteem, so we must begin by understanding what *self-esteem* means.

Unfortunately, like so many other terms in psychology, there is no generally agreed-upon definition. And the assumption that we all know what it means is mistaken. If we were to ask anyone what *self-esteem* means, we might receive an answer such as, "I feel competent, sure of myself," or "I like myself," or "Thinking I'm superior to other people." The first two statements would not be wrong but would be incomplete; the third would simply be false.

A person who does not feel competent in the performance of some particular task, such as flying an airplane, designing a computer program, or operating a business, does not necessarily suffer from poor self-esteem. But a physically healthy person who feels fundamentally inadequate to the normal challenges of life, such as earning a living, most certainly does. A person who feels undeserving of some particular award or honor, such as the Nobel Prize or universal adulation for having dashed off a fairly simple love song, again does not necessarily lack good self-esteem. But a person who feels undeserving of happiness, who feels unworthy of any joy or reward in life, surely has a self-esteem deficiency.

Self-esteem is a concept pertaining to a *fundamental* sense of efficacy and a *fundamental* sense of worth, to competence and worthiness *in principle*. "I trust my mind to make the choices and decisions that will guide my life" is a very different statement, in terms of self-esteem, from "I feel very confident to deal with the problems posed by molecular biology." "I feel entitled to assert my own legitimate needs and wants" is very different from "I am entitled to 10 million dollars."

High self-esteem can best be understood as the integrated sum of self-confidence and self-respect. *Self-confidence* is consciousness evaluating the efficacy of its own operations when applied to the task of understanding and dealing with reality. Am I competent to know? Am I competent to choose? To chart the course of my life? To satisfy my needs? *Self-respect* is the feeling of personal worth. Is it appropriate that I should be happy? That others should find me lovable? That I should be treated with respect? That my needs and wants should matter to those who are close to me?

In sum, self-esteem is an evaluation of my mind, my consciousness, and, in a profound sense, my person. It is not an evaluation of particular successes or failures, nor is it an evaluation of particular knowledge or skills. Thus, I can be very confident of myself at the fundamental level and yet be uncertain of my abilities in specific social situations. And, conversely, I can outwardly revel in my social savoir-faire, yet inwardly be self-doubting and insecure.

Going still further, I can be universally loved and yet not love myself. I can be universally admired and yet not admire myself. I can be widely regarded as brilliant and yet think myself intellectually inadequate. I can be a high achiever and yet feel like a failure, because I have not lived up to my own standards.

Living up to my own standards is, as we shall see when we consider the factors that enhance or diminish self-esteem, an essential condition of high self-esteem. The notion that my self-esteem is simply a function of how others see and evaluate me is false.

I have said that positive self-esteem is the experience that I am competent to live and worthy of happiness—or, to express the same thought a little differently, that I am appropriate to life and to its requirements and challenges. It would be more precise to say that positive self-esteem is the *disposition* to experience myself in this way, since, like any other feeling or state, it is not experienced with equal intensity at all times. Self-esteem is an orientation toward the self. Self-esteem is the ultimate *ground of consciousness*, ground to all particular experience; this is the single most important thing to be understood about its role in human psychology.

To experience that I am competent to live means that I have confidence in the functioning of my mind. To experience that I am worthy of living means that I have an affirmative attitude toward my right to live and to be happy.

In contrast to this experience, to have poor self-esteem is to feel that I am inappropriate to life, that I am wrong—not wrong about an issue or a piece of knowledge, but *wrong as a person*, wrong in my being. I thus respond to the challenges and joys of existence with a fundamental sense of inadequacy and unworthiness.

Of course, I may elect to judge myself by such relatively superficial criteria as success or failure at specific tasks, my ability to elicit love, admiration, or approval, and so forth. But to do so is already to have a problem in self-esteem, as we shall see when I discuss pseudo-self-esteem.

Besides which, the people we are most likely to admire are precisely those who manage to persevere in faithfulness to their own vision, without a good deal of positive reinforcement, without the understanding of others, their approval, or their applause—in fact, often in the face of hostility and opposition. When we see those who possess a fundamental certainty about themselves that remains relatively untouched by the vicissitudes of life, we sense that an unusual psychological achievement is involved; we may or may not identify that what we are looking at is high self-esteem.

To the extent that we trust the efficacy of our mind, we persevere when faced with difficult or complex challenges. And we are likely to succeed more often than fail, confirming and reinforcing our sense of efficacy. High self-esteem seeks the stimulation of demanding goals. To the extent that we doubt the efficacy of our minds, we do not persevere. And we are likely to fail more often than succeed, confirming and reinforcing our negative self-evaluation. Low self-esteem typically seeks the safety of the familiar and undemanding.

For example, two persons go to work in the same office. The first seeks to learn everything relevant to the job for which he has been hired, to expand his knowledge continually, and to keep searching for more effective ways to do the tasks he has been given. The second is concerned primarily with not drawing negative attention to himself; beyond that, his policy is to get by with as little effort as possible; to him, a job is a refuge, not an opportunity. The first will not be bewildered by his success; the second may profess to be bewildered by his failure.

If I enjoy healthy self-esteem, I value rather than am threatened by that same trait in others. People with poor self-esteem end up in the company of their own kind; shared fear and insecurity reinforce negative self-assessments.

And if I feel lovable and deserving of respect, I treat others well and expect them to treat me well. But if I feel unlovable and undeserving of respect and I am treated poorly, I put up with it and feel it is my fate.

Low self-esteem tends to generate depression and anxiety. To feel that I am significantly devoid of efficacy and worth is almost inevitably to experience existence as frightening and futile.

And while good self-esteem is only one of the elements necessary for happiness and does not necessarily guarantee happiness in and of itself, a high level of self-confidence and self-respect is intimately related to the ability to enjoy life and to find sources of satisfaction in our existence.

High self-esteem is a powerful force in the service of life.*

---

*An excellent review of some of the most significant research concerning how the level of our self-esteem affects our interpersonal relationships may be found in D. E. Hamachek's *Encounters with Others: Interpersonal Relationships and You.*

We need to distinguish the concept of positive self-esteem from the concept of pride, since the two are often confused. Self-esteem, as we have seen, pertains to an inner conviction of our fundamental efficacy and worth. Pride pertains to the more explicitly conscious pleasure we take in ourselves on the basis of and in response to specific achievements or actions. Positive self-esteem is "I can." Pride is "I have," and the deepest pride we can experience is that which results from the achievement of self-esteem, for self-esteem is a value that has to be earned—and has to be maintained.

Pride is a positive emotional experience, just as self-esteem is. It is not a vice to be overcome but a virtue to be attained—a form of honoring the self. If, however, one subscribes to the view that human beings are unworthy by nature (for example, if one thinks of humanity as "all equally miserable sinners in the sight of God"), then of course one speaks of "the sin of pride" and warns that "pride goeth before a fall." But this is a perspective I do not share; indeed, I regard it as malevolent and antilife.

Is it possible to possess too high a level of self-esteem? Not if we understand that we are speaking of authentic self-esteem, a genuine, organic experience, and not some overinflated pretense at self-value aimed at concealing a deficiency.

No one would ask, "Is is possible to enjoy too high a level of physical health?" Health is an unqualified desirable. So is positive self-esteem.

Genuine self-esteem is not competitive or comparative. Neither is genuine self-esteem expressed by self-glorification at the expense of others, or by the quest to make oneself superior to all others or to diminish others so as to elevate oneself. Arrogance, boastfulness, and the overestimation of our abilities reflect inadequate self-esteem rather than, as some people imagine, too high a level of self-esteem.

In human beings, joy in the mere fact of existing is a core meaning of healthy self-esteem. It is a state of one who is at war neither with self nor with others.

When we meet a person for the first time, often one of our earliest impressions, or assessments, concerns that person's self-appraisal, although we are usually not aware of this. We are not always right, of course, and we may revise our estimate when we know the person better. But from the beginning, almost like animals, we intuit one another's level of comfort and happiness with the self—one another's level of self-confidence and self-respect. The way we respond depends not only on the other person's level of self-esteem but also on our own.

Since this process of appraisal is usually subconscious, or largely so, even for psychotherapists, I have found it personally challenging to articulate at least some of the overt criteria by which I judge when I don't know the intimate details of another person's life.

Curious to compare my criteria with those of other professionals, I solicited responses from psychologists across a fairly wide intellectual spectrum—from transpersonal psychologists to humanistic psychologists to psychoanalysts to clinicians of a behavior-therapy orientation. I found a good deal of correlation, although different persons inevitably emphasized different traits or characteristics.

Listed below are a number of behaviors, usually easily discernible, that pertain to positive self-esteem.

1. The individual's face, manner, way of talking and moving project joy in being alive, a simple delight in the fact of being.

2. The individual is able to speak of accomplishments or shortcomings with directness and honesty.

3. The individual is comfortable in giving and receiving compliments, expressions of affection, appreciation, and the like.

4. The individual is open to criticism and comfortable about acknowledging mistakes.

5. The individual's words and movements have a quality of ease and spontaneity.

6. There is harmony between what the individual says and does and how he or she looks, sounds, and moves.

7. The individual exhibits an attitude of openness to and curiosity about new ideas, new experiences, new possibilities of life.

8. The individual is able to see and enjoy the humorous aspects of life, in self and in others.

9. The individual projects an attitude of flexibility in responding to situations and challenges, a spirit of inventiveness and even playfulness.

10. The individual is comfortable with assertive (not belligerent) behavior.

11. The individual preserves a quality of harmony and dignity under conditions of stress.

Of course, this list is by no means exhaustive, and not every person of high self-esteem exhibits each of these traits to the same degree; but the list does reflect some of the essential indicators by which one can assess how a person feels about him- or herself.

We respond to the sum total of what a person presents. For example, a relaxed, well-balanced posture and hard, chronically staring eyes tell a conflicting story. No single trait or characteristic, judged out of context, is ever conclusive.

In addition to the foregoing, and supplemental to it, there are specifically physical indicators of a person's level of self-esteem (subject to the same qualifications made in the above paragraph about psychological indicators).* These are:

1. Eyes that are alert, bright, lively.

2. A face that is relaxed and (barring illness) exhibits natural color and good skin vibrancy.

3. A chin that is held naturally in alignment with the body.

4. A jaw that is relaxed.

5. Shoulders that are relaxed and erect.

6. Hands that are relaxed, graceful, and quiet.

7. Arms that hang in a relaxed, natural way.

---

*This list of physical indicators is adapted from one sent to me by George Leonard and prepared by two of his colleagues, Joel and Susan Kirsch. Most of the professionals with whom I spoke mentioned some of the physical indicators on this list. The Kirsches named them all.

8. A posture that is relaxed, erect, well balanced.

9. A walk that is purposeful (without being agressive and overbearing).

10. A voice that is modulated, with an intensity appropriate to the situation, and with clear pronunciation.

Observe that the theme of relaxation occurs again and again. Relaxation implies that the individual is not hiding him- or herself, is not at war with who he or she is, whereas chronic tension conveys a message of some form of internal split, some form of self-denial or self-repudiation, some aspect of the self being disowned or held on a very tight leash.

The human voice is often a profoundly eloquent indicator of an individual's level of self-esteem. People with high self-esteem are willing to take responsibility for what they say; therefore, they are willing to be heard; therefore, they are willing to speak clearly, not unnecessarily loudly or aggressively. Their speech is *appropriate*.

It is easier to grasp that self-esteem is important in human life than to grasp why it should be. Why does the need for self-esteem arise in the first place? Lower animals do not have such a need; why do humans? What are the distinctive facts of our nature that give rise to this need? Why must we judge ourselves at all?

We cannot fully understand the meaning of self-esteem until we have answered these questions. We cannot appreciate the standard by which self-esteem is to be gauged—and the steps by which one builds or rebuilds it—until we understand the roots of the need, the reasons for its existence.

The reasons are far from self-evident—and yet, in all the psychological literature, I have never even found the problem addressed.

This is the issue to which we shall now turn.

2
The Need for Self-Esteem

Our specific level of evolutionary development as thinking beings makes the process of self-evaluation inevitable and supremely important to us. From this process, we need to emerge with positive self-esteem. Since thinking is involved here and since thinking is an act of choice, attaining positive self-esteem is often a struggle of heroic proportions.

In this chapter I will justify the concept of the heroic, as well as the concept of self-esteem, by exploring our ability to think, our choice to do so, and the consequences for our existence.

For every organism that possesses it, consciousness is the basic means of survival—the ability to be aware of the environment in some form, at some level, and to act appropriately. Here I use *consciousness* in its primary meaning: the state of being conscious or aware of some aspect of reality.

Like every other species that possesses awareness, we depend for our survival on the guidance of *our* distinctive form of consciousness, our conceptual faculty. To learn to grow food, to construct a bridge, to grasp the healing possibilities of some drug, to conduct a scientific experiment, to understand the teachings of a sage—all require a process of thought.

To respond appropriately to the complaints of a child or a spouse, to recognize that there is a disparity between our behavior and our professed feelings, to learn how to deal with hurt and anger in ways that will heal rather than destroy—all require a process of thought.

Even to know when to abandon conscious efforts at problem

solving and turn the task over to the subconscious, to know when to allow conscious thinking to stop, requires a process of thought.

The problem and the challenge are that we are not programmed to think automatically just because thinking is a necessity of successful existence. This brings us to the central issue: the choice to think.

To use our consciousness appropriately in any given situation is, as I have said, neither "instinctive" nor automatic. We are not wired so as always to choose awareness over blindness, knowledge over ignorance, fact over delusion, truth over falsehood. The design of our nature contains an extraordinary option—that of seeking awareness or avoiding it, seeking truth or avoiding it, focusing our mind or unfocusing it. In other words, *we have the option of subverting our means of survival and well-being.*

It is at this most fundamental level that the issue of honoring the self first arises: Shall I assert consciousness or flee from it? Shall I take responsibility for consciousness or pretend no such responsibility exists?

This freedom is in a sense discontinuous with the rest of the biological world, where everything seems to happen by automatic patterns and rhythms. In human beings, both life and consciousness reach their most highly developed form. Going beyond the sensory-perceptual mode in which consciousness of the external world regulates behavior, human behavior ascends to the conceptual mode—to the level of abstractions, principles, explicit reasoning, propositional speech, and *self-consciousness.*

Now we are at the heart of the matter: the *self-conscious* level of organismic self-regulation. On the sensory-perceptual level of consciousness that human beings share with animals, awareness is the controlling and regulating goal of an automatic integrative process, by nature's programming. But on the higher levels of consciousness, on the conceptual plane, the exercise of mind is volitional, which means it is *our responsibility.*

We activate and direct the process by setting the goal—*awareness*—and that goal acts as the regulator and integrator of our mental activity (much of which happens, needless to say, at the subconscious level).

For example, I wake up in the morning, go to my desk, and

am confronted with a vast array of papers, notes, research materials. I sit down, dimly aware that my mind is far from fully in focus. I look at my work and think to myself, "Get going." In other words, I establish the goal of awareness by telling myself, in effect, "Grasp this. See where you left off, re-create your context, grasp what the situation now requires—and proceed." I activate the appropriate mental state.

Since I discuss this issue in considerable detail in *The Psychology of Self-Esteem*, it is not necessary to repeat all the details here. Instead, I will confine myself to some necessary amplifications and clarifications.

In my earlier book I implied that the choice of awareness means the choice of a highly focused form of consciousness. In fact, sometimes our choice is a more diffuse form of awareness, but if the intention is contact with rather than evasion of reality, I describe that state of mind, too, as *focused*.*

To be in mental focus does not mean that we must be engaged in the task of problem solving every moment of our waking existence. We may choose to meditate, for example, emptying our mind of all thought to make ourselves available to new possibilities of relaxation, rejuvenation, creativity, insight, or some form of transcendence. This can be an entirely appropriate mental activity—in fact, in some contexts, a highly desirable one. And of course there are still other alternatives to problem solving, such as creative daydreaming or abandonment to erotic sensation. In matters of mental functioning, *context determines appropriateness*.

The possibility of choice in this area is what generates the need for self-esteem. And the kinds of choices we make determine the kind of self-esteem we possess.

We can choose not only to avoid the effort of purposeful awareness in general but to avoid specific lines of thought that we find disconcerting or painful. Perceiving qualities in our friends, our spouse, or ourself that clash with our standards, we can sur-

---

*Jungian psychologists use the concept of *focused consciousness* in a much narrower sense than I do and identify it with the masculine mode of cognition, as opposed to *diffused consciousness*, which they identify with the feminine. I want to emphasize that that is not the context in which I write. When I speak of the choice to focus or not to focus, I mean seeking to expand consciousness in some way or allowing consciousness to remain at inappropriately low levels of intensity and clarity.

render our mind to blankness or switch it hastily to some other concern, refusing to identify the meaning or implications of what we have noted. Dimly apprehending, in the midst of an argument, that we are being ridden by unexamined feelings and are maintaining a position for reasons other than those we are stating, reasons we know cannot bear close scrutiny, we can refuse to pause on this knowledge, refuse to integrate it; we can push it aside and continue to shout with righteous indignation. Grasping that we are pursuing some course of action in blatant defiance of reason, we can cry to ourselves, in effect, "Who can be sure of anything?"—and continue on our way.

In such cases, we may be doing more than defaulting on the responsibility of making awareness our goal. We may be actively seeking unawareness as our goal, practicing evasion in a context where awareness clearly is needed.

Sometimes the awareness we are evading is that we are not translating our thinking and knowledge into action, as if to imply that as long as we are "thinking," we do not have to *do* anything—a viewpoint that clear thinking can hardly sustain.

A woman, for example, becomes aware of the fact that she has treated her daughter unfairly and cruelly in some matter. She knows that she has left her daughter hurt and bewildered. The woman "thinks" about her own behavior—about its reasons, and about the necessity of behaving differently in the future—yet she does nothing. She is dimly aware that she does not find it easy to admit she has made a mistake. "I'm thinking about it," she keeps telling herself. She does not speak to her daughter of what she is aware of or what she is experiencing; she pretends their situation is normal. She does not confront her daughter, and she does not confront her own resistance to confronting her daughter—all the while insisting that she is "still thinking."

Since evasion is so important to the issue of self-esteem, I need to stress that it pertains specifically to situations of avoiding awareness where we perceive that clearer awareness is possible to us and decline to pursue it. If we do not choose to think about some issue that does not seem relevant to our interests or needs or context, we are not practicing evasion. If we do not think about some issue because we do not know how to start or where to go, or if we do not think about some issue because we genuinely believe our effort will be futile, we may not be practicing evasion.

The choice to think is truly heroic in some cases. For instance, if we choose to think and we come up against facts we cannot handle, what then? If we choose to think and our thinking leads us to conclusions that threaten to disrupt the routine of our life, what then? If we choose to think and our conclusions lead us far from the mainstream beliefs of others, what then? If we choose to think and we begin noticing traits and characteristics of ourselves we do not admire, what then? If we choose to think and we see what we do not wish to see, what then? Or what others do not wish to see—what then?

Temptations to avoid thinking exist in abundance. But that does not invalidate the fact that thinking is our basic means of survival and that we must choose to think. We possess freedom of will.

While the doctrine of psychological determinism, which denies free will, has enjoyed a long and influential vogue in psychology, it has never possessed a strong scientific or philosophical foundation. It rests on a series of misconceptions, non sequiturs, and contradictions that I explore in *The Psychology of Self-Esteem*.

Psychological determinism denies the existence of any element of freedom or volition in human consciousness. It holds that in relation to our actions, decisions, values, and conclusions, we are ultimately and essentially passive; that we are merely reactors to internal and external pressures; that those pressures determine the course of our actions and the content of our convictions, just as physical forces determine the course of every particle of dust in the universe.

Aside from other objections that may be raised, determinism contains a central and insuperable contradiction—a contradiction implicit in any variety of determinism, whether the alleged determining forces be physical, psychological, environmental, or divine. The determinist view of mind maintains that whether an individual thinks or not, takes cognizance of the facts of reality or not, places facts above feelings or feelings above facts—all are determined by forces outside his or her control; at any given moment or situation, the individual's method of mental functioning is the inevitable product of an endless chain of antecedent factors.

We are neither omniscient nor infallible. We must work to achieve our knowledge. The mere presence of an idea inside our

23

mind does not prove that the idea is true; many ideas that are false may enter our consciousness. But if we believe what we *have* to believe, if we are not free to test our beliefs against reality and to validate or reject them—if the actions and content of our mind, in other words, are determined by factors that may or may not have anything to do with reason, logic, and reality—then we can never know if our conclusions are true or false.

Knowledge consists of the correct identification of facts; and in order for us to know that the contents of our mind *do* constitute knowledge, in order for us to know that we have identified the facts correctly, we require a means of testing our conclusions against reality and checking for contradictions. This means is the process of reasoning; it is thus that we validate our conclusions. But this validation is possible only if our capacity to judge is free—that is, nonconditional.

Free will—in the widest meaning of the term—is the doctrine that human beings are capable of performing actions that are not determined by forces outside their control, that we are capable of making choices that are not necessitated by antecedent factors. The specific concept of free will being developed here differs from other theories in that it locates our freedom specifically in the choice to seek or avoid awareness.*

Freedom does not mean causelessness; this point must be stressed. A volitional choice is not causeless. It is caused by the person who makes the choice, and the choice entails an enormity of issues:

Focusing versus nonfocusing.

Thinking versus nonthinking.

Awareness versus unawareness.

Clarity versus obscurity or vagueness.

Respect for reality versus avoidance of reality.

---

*It is closest to the concept of volition proposed by Ayn Rand but differs from hers in that Rand identifies the choice to focus exclusively with the choice to think, to engage in a process of explicit reasoning, whereas, as I have already indicated, my own view of the choice to focus is considerably broader.[63, 64]

Respect for facts versus denial of facts.

Respect for truth versus rejection of truth.

Perseverance in the attempt to understand versus abandonment of the attempt to understand.

Loyalty in action to our professed convictions versus disloyalty (this is the issue of integrity).

Honesty with self versus dishonesty.

Self-confrontation versus self-avoidance.

Receptivity to new knowledge versus closed-mindedness.

Willingness to see and correct mistakes versus perseverance in error.

Concern with congruence versus disregard of contradictions.

Reason versus irrationalism; respect for logic, consistency, coherence, and evidence versus disregard.

From the time that a child acquires the capacity for conceptual functioning and self-awareness, he or she becomes increasingly aware—implicitly, nonverbally—of a responsibility for the regulation of mental activity. The above list covers the issues that that regulation concerns.

While focusing is not synonymous with reasoning, we can see how central the role of reason and rationality is. Reason is the faculty and process by which human beings integrate data given or present in consciousness, in accordance with the law of non-contradiction. By this definition, free will entails the choice to be rational or to be irrational—which ultimately means the choice to respect reality or to defy it.

Our freedom is neither absolute nor unlimited, however. There are many factors that can make the appropriate exercise of our consciousness easier or harder. Some of these factors may be genetic, biological. Others are developmental. The environment can support and encourage the healthy assertion of consciousness, or it can oppose and undermine it. We will consider the role of the environment at a later point.

Within the mind itself, there may be obstructions to thinking. Subconscious defenses and blocks may make us oblivious even of the need to think about a particular issue. Consciousness is a continuum; it exists on many levels. And unresolved problems at one level may subvert operations at another. For example, if I block my feelings about my parents—if I cut off access to those feelings through denial, disowning, repression—and then try to think about our relationship, I have disconnected myself from so much pertinent material that I can easily become muddled and discouraged and give up.

Clearly, the desire to be more aware does not guarantee that the results of our efforts will be successful. We are free to try; there is never a guarantee of success. If there were such a guarantee, fewer people would avoid the responsibility of thinking. Uncertainty is built into the very essence of our existence, and *it is this uncertainty and freedom that create the need for self-esteem.*

Self-esteem, we have seen, is the integrated sum of self-confidence and self-respect. Our need for self-esteem is our need to know that the choices we exercise are appropriate to reality, appropriate to our life and well-being. It is our need to know that we have made ourselves competent to live. Since reality continuously confronts us with alternatives, since we must choose our goals and actions, since we are constantly obliged to make decisions concerning our interactions with the environment, our sense of efficacy and security requires the conviction that we are *right in our method* of choosing and of making decisions; right in our characteristic manner of using our consciousness; right *in principle*, appropriate to reality.

Self-confidence is confidence in the reliability of our mind as a tool of cognition. Self-confidence is not the conviction that we can never make an error. It is the conviction that we are able to think, to judge, to know (and to correct our errors)—that we are genuinely committed to perceiving and honoring reality to the fullest extent of our volitional power. To doubt the efficacy of our basic means of survival is to be interrupted or paralyzed (to varying degrees) in our efforts to cope with the challenges of life—thus condemned to feelings of anxiety and helplessness; thus sentenced to feelings of being less than fit to live.

Regarding our need for *self-respect*: as we develop, as we progressively become aware of our power to choose our actions, as we acquire our sense of being a person, we experience the need

26

to feel that we are right as a person, right in our characteristic manner of acting—in a word, that we are *good*. We learn the concept from adults, but the need is inherent in our nature. A child may not be aware of the relation of the issue of being right or good to the issue of life or death; a child may be aware of it only in relation to the alternatives of joy or suffering, self-delight or self-repudiation. To be right as a person is to be fit for happiness; to be wrong is to be threatened by pain. To be worthy as a person is to be worthy of joy; to be unworthy as one is to be unworthy of the other.

Inherent in our existence as human beings are such questions as: What kind of entity should I seek to become? By what principles should I guide my life? What values are worthy of pursuit? I say "inherent in our existence" because the concern with right and wrong is not merely the product of social conditioning, as behaviorists have tried to persuade us; a concern with morality or ethics arises naturally in the early stages of our development, much as our other intellectual abilities develop, and progresses in step with the normal course of our maturation.[41, 60]

We cannot exempt ourselves from the realm of values and value judgments. Whether the values by which we judge ourselves are conscious or subconscious, rational or irrational, consistent or contradictory, life serving or life threatening, every one of us judges him- or herself by *some* standard. And to the extent that we fail to satisfy that standard, our self-respect suffers.

We are the one species that is able to form a judgment about what is best for us to do—*and then proceed to do the opposite.* We are the one species free to disregard our own knowledge or to betray our own values. The concept of hypocrisy is not applicable to lower animals; neither is the virtue of integrity. In order for us to understand our need for the experience of personal worth, it is essential to grasp this fact.

As we shall discuss later, parents and the family environment play a significant role in the development of a child's values, self-concept, and self-esteem. And while it is false to hold that a child's self-esteem is merely a reflection of the appraisals received from others, I do not wish to deny that those appraisals constitute an important part of the child's life experience, with consequences for the child's psychology.[2, 82]

A human being *needs* self-respect, *needs* the experience of

27

worthiness, fully as much as he or she needs self-confidence. We must act to achieve our goals—and in order to act, we must value ourselves as beneficiaries of our actions. To fight for our happiness, we must consider ourselves worthy of happiness. Lacking the sense of that worthiness, we will fail in those acts of self-assertion that our well-being requires. In key areas of life we will be interrupted or paralyzed (to varying degrees)—condemned to feelings of being inappropriate to life.

We make ourselves worthy of living by making ourselves *competent* to live. If we default on the responsibility of thought and reason, if we turn our backs on reality and facts, thus undercutting our competence to live, we will not retain a sense of worthiness. If we betray our integrity, if we betray our moral convictions, if we turn our back on our own standards, thus undercutting our sense of worthiness, we do so by evasion; by the refusal to see what we see and know what we know, we commit treason to our own (correct or mistaken) judgment, and thus we do not retain our sense of competence.

This judgment passed on our mental behavior is typically experienced as an assesssment of our "essence." Behavior at this level of intimacy is experienced as "who I am." It is experienced as almost inseparable from an individual's sense of self. Whereas it is relatively easier to perceive external behavior as an expression of self but not identical with self, internal behavior—choices and mental operations—is normally intrinsic to the self-experience.

But we can and do disidentify self with particular choices and operations when we say, for instance, "I regret that I chose to be so irresponsible in that matter, and I am determined to function differently in the future."

The self continually evolves, continually shapes itself, continually affects the way it is experienced—by the continuing stream of choices and decisions it makes in the course of living. That is why change and growth are possible. We are not obliged to remain the prisoners of yesterday's errors, or yesterday's defaults on the responsibility of appropriate consciousness.

Our choices do have psychological consequences. The way we choose to deal with reality, truth, facts—our choice to honor or dishonor our own perceptions—registers in our mind, for good or for bad, and either confirms and strengthens our self-esteem or denies and weakens it.

28

Self-esteem is the reputation we acquire with ourselves.

It is apparent by now that the "self" we are esteeming is our mind—our *mind* and its characteristic manner of operation. This needs to be stressed because *self* is a term that acquires somewhat different meanings according to context.

Sometimes when we speak of "my self," we mean "my person, the totality of my being, including my body." In a psychological context, *self* is used most often to mean the totality of those mental characteristics, abilities, processes, beliefs, values, and attitudes that I may or may not consciously recognize as mine. Thus, much of the territory of the self may be subconscious.

The concept of *mind* has a narrower application than that of *consciousness* and is associated specifically with the ability to represent and manipulate reality symbolically, to form and use concepts, to reason, and to construct propositional speech. *Mind* designates human consciousness (or the human form of consciousness), in contradistinction to the forms of consciousness exhibited by lower animals.[6]

Ego (the Latin word for "I") is the unifying center of consciousness, the irreducible core of self-awareness—that which generates and sustains a sense of self, of personal identity. Our ego is not our thoughts, but that which thinks; not our judgments, but that which judges; not our feelings, but that which recognizes feelings; the ultimate witness within; the ultimate context in which all our narrower selves or subpersonalities exist. Thus, *self-esteem* might better be termed *ego esteem*. When we say of someone that he or she has "a strong ego" or "a healthy ego," we generally mean to imply that that person enjoys good self-esteem.

Self-concept pertains to an individual's ideas, beliefs, and images concerning his or her (real or imagined) traits and characteristics, liabilities and assets, limitations and capabilities. As such, it is wider than self-esteem; it contains self-esteem as one of its components. We may think of self-esteem as a circle enclosed within the larger circle of self-concept. Or we may think of self-esteem as the evaluative component of self-concept.

One of the most powerful influences on self-esteem development is parental upbringing. We turn next to a discussion of some of the key issues in child-parent relationships that tend to affect the quality of self-esteem that evolves. We deal here with influences, not determinants. Ultimately, it is we ourselves who generate the level of our self-confidence and self-respect. After we have dealt with parental and related environmental factors, we will be ready to take up directly our own crucially decisive role in raising or lowering self-esteem.

3
Self-Esteem and Child-Parent Relationships

Every organism depends on its environment, to some extent, for successful growth. While we are able to transcend an adverse environment, our ability is not unlimited, and it is important to understand the kinds of interactions that support or subvert the emergence of self-confidence and self-respect.

Let me begin with a general observation. A child needs to make sense out of his or her world, and when that need is frustrated again and again, a tragic sense of self and of life is often the result.

I recall discussing this issue one day with the distinguished family therapist Virginia Satir, who gave an exquisite and appalling illustration of the kind of craziness with which so many of us grow up. Imagine, she said, a scene among a child and a mother and father. Seeing a look of unhappiness on mother's face, the child says, "What's the matter, mommy? You look sad." Mother answers, her voice tight and constricted, "Nothing's the matter. I am fine." Then father says angrily, "Don't upset your mother!" The child looks back and forth between mother and father, utterly bewildered and unable to understand the rebuke. He begins to weep. Then mother cries to father, "Now look what you've done!"

Let us look at this scene more closely. The child correctly perceives that something is bothering mother and responds appropriately. Mother acts by invalidating the child's (correct) perception of reality. Perhaps she does so out of the desire to "protect" him, perhaps because she herself does not know how to handle her unhappiness. If she had said. "Yes, mommy is feeling a little

31

sad right now; thank you for noticing," she would have validated the child's perception. By acknowledging her own unhappiness simply and openly, she would have reinforced the child's compassion and taught him something profoundly important concerning a healthy attitude toward pain. Father, perhaps to "protect" mother, perhaps out of guilt because mother's sadness concerns him, rebukes the child, adding to the incomprehensibility of the situation. If Mother is not sad, why would a simple inquiry be upsetting? And why should it be upsetting in any event? The child, feeling hurt and helpless, begins to cry. Now mother screams at father, implying that she does not approve of what he has done in rebuking the child. Contradictions compounded, incongruities within incongruities. How is the child to make sense out of the situation?

The child may run outside, frantically looking for something to do or someone to play with, seeking to erase all memory of the incident as quickly as possible, repressing feelings and perceptions. And if the child flees into unconsciousness to escape the terrifying sense of being trapped in a nightmare, do we blame his well-meaning parents for behaving in ways that encourage him to feel that sight is dangerous and that there is safety in blindness?

An ordinary story, without villains. No one is likely to imagine that the parents are motivated by destructive intentions. But in choosing to deny simple reality, they give the child the impression that he exists in an incomprehensible world where perception is untrustworthy and thought is futile.

In considering the many parental messages that may have a detrimental effect on a child's self-esteem, there is probably none I encounter more often in the course of my work than some version of "You are not enough." Unfortunately, early in life all too many of us receive this message from parents and teachers. You may have potential, but you are unacceptable as you are. You need to be fixed. ("Here, let me adjust your hair," "Your clothes aren't right," "Smile," "Let me rearrange your posture," "Stand straighter," "Lower your voice," "Don't be so excited," "Don't play with that toy, play with this toy," *"What's the matter with you?"*) One day you may be enough, but not now. You will be enough only if and when you live up to our expectations.

Sometimes the message "You are not enough" is communicated not by criticism but by excessive praise. If a child feels overpraised, if his or her accomplishments are perceived exaggeratedly by loving parents ("Listen to Jimmy play the piano! We've got a Horowitz in the family!"), the result is a feeling of psychological invisibility and the sense that who I *really* am is not enough.[28, 29, 30]

The tragedy of many people's lives is that in accepting the verdict that they are not enough, they may spend their years exhausting themselves in pursuit of the Holy Grail of enoughness. If I make a successful marriage, then I will be enough. If I make so many thousand dollars a year, then I will be enough. One more promotion, and I will be enough. One more sexual conquest, one more doubling of my assets, one more person telling me I am lovable—then I will be enough. But I can never win the battle for enoughness on these terms. The battle was lost on the day I conceded there was anything that needed to be proved. I can free myself from the negative verdict that burdens my existence only by rejecting this very premise.

Children who experience being loved and accepted as they are, who do not feel their basic worth is continually on trial in their parents' eyes, have a priceless advantage in the formation of healthy self-esteem, as the work of Virginia Satir, Haim Ginott, and Stanley Coopersmith (to cite only three eminent specialists in this field) eloquently testifies.[76, 77, 28, 29, 30, 14]

Interestingly enough, the best work that psychologists in general have done with regard to self-esteem has been in the area of child-parent relations, with the emphasis on what parents can do to contribute to the growth of healthy self-esteem. Stanley Coopersmith's *The Antecedents of Self-Esteem* is the most scholarly and the best-researched study in this area.

One of the most interesting facts of the Coopersmith study is a negative finding: namely, that a child's self-esteem is not related to family wealth, education, geographic living area, social class, father's occupation, or always having mother at home. Stated in the positive, what is significant is the quality of the relationship that exists between the child and the significant adults in his or her life.

Coopersmith found four conditions most often associated with high self-esteem in children:

1. The child experiences full acceptance of thoughts, feelings, and the value of his or her being.

2. The child operates in a context of clearly defined and enforced limits that are fair, nonoppressive, and negotiable—but the child is not given unrestricted "freedom." In consequence, the child experiences a sense of security as well as a clear basis for evaluating his or her behavior. Further, the limits generally entail high standards, as well as confidence that the child will be able to meet them, with the consequence that the child usually does.*

3. The child experiences respect for his or her dignity as a human being. The parents take the child's needs and wishes seriously. The parents are willing to negotiate family rules within carefully drawn limits. In other words, authority, but not authoritarianism, is in operation.

   As an expression of this same overall attitude, they are less inclined to resort to punitive discipline (and there tends to be less need for punitive discipline), and more inclined to put the emphasis on rewarding and reinforcing positive behavior.

   The parents show an interest in the child, his or her social and academic life, and they are generally available for discussion when and as the child desires it.

4. The parents themselves tend to enjoy a high level of self-esteem. Since the way we treat others generally reflects the way we treat ourselves, this last finding is hardly surprising.

Yet some children have emerged from the most appallingly oppressive childhood environments with their sense of self heroically intact and their self-esteem high. Other children, from warm, supporting environments in which a sense of self seems to have

---

*Haim Ginott also stresses the need for limits if the child is to develop healthily and self-confidently, as contrasted with those psychologists who believe that the child's well-being is best served by unrestricted permissiveness.[28, 29, 30] Research does not support this latter assumption. Limits, provided they are reasonable, give the child a much-needed sense of security and stability, as Coopersmith's study shows.

been admirably nurtured by parents, grow up ridden with self-doubts and insecurities.[82]

After carefully elucidating such antecedents of self-esteem as his studies could disclose, Coopersmith goes on to observe, "We should note that there are virtually no parental patterns of behavior or parental attitudes that are common to all parents of children with high self-esteem."

Parents and teachers are not omnipotent with regard to a child's self-esteem, but neither are they powerless. Let us continue, therefore, to consider the nature of such influence as they have the ability to exercise.

I often tell parents, "Be careful what you say to your children. They may agree with you." Before calling a child "stupid" or "clumsy" or "bad" or "a disappointment," it is important for a parent to consider the question, "Is this how I wish my child to experience him- or herself?"

If a child is repeatedly told that he or she mustn't feel this, mustn't feel that, the child is being encouraged to deny and disown feelings or emotions in order to please or placate parents. Normal expressions of excitement, anger, happiness, sexuality, longing, and fear are treated as sinful or otherwise distasteful to parents, and the child may disown and repudiate more and more of his or her self in order to belong, to be loved, to avoid the terror of abandonment.

Overprotective parents may also cripple self-esteem in a child. Forbidden the risk taking and exploration essential for healthy development, the child intuits that he or she is inadequate to the normal challenges of life, is inherently unfit for independent survival.

Sometimes, when a child's parent dies or the parents divorce, the child feels painfully abandoned and may conclude, "Somehow it's my fault." Unless the child is helped to understand that the death or divorce was in no way caused by his or her behavior, a verdict of "I am not enough" may spread like a poison within the child's psyche.

To a child who has had little or no experience of being treated with respect—of being seen, attended to, listened to, trusted—such self-disrepect feels natural. We tend to go on giving ourselves the messages that our parents once gave us.

35

Some years ago (1969–1970), thinking about and researching the essential nutrients for healthy growth and self-esteem, I developed a set of questions that I then proceeded to explore intensively with a number of psychotherapy clients. The list was refined to the items presented below, all of which were found to have significance for the emergence (or nonemergence) of self-confidence and self-respect.*

The questions were, in effect, a device for journeying into the childhood origins of their self-concept in general and their self-esteem in particular.

The clients were asked first to answer the questions as best they could, then to cite examples in support of their answers, then to describe exhaustively all the emotions that the memory of those examples invoked, and, finally, to meditate on the conclusions drawn from these childhood experiences.

I was not (and am not) assuming that all their important conclusions from childhood were drawn on the basis of experiences with their parents. I merely considered this one worthwhile avenue of investigation.

The significance of these questions will be most apparent if the reader attempts to answer them personally.

1. When you were a child, did your parents' manner of behaving and of dealing with you give you the impression that you were living in a world that was rational, predictable, intelligible? Or a world that was contradictory, bewildering, unknowable?

2. Were you taught the importance of learning to think and of cultivating your intelligence? Did your parents provide you with intellectual stimulation and convey the idea that the use of your mind can be an exciting adventure?

3. Were you encouraged to think independently, to develop your

---

*I described some of my experiences in working with a somewhat shorter version of this list in *Breaking Free*. While *Breaking Free* does not in any important way reflect my approach to psychotherapy as I practice it today or have practiced it for some years past, the information generated by working with the list of questions continues to be valuable and is certainly supported by the research and findings of others.

critical faculty? Or were you encouraged to be obedient rather than mentally active and questioning? (Supplementary questions: Did your parents project that it was more important to conform to what other people believed than to discover what is true? When your parents wanted you to do something, did they appeal to your understanding and give you reasons, when possible and appropriate, for their request? Or did they communicate, in effect, "Do it because I say so"?)

4. Did you feel free to express your views openly, without fear of punishment?

5. Did your parents communicate their disapproval of your thoughts, desires, or behavior by means of humor, teasing, or sarcasm?

6. Did your parents treat you with respect? (Supplementary questions: Were your thoughts, needs, and feelings given consideration? Was your dignity as a human being acknowledged? When you expressed ideas or opinions, were they taken seriously? Were your likes and dislikes, whether or not they were acceded to, treated with respect? Were your desires responded to thoughtfully and, again, with respect?)

7. Did you feel that you were psychologically visible to your parents, seen and understood? Did you feel real to them? (Supplementary questions: Did your parents seem to make a genuine effort to understand you? Did your parents seem authentically interested in you as a person? Could you talk to your parents about issues of importance and receive concerned, meaningful understanding from them?)

8. Did you feel loved and valued by your parents, in the sense that you experienced yourself as a source of pleasure to them? Or did you feel unwanted, perhaps a burden? Did you feel hated? Or did you feel that you were simply an object of indifference?

9. Did your parents deal with you fairly and justly? (Supplementary questions: Did your parents resort to threats in order to control your behavior—either threats of immediate punitive action on their part, threats in terms of long-range consequences for your life, or threats of supernatural pun-

ishments, such as going to hell? Were you praised when you performed well, or merely criticized when you performed badly? Were your parents willing to admit it when they were wrong? Or was it against their policy to concede that they were wrong?)

10. Was it your parents' practice to punish you or discipline you by striking or beating you?

11. Did your parents project that they believed in your basic goodness? Or that they saw you as bad or worthless or evil?

12. Did your parents convey the sense that they believed in your intellectual and creative potentialities? Or did they project that they saw you as mediocre or stupid or inadequate?

13. In your parents' expectations concerning your behavior and performance, did they take cognizance of your knowledge, needs, interests, and circumstances? Or were you confronted with expectations and demands that were overwhelming and beyond your ability to satisfy?

14. Did your parents' behavior and manner of dealing with you tend to produce guilt in you?

15. Did your parents' behavior and manner of dealing with you tend to produce fear in you?

16. Did your parents respect your intellectual and physical privacy?

17. Did your parents project that it was desirable for you to think well of yourself—in effect, to have self-esteem? Or were you cautioned against valuing yourself, encouraged to be "humble"?

18. Did your parents convey that what a person made of his or her life, and what you, specifically, made of your life, was important? (Supplementary questions: Did your parents project that great things are possible for human beings, and specifically that great things are possible for you? Did your parents give you the impression that life could be exciting, challenging, a rewarding adventure?)

19. Did your parents instill in you a fear of the world, a fear of

other people? Or were you encouraged to face the world with an attitude of relaxed, confident benevolence?

20. Were you urged to be open in the expression of your emotions and desires? Or were your parents' behavior and manner of treating you such as to make you fear emotional self-assertiveness and openness or to regard it as inappropriate?

21. Were your mistakes accepted as a normal part of the learning process? Or as something you were taught to associate with contempt, ridicule, punishment?

22. Did your parents encourage you in the direction of having a healthy, affirmative attitude toward sex and toward your own body? A negative attitude? Or did they treat the entire subject as nonexistent?

23. Did your parents' manner of dealing with you tend to develop and strengthen your sense of your masculinity or femininity? Or to frustrate and diminish it?

24. Did your parents encourage you to feel that your life belonged to you? Or were you encouraged to believe that you were merely a family asset and that your achievements were significant only insofar as they brought glory to your parents? (Supplementary question: Were you treated as a family resource, or as an end in yourself?)

The relevance of these questions to self-esteem is so apparent that additional comment scarcely seems needed. Almost everything psychology has learned about the environmental conditions that support healthy self-esteem is reflected in the above selection of issues. All significantly affect a child's sense of self.

An important question in the above list that I want to pause on is question 7, the issue of whether or not a child feels visible to his or her parents.

A child has a natural desire to be seen, heard, understood, and responded to appropriately. This is the need for *psychological visibility*.

When we discuss psychological visibility we are, of course, always operating within the context of degree. From childhood on, we receive from human beings some measure of appropriate feedback; without it, we could not survive. Statistically, however, in their early years few children experience a high degree of appropriate visibility from adults.

A child who experiences his or her excitement as good, as a value, but is punished or rebuked for it by adults undergoes a bewildering experience of invisibility and disorientation. Similarly, a child who is praised for "always being an angel" but knows this is not true also experiences invisibility and disorientation.

Working with clients in psychotherapy and with students at my Intensive Workshops on "Self-Esteem and the Art of Being," I am often struck by the frequency with which the pain of invisibility in their home life as children is clearly central to their developmental problems and to their insecurities and inadequacies in their adult relationships.

I do not wish to imply that we first acquire an independent sense of identity and *then* seek visibility through interaction with others. Obviously, our relationships and the responses and feedback we receive contribute to the sense of self we acquire. All of us, to a profoundly important extent, experience who we are in the context of our relationships. When we encounter a new human being, our personality contains, among other things, the consequences of many past encounters, many experiences, the internalization of many responses and instances of feedback from others. And we keep growing through our encounters.

We need the experience of visibility. We normally have, of course, a sense of our own identity, but it is experienced more as a diffuse feeling than as an isolated thought. Our self-concept is not a single concept but a cluster of images and abstract perspectives on our various (real or imagined) traits and characteristics.

In the course of our life, our values, goals, and missions are first conceived in our mind. To the extent that our life is successful, we then translate them into action and objective reality. They become part of the "out there" of the world that we perceive.

But our most important value—our character, soul, psychological self, spiritual being, whatever name one wishes to give it—can never be perceived as part of the "out there." We can never objectify it apart from our own consciousness. Yet we desire and need the fullest possible experience of the reality and objectivity of that compound of consciousness, our self, because our concept of who we are, of the person we have evolved into, is central to all our motivation.

In interaction with other human beings—first as a child, when our sense of identity is in the early stages of emerging, and then in more complex ways appropriate to adulthood—we seek this experience of visibility.

One of the reasons I so much admire the work of the late child psychologist Haim Ginott is that Ginott was a genius at teaching parents and teachers how to interact with children in ways that provide an experience of enriched visibility and self-esteem.[20, 28, 29, 30]

A favorite adecdote of mine, taken from Ginott's *Between Parent and Teenager,* illustrates some of the principles I have been discussing above and has special relevance for the issue of visibility:

David, age seventeen, was interviewed for a summer job, but was rejected. He returned home disappointed and depressed. Father felt sympathy for his son and conveyed it effectively.
  Father: You really wanted this job, didn't you?
  David: I sure did.
  Father: And you were so well-equipped for it, too.
  David: Yeah! a lot of good that did me.
  Father: What a disappointment.
  David: It sure is, Dad.
  Father: Looking forward to a job and having it slip away just when you need it is tough.
  David: Yeah, I know.
  There was silence for a moment. Then David said: "It's not the end of the world. I'll find another job."

Let us pause on this interaction a moment.

It is very likely that at the same time the boy is feeling disappointed and depressed, he is *resisting* the feeling of disappointment and depression; he is tensing his body against it to shut off and deny his emotions. By recognizing what the boy would necessarily feel, by naming it in words, and by communicating benevolent acceptance and respect, the father is in effect permitting the boy to experience his emotions fully, to accept and integrate them into conscious awareness.

We do not fully explain the healing effect of the father's response if we say merely that the boy feels better because he received sympathy. He feels better because his feelings do not remain trapped within him. He is able to assimilate the painful experience and therefore move beyond it; his natural, healthy sense of reality is now able to assert itself.

Most parents do not respond to such situations like the father in Ginott's example; they respond instead in a manner likely to prolong and aggravate the depression. Ginott gives seven examples of common types of destructive response perpetrated by parents, which I would like to quote:[29]

> "What did you expect? To get the first job you wanted? Life is not like that. You may have to go to five or even ten interviews before you are hired."
>
> "Rome was not built in one day, you know. You are still very young, and your whole life is in front of you. So, chin up. Smile and the world will smile with you. Cry and you will cry alone. I hope it will teach you not to count your chickens before they are hatched."
>
> "When I was your age I went looking for my first job. I shined my shoes, got a haircut, put on clean clothes, and carried the *Wall Street Journal* with me. I knew how to make a good impression."
>
> "I don't see why you should feel so depressed. There is really no good reason for you to be so discouraged. Big deal! One job did not work out. It's not worth even talking about."
>
> "The trouble with you is that you don't know how to talk with people. You always put your foot in your mouth. You lack poise, and you are fidgety. You are too eager, and not patient enough. Besides, you are thin-skinned and easily hurt."
>
> "I am so sorry, dear, I don't know what to tell you. My heart breaks. Life is so much a matter of luck. Other people have all the luck. They know the right people in the right places. We don't know anyone, and no one knows us."
>
> "Everything happens for the best. If you miss one bus, there will soon be another, perhaps a less crowded one. If you don't get one job, you'll get another—perhaps even a better one."

All such responses have this in common: they encourage the

child to deny and repress feelings; they convey lack of confidence in the child's ability to arrive at a healthy, balanced perspective; they alienate the child from his or her experience; and they leave the child feeling invisible. These are the kind of responses that most of us received over and over again in the course of growing up. None of them serves the needs of healthy development or positive self-esteem.

A child who experiences invisibility in the early years of life and who feels badly frustrated with regard to other basic needs—physical contact, for example, or affection, or respect, or recognition, or love, or confidence in his or her strengths—is caught in a universe that is not only painful but bewildering. The child has almost no way to understand his or her suffering, which makes the suffering harder to bear. In addition to feeling pain, the child feels helpless.

A child of four or five can hardly be expected to think, "I understand why daddy won't play with me or allow me to sit on his knee. No need for me to take it personally. It's just that daddy's father was a terribly repressed man, cut off from his own feelings and emotions. He was so cold and unfeeling in the way he brought up daddy that when daddy was a little boy, he shut down emotionally, he numbed himself in order not to feel the pain. He's kept himself numb through his whole life, and now he doesn't know what to do. It's not that he intends to hurt me. But if he were to open himself to me and to my needs, he would have to reconnect with a small, lonely, abandoned little boy in himself—and that would be too painful for daddy."

A little girl can hardly be expected to say, "I understand why mommy shouts and screams so much. It's not really me she's angry at. It's just that daddy almost never makes love with her, and his coldness and lack of affection is tormenting her unbearably—and she doesn't know what to do. Her nerves are torn to shreds. So she explodes over anything and everything. And it's easier to get mad at me than at daddy."

No, this is not the typical thinking of children. From their point of view, what is happening is incomprehensible. All they know for certain is that they hurt.

And to believe that their hurt bears no important relation to their own actions but is merely the end product of unsolved problems residing within their parents would only generate an intensfied feeling of powerlessness. They cannot solve their parents' problems. So what are they to do?

At this point, the need for intelligibility and the need for an experience of efficacy in effect conspire against the child. They often lead the child to a solution that yields short-term benefits while laying the foundation for a long-term disaster in which self-esteem turns against itself. The need for the experience of efficacy turns into a tool of self-destruction.

The solution consists of some variant of the idea "There's something wrong with me. It's my fault. I'm bad in some way. I'm wrong somehow. I'm not enough. I'm unlovable. I'm undeserving." For the child, this self-condemnation is a *survival strategy*—the self is attacked at one level in order to protect some sense of efficacy at another.

An analogy may prove helpful. When human beings developed the notion of a God who is omnisicient and omnipotent, they quickly added the attribute all-good. It would be too terrifying to imagine a capricious or sadistic God. Therefore, if disaster befalls, the fault must be ours. Someone or something must be sacrificed to appease this God.

A child's relationship to his parents is in some way like our relationship to this God.

So if I suffer, let me believe I have committed some offense, even though I don't understand what it is. It is too terrifying to imagine that my parents do not know what they are doing. I will disown what I see, repress what I feel—and take the guilt upon myself. And if only I can discover the actions that will please my parents, *then* will I receive the kindness and nurturing I crave.

The problem is compounded by the fact that when we begin to think that we are bad, we usually proceed to prove ourselves right. We strike a younger sibling, we smash a friend's toy, we tell lies, we get pregnant at the age of fourteen, we get arrested for reckless driving at the age of sixteen, and so on.

In the early years of practicing psychotherapy, I recall being puzzled by the intense attachment that clients seemed to have for their own guilt. They would come to therapy, talk about feeling bad or unworthy or unlovable or undeserving, and when I would ask, in effect, "What's so bad about you?" they were rarely able to cite instances of wrongdoing that were remotely commensurate with the degree of their self-condemnation. When I suggested that perhaps they were being too hard on themselves, they looked at me as if I were annoying, irrelevant, and insensitive to the reality of the situation—which I was. I had not yet discovered the functional utility of their self-condemnation, within the context of their private model of self-in-the-world.

Slowly I began to realize the survival value of their self-blame. Unless they came to see not only that their strategy was obsolete but that superior alternatives for living were possible for them, they would not abandon the only life belt they had ever known.

When I began working with the sentence-completion technique, I found the way to demonstrate easily, to myself and my clients, the functional utility of much of their self-condemnation. The essence of the sentence-completion technique is that the client is given a sentence stem by the therapist and asked to keep repeating the stem, adding a different ending each time, generally going as rapidly as possible, without worrying whether each ending is literally true and without worrying whether one ending might conflict with another.*

Whenever I suspected the presence of the problem I have been discussing, I asked the individual to work with the stem "If it turns out I'm not a bad person and never was—." Here are the kind of endings I hear over and over again.

> *If it turns out I'm not a bad person and never was—*
> Then I don't understand mother.
> What has my whole life been about?
> My father was crazy!
> I don't understand anything or anybody!
> No, no, this is too frightening even to think about!
> Then what was the matter with my parents?
> I want to kill mother!
> I feel rage!

---

*The sentence-completion technique is described in some detail in *The Romantic Love Question & Answer Book* and in *If You Could Hear What I Cannot Say*

I feel fear!
I feel my whole life has been a sham!
I'm so hurt and angry!
Then it's all been so unfair!
Then I'm an orphan, and I've always been an orphan!
Then why did they do the things they did?
How am I ever going to understand anything?
I'm alone, I'm alone, I'm alone.

The child within us, who long ago turned to self-condemnation to make sense out of the world and to survive, can have great difficulty, even now, relinquishing the notion of "badness." We cling to the strategy of self-blame, perpetuating it by behaviors we ourselves condemn, not ever noticing that the need for the strategy has long passed, that the strategy that may have helped us at age five is killing us at age thirty-five, forty-five, fifty-five, or sixty-five.

When clients in therapy come to understand this, they begin to realize that the most courageous task life may ever ask of them is to relinquish their attachment to the vision of themselves as inadequate, unworthy, not enough. Because on the day they give up that strategy, they will stand face to face with the fact of their own aloneness and with a need to accept responsibility for their own existence as adults.

When I propose, without explanation, that clients experiment with the following stem, they typically respond with such endings as these, which speak for themselves.

If I were to admit how much I secretly like myself—
    I couldn't pretend to be helpless anymore.
    I would no longer be my parents' child.
    My family would hate me.
    I'd be on my own.
    I'd have to do something with my life.
    I'd realize that the way I'm living is ridiculous.
    I'd have more energy.
    I'd take more risks.
    I'd want more out of life.
    I wouldn't put up with being treated badly.
    I'd have more ambition.

I'd have to change.
I'd have to be more vulnerable.
I'd be scared.
I'd be free.

As adults, there are many additional payoffs to self-blame. People can tell themselves that they have higher standards than others. They can manipulate others into feeling sorry for them and assuring them that they are better than they think. They can send out the signal (to themselves as well as to others) "Expect nothing of me—I'm inadequate." They can remain where they are, stuck, paralyzed, passive, unresponsible, and unresponsive to the challenges of life.

Just as one of the greatest gifts a parent can give a child is projection of a belief in the child's competence and worth, so one of the greatest gifts we can often give another human being is not to buy at face value his or her negative self-esteem. When we deal with human beings as if we expect them to be rational, we increase the probability that they will be honest. And the same principle holds true for self-responsibility or any other virtue we wish to encourage. If, on the other hand, we deal with people as if we expect the worst, we tend to get it.

This principle has been most intensively studied in the context of parent-child and teacher-student relationships. But it applies to all human encounters. Virtually everything discussed in this chapter describes principles that apply to all caring relationships. I might go farther and say to all truly human relationships.

One of the characteristics of good relationships—love relationships or friendships—is that they have a mutually enhancing effect on feelings of self-worth.

But sometimes people confuse the desire to feel seen, visible, understood, or appreciated with the desire to be "approved of" or "validated." These are not quite the same thing. The desire to be validated, confirmed, approved of, in our being and behavior, is normal. I call such a desire irrational or pathological only when it gains such ascendancy in our hierarchy of values that we will sacrifice honesty and integrity in order to achieve it, in which case we clearly suffer from poor self-esteem.

I want to emphasize that the desire for visibility is not an expression of a weak or uncertain ego or of low self-esteem. On the contrary, the lower our self-esteem, the more we feel (at least in part) the need to hide, and the more ambivalent our feelings toward visibility are likely to be—we both long for and are terrified by it. The more we take pride in who we are, the more transparent we are willing to be. I might also add: the more transparent *we are eager to be.*

One of the characteristics of a self-esteem deficiency is an excessive preoccupation with gaining the approval and avoiding the disapproval of others, a hunger for validation and support at every moment of our existence. Some people dream of finding this validation and support in "love." But because the problem is essentially internal, because the person does not believe in him- or herself, no outside source can ever satisfy this hunger, except momentarily. The hunger is not for visibility; it is for self-esteem. And this cannot be supplied by others.

To the extent that we have successfully evolved toward good self-esteem, we hope and expect that others will *perceive* our value, not *create* it. We want others to see us as we actually are—even to help us see ourselves more clearly—but not to invent us out of their own fantasies. Even if the other person's fantasies concerning us are complimentary, we feel invisible, unseen; we feel unreal to the person who may be professing to adore us. In the responses of others, we long for *appropriateness.*

The unfortunate truth is that most human beings, from childhood on, are the recipients of many inappropriate responses. They are the survivors of many occasions when they were transparently lied to, when their person was not respected, their dignity not acknowledged, their thoughts met with indifference, their feelings denied or condemned. And because this state of affairs is so widespread, when we meet a person of high self-esteem we are probably looking at a heroic attainment. We are probably looking at a person who knows how to honor the self, even without support.

Some psychologists look for the "causes" of a person's behavior exclusively in the person's history, believing that there are a number of people in our past who made us what we are today. If they see a person with good self-esteem, they want to know who "made" him or her that way. And if they see a person with poor self-esteem, they want to know who is responsible, since they assume it is not the person they are looking at. They overlook that we are not merely passive reactors but active contestants in the drama of our lives.

Which leads me to the story with which I would like to conclude this chapter.

Once upon a time there were two brothers who aroused the interest of a psychologist. One brother was an alcoholic, while the other hardly touched liquor at all. The psychologist, curious as to the "causes" of this difference, undertook to interview each man separately.

To the alcoholic he said, "You've been an alcoholic for most of your adult life. Why do you suppose that is?" The man responded, "That's easy to explain. You see, my father was an alcoholic. You might say I learned to drink at my father's knee."

To the man who hardly touched liquor at all the psychologist said, "You don't like to drink. How come?" The man responded, "That's easy to explain. You see, my father was an alcoholic. You might say I learned very early in life that alcohol can be poison."

Ultimately, we are responsible for the life decisions we make. We are responsible for the conclusions we draw from our experience. The kind of decisions and conclusions we arrive at inevitably reflect the mental operations through which we process the events of our life. Those mental operations are the single most decisive factor to our level of self-esteem. Let us turn, therefore, to the internal sources of self-appraisal.

4

Generating Positive Self-Esteem

Since the need for self-esteem arises from the fact that the function of our consciousness is volitional, it follows that we should judge ourselves by that which is in our volitional control—for example, our rationality, honesty, integrity. To judge ourselves by that which is beyond our volitional control—for example, that which depends on the will and choices of others—is subversive to healthy self-esteem.

Recognizing that self-esteem pertains to the issue of our fundamental appropriateness to life and, therefore, to our mental operations, we can readily appreciate the error of measuring our worth by such standards as our popularity, influence, affluence, material possessions, or good looks.

Since we are social beings, some measure of esteem from others is necessary; but to tie our self-assessment to the good opinion of others is to place ourselves at their mercy in the most humiliating way. And what are we to do when the persons whose esteem we desire have different expectations, so that to gain the approval of one of our significant others is to risk the disapproval of another?

Or again, we may take pleasure in an attractive appearance, but to tie our self-esteem to our appearance is to be in growing terror with every passing year as the marks of age inevitably advance upon us. And if our good looks are far superior to our behavior, they will hardly heal the psychic wounds inflicted by dishonesty, irresponsibility, or irrationality.

In choosing to focus on and emphasize the volitional function of consciousness, I have no wish to ignore or deny the powerful role of the subconscious, by which I mean the wide range of mental processes and contents that lie outside awareness. Clearly the self includes more than that of which we are consciously aware, and we are influenced in any number of ways by factors operating beneath explicit awareness. This is one of the reasons why our free will is not unlimited. Nonetheless, our psychological freedom is a powerful force within our psyche. If conscious intentions and goals counted for nothing, we would all be existentially and intellectually impotent. Admittedly, our freedom exists within limits. Admittedly, we can be under the sway of forces we do not recognize or understand. But in the possibility of self-awareness and self-monitoring lies the possibility of change and evolution— and some reasonable measure of control over our existence.

A commitment to awareness—the will to understand—is the central pillar of positive self-esteem.

The potential range of our awareness depends on the extent of our intelligence, on the breadth of our abstract capacity. But the principle of commitment to awareness, or the will to understand, remains the same on all levels of intelligence. It entails the behavior of seeking to integrate, to the best of our knowledge and ability, that which enters our mental field—as well as the effort to keep expanding that field.

The beginning of self-assertion is the assertion of consciousness itself, the act of seeing and of seeking to grasp that which we see, of hearing and of seeking to grasp that which we hear—of responding to life actively rather than passively. This is the foundation of honoring the self.

We have already seen that many children undergo experiences that place enormous obstacles in the way of the healthy development of this attitude. A child may find the world of parents and other adults incomprehensible and threatening. The self is not nurtured but attacked. After a number of unsuccessful attempts to understand adult policies, statements, and behavior, some children give up—and take the blame for their feelings of helplessness. Often they sense, miserably, desperately, and inarticulately, that there is something terribly wrong—with their elders, or with themselves, or with *something*. What they often come to feel is: "I'll never understand people; I'll never be able to do what they expect of me; I don't know what's right or wrong, and I'm never going to know."

The child who continues to struggle to make sense out of the world and the people in it, however, is developing a powerful source of strength, no matter what the anguish or bewilderment experienced. Caught in a particularly cruel, frustrating, and irrational environment, he or she will doubtless feel alienated from many of the people in the immediately surrounding world, and legitimately so. But the child will not feel alienated from reality, will not feel, at the deepest level, incompetent to live—or at least he or she has a relatively good chance to avoid this fate.

The growing individual who retains a commitment to awareness learns subjects, acquires skills, accomplishes tasks—reaches goals. And of course these successes validate and reinforce the choice to think. The sense of being appropriate to life feels natural.

A commitment to awareness, then—a commitment to thinking as a way of life—is both a source and an expression of positive self-esteem. But often we associate positive self-esteem only with the final result—with knowledge, success, the admiration and appreciation of others—and miss the cause: all the choices that, cumulatively, add up to what we call a commitment to awareness, the will to understand. Thus we can deceive ourselves about the actual sources of positive self-esteem.

The concept of the will to be efficacious is an extension of the will to understand. It places its emphasis on the aspect of perseverance in the face of difficulties: continuing to seek understanding when understanding does not come easily, pursuing the mastery of a skill or the solution to a problem in the face of defeats, maintaining a commitment to goals while encountering many obstacles along the way. The will to be efficacious is the refusal to identify our ego or self with momentary feelings of helplessness and defeat.

All of us know times of bewilderment, despair, and a painful sense of impotence or inadequacy. The question is, Do we allow such moments to define us?

I remember as a child being enormously bewildered by the behavior of adults, by what I perceived as the strangeness and superficiality of their values, by the lack of congruence between statements and feelings, by an anxiety that seemed to saturate much of the atmosphere around me, and by the overwhelming sense that often the adults did not know what they were doing, that they were lost and helpless while pretending to be in control. This experience was painful and at times frightening. I desperately wanted to understand why human beings behaved as they did. Somewhere in my mind, at quite a young age, there must have been the conviction that knowledge is power, safety, security, and serenity. Doubtless this conviction played a significant role in my choice of profession.

Many years ago I witnessed an encounter between two colleagues, a psychologist and a psychiatrist, that was important for my own understanding of the issue I am discussing. The two men were first cousins and had grown up in similar environments. They shared many painful memories of the behavior of their elders and other relatives. "You survived all that in a way I didn't," the psychiatrist said to the psychologist. "They didn't get to you. I always wondered what made you persevere. Because I didn't. I gave up in some way."

The psychologist answered, "I do recall feeling quite overwhelmed many times. But somewhere deep in my body was a voice saying, 'Don't give up. Hang on.' Hang on to staying conscious, I suppose. Hang on to trying to understand. Don't give up the conviction that it's possible to be in control of your life. Obviously those weren't the words I used as a child, but that was the meaning. That's what I clung to."

"The will to be efficacious," I volunteered impulsively. The will to be efficacious—here was a concept that helped me explain something I had observed in my clients and students, the principle to help me understand the difference between those who felt fundamentally defeated by life and those who did not.

The will to be efficacious—the refusal of a human consciousness to accept helplessness as its permanent and unalterable condition.

It is impressive to see a person who has been battered by life in many ways, who is torn by a variety of unsolved problems, who may be alienated from many aspects of the self—and yet who is still fighting, still struggling, still striving to find the path to a fulfilling existence, moved by the wisdom of knowing, "I am more than my problems."

Having the will to be efficacious does not mean that we deny or disown feelings of inefficacy when they arise; it means that we do not accept them as permanent. We can feel temporarily helpless without defining our essence as helplessness. We can feel temporarily defeated without defining our essence as failure. We can allow ourselves to feel temporarily hopeless, overwhelmed, while preserving the knowledge that after a rest, we will pick up the pieces as best we can and start moving forward again. Our vision of our life extends beyond the feelings of the moment. Our concept of self can rise above today's adversity. This is one of the forms of heroism possible to a volitional consciousness.

At this point a question might arise: Can one be of modest intelligence and still enjoy good self-esteem?

No study has ever suggested that good self-esteem correlates with IQ. And this is not surprising. Self-esteem is a function, not of our native endowment, but of our manner of using our consciousness—the choices we make concerning awareness, the honesty of our relationship to reality, the level of our personal integrity.

To repeat, self-esteem is neither competitive nor comparative. Its context is always the individual's relationship to self and to the choices of self. A person of high intelligence and high self-esteem does not feel *more* appropriate to life or *more* worthy of happiness than a person of high self-esteem and more modest intelligence.

An analogy may prove helpful. Two persons may be equally healthy and physically fit, but one is stronger than the other; the one who is stronger does not experience a higher level of physical well-being; one can merely do some things the other cannot. Looking at them from the outside, we may say that one enjoys certain advantages over the other. But this does not mean that there is a difference in the internal feeling of wellness and aliveness.

Just as brain endowment is far from the most significant issue with regard to the will to understand and the will to be efficacious, so is it far from the most significant consideration relative to another of the key pillars of healthy self-esteem: independence.

Intellectual independence is implicit in the commitment to awareness or the will to understand. A person cannot think through the mind of another. We can learn from one another, but knowledge

54

entails understanding, not mere repetition or imitation. We can either exercise our own mind or pass on to others the responsibility of knowledge and evaluation and accept their verdicts more or less uncritically. The choice we make is crucial for the way we experience ourselves and for the kind of life we create.

That we are sometimes influenced by others in ways we do not recognize hardly alters the fact that there is a distinction between the psychology of those who try to understand things for themselves, think for themselves, judge for themselves, and those to whom such a possibility rarely occurs. What is crucial here is the matter of intention, the matter of an individual's goal.

I recall a client in therapy once saying to me, "I can't understand why I'm always relying on the opinions of other people." I asked her, "As you were growing up, did you ever *want* to be independent, did you ever think of learning to be independent— did you ever make independence your goal?" She pondered for a moment, then replied, "No." I said, "No need to be surprised, then, that you didn't arrive there."

To speak of "thinking independently" is useful because the redundancy has value in terms of emphasis. Often what people call "thinking" is merely recycling the opinions of others. So we can say that thinking independently—about our work, our relationships, the values that will guide our life, the goals we will set for ourselves—enhances self-esteem. And healthy self-esteem results in a natural inclination to think independently.

Seeing only the tail end of the process I am describing, a person might say, "It's easy for him to think independently. Look at how much self-esteem he has." But self-esteem is not a given; it is acquired. And one of the ways it is acquired is by thinking independently when it may not be easy to do so, when it may even be frightening, when the person doing the thinking is struggling with feelings of uncertainty and insecurity and is choosing to persevere nonetheless. It is not always easy to stand by our own judgment, and if it has become easy, that itself is a psychological victory—because in the past there were certainly times when it was not easy, when the pressures against independent thought were considerable, and when we had to confront and endure anxiety.

When a child finds that his or her perceptions, feelings, or judgments conflict with those of parents or other family members, and the question arises of whether to heed the voice of self or to disown it in favor of the voice of others; when a woman believes that her husband is wrong on some fundamental issue, and the question arises of whether to express her thoughts or to suppress them and thus protect the "closeness" of the relationship; when an artist or scientist suddenly sees a path that would carry him or her far from the consensual beliefs and values of colleagues, far from the mainstream of contemporary orientation and opinion, and the question arises of whether to follow that lonely path wherever it leads or to draw back—the issue and the challenge in all such situations remain the same. Should one honor one's inner signals or disown them? Independence versus conformity, self-expression versus self-repudiation, self-assertion versus self-surrender.

Innovators and creators are persons who can to a higher degree than average accept the condition of aloneness. They are more willing to follow their own vision, even when it takes them far from the mainland of the human community. Their anxiety, to whatever extent it exists, does not deter them. This is one of the secrets of their power. That which we call "genius" has a great deal to do with courage and daring, a great deal to do with sheer nerve.

We are social animals. While it may sometimes be necessary, we do not normally enjoy long periods of being alienated from the thinking and beliefs of those around us, especially those we respect and love. One of the most important forms of heroism is the heroism of consciousness, the heroism of thought: the willingness to tolerate aloneness.

Like every other psychological trait, independence is a matter of degree. Although no one is perfectly independent and no one is hopelessly dependent all of the time, the higher the level of our independence and the more willing we are to think for ourselves, the higher the level of our self-esteem.

Part of thinking independently is learning to differentiate between facts on the one hand and wishes and fears on the other. The task is sometimes difficult because thoughts themselves are invariably touched or even saturated with feeling.

Still, on many occasions we can recognize that the desire to perform some action is not proof that we should perform it: running out of the room in the midst of an argument when we become upset, for example. And the fact that we may be afraid to perform some action is not proof that we should avoid performing it: going to a physician for a checkup when there are signs of illness, for another example.

If we make a purchase we know we cannot afford and avoid thinking about impending bills we will not be able to pay, we have surrendered our consciousness to our wishes. If we ignore signs of danger in a marriage and then profess to be bewildered and dismayed when the marriage finally explodes, we have paid the penalty for sacrificing consciousness to fear.

As far as our self-esteem is concerned, the issue is not whether we are flawless in executing the task of distinguishing among facts, wishes, and fears and choosing consciousness over some form of avoidance. Rather, the issue is one of our underlying intention. When we describe a person as "basically honest," in the sense meant here, we do not mean that he or she is impervious to the influence of wishes and fears, but rather that there is a pronounced and evident *desire* and *intention* to see things as they are. We cannot always know for certain whether or not we are being rational or honest; but we can certainly be concerned about it, we can certainly care. We are not always free to succeed in our thinking, but we are always free to try.

The accumulated sum of our choices in this matter yields an inner sense of basic honesty or dishonesty—a fundamental responsibility or irresponsibility toward existence. From childhood on, some individuals are far more interested in and respectful of such questions of truth than others. Others operate as if facts need not be facts if we do not choose to acknowledge them, as if truth is irrelevant and lies are lies only if someone finds them out.

As I write these lines, I recall a news article I read recently about a medical researcher of high repute who was discovered to have been faking his data for years while piling up grant after grant and honor after honor. There is no way for self-esteem not to have been a casualty of such behavior, even before his fakery was revealed. He knowingly chose to live in a world of essential unreality, where his achievements and prestige were equally unreal.

Contrast this with the psychology of scientists who patiently and assiduously seek out evidence that will *disprove* their hypotheses. They understand that the unreal has no value.

The task of consciousness is to perceive that which exists, to the best of our ability. To honor reality—the perception of that which exists—is to honor consciousness; to honor consciousness is to honor the self.

All of the foregoing leads us very naturally to still another pillar of healthy self-esteem: integrity.

As we grow older and develop our own values and standards, the maintenance of personal integrity assumes increasing importance for our self-evaluation. *Integrity* means the integration of convictions, standards, beliefs—and behavior. When our behavior resonates with our professed values, and philosophy and action are integrated, we have integrity.

When we behave in ways that conflict with our judgments of what is appropriate, we lose face in our own eyes. We respect ourselves less. If the policy becomes habitual, we trust ourselves less—or cease to trust ourselves at all.

In their eagerness to disassociate themselves from philosophy in general and ethics in particular, psychologists are often uncomfortable about anything that sounds like a reference to morality in the context of psychotherapy or psychological well-being. In consequence, they can miss the obvious fact that integrity is, in effect, one of the guardians of mental health and that it is cruel and misleading to encourage people to believe that practicing "unconditional positive regard" toward themselves will bring them to undiluted self-love, irrespective of the question of their personal integrity.

Sometimes an individual seeks to escape from the burden of integrity by disavowing, or professing to disavow, all values and standards. The truth is, human beings cannot successfully regress to a lower level of evolution; we cannot draw back to a time before thinking in principles and long-range planning were possible. We are conceptual beings, and we cannot function successfully as anything less. We need values to guide our actions. We need principles to guide our lives. Our standards may be appropriate or inappropriate to the requirements of our life and well-being, but to live without standards of any kind is impossible. So profound a rebellion against our nature as the attempt to discard all values, principles, and standards is itself an expression of impoverished self-esteem and a guarantee the impoverishment will be ongoing.

While it is easy enough to recognize, at a commonsense level, the relationship between self-esteem and integrity, the issue of living up to our standards is not always as simple as it may first appear. What if our standards are mistaken or irrational?

We may accept a code of values that does violence to our needs as living organisms. For example, certain religious teachings implicitly or explicitly damn sex, damn pleasure, damn the body, damn ambition, damn material success, damn (for all practical purposes) the enjoyment of life on earth. This acceptance of life-denying standards is an enormous problem and one to which we shall have to return.

Once we see that living up to our standards appears to be leading us toward self-destruction, the time has obviously come to question our standards, rather than simply resigning ourselves to living without integrity. We must summon up the courage to challenge some of our deepest assumptions concerning what we have been taught to regard as the good.

To cite a number of random examples of the kind commonly encountered in the practice of psychotherapy: women who struggle with the moral dilemmas created by the Catholic church's prohibition of birth control devices and abortion; employees in government agencies who, appalled by the magnitude of bureaucratic corruption, feel themselves caught in conflict between their notion of patriotism and good citizenship on the one hand and the demands of individual conscience on the other; hard-working, ambitious businessmen who had been encouraged at the start of their careers to be productive and industrious but who, when they finally committed the sin of succeeding, were confronted with the disorienting biblical pronouncement that it shall be easier for a camel to pass through the eye of a needle than for a rich man to enter the kingdom of heaven; wives who suddenly sense that the traditional view of woman-as-servant-to-man is a morality of self-annihilation; young men struggling with the dilemma of complying with or fleeing from military conscription; former nuns and priests disenchanted with the religious institutions to which they

had given their allegiance and striving to define their values outside the context of a tradition they could no longer accept; rabbis
or former rabbis with precisely the same problem; young persons
rebelling against the values of their parents and not knowing what
vision of the good to live by instead.

Such conflicts and the manner in which they are resolved or
left unresolved necessarily affect the quality of the individual's
self-esteem beccause they affect the experience of integrity. And
integrity is a prerequisite of high self-esteem.

No discussion of the central pillars of healthy self-esteem
would be complete that did not acknowledge the profoundly important role of self-responsibility as a basic life orientation. Self-
responsibility is essential to self-esteem, and it is also a reflection
or manifestation of positive self-esteem. The relation between self-
esteem and its pillars is always reciprocal.

Working with clients in psychotherapy, I often see that the
most radical transformation occurs after the client's realization
that no one is coming to the rescue. "When I finally allowed myself
to face fully my own responsibility for my life," more than one
client has said to me, "I began to grow. I began to change. And
my self-esteem began to rise."

I am responsible for my choices and my actions. Not responsible as the recipient of moral blame or guilt, but responsible as
the chief causal agent in my life and behavior. Further, self-
responsibility means acceptance of my basic aloneness and acceptance of responsibility for the attainment of my own goals.

The appreciation of self-responsibility can be an exhilarating
and empowering experience. It places our life back in our own
hands. For example, a client in therapy learns to question, "Why
and how do I make myself so passive? What do I tell myself to
keep myself so passive?" rather than bemoaning, "Why am I so
passive?" Instead of asserting that he can't care about anything,
the client learns to explore why and how he prevents himself from
experiencing strong feelings about anything. "Why," in this context, means, "For what purpose?" Instead of saying, "Why does
the back of my neck become painfully tense?" the client learns to
say, "What feelings am I trying to avoid experiencing by tensing
my neck muscles?" Instead of complaining that people are so often

taking advantage of her, the client learns to say, "Why and how do I invite or encourage people to take advantage of me?" Instead of complaining, "No one understands me," the client asks, "Why and how do I make it difficult for people to understand me?" Instead of saying, "Why do women always turn away from me?" the client confronts the question, "Why and how do I cause women to turn away from me?" Instead of moaning, "I always fail at whatever I attempt," the client begins to consider, "Why and how do I always cause myself to fail at whatever I attempt?"

I do not mean to imply that a person never suffers through accident or through the fault of others, nor that a person is responsible for everything in life that may happen to him or her. We are not omnipotent.

But self-responsibility is clearly indispensable to good self-esteem. Avoiding self-responsibility victimizes us with regard to our own life; it leaves us helpless. It is just this view from which many people need to emancipate themselves if they are ever to evolve to a nontragic sense of life.

Much more remains to be said about the conditions of successful self-esteem—more than can be contained in this chapter. But everything I have discussed thus far is traceable back to mental operations, and this will continue to be true in the material that follows. This is the essential point at the base of the entire presentation. Self-esteem is rooted internally, rather than in external successes or failures.

The failure to understand this principle causes an incalculable amount of unnecessary anguish and self-doubt. If we judge ourselves by criteria that entail factors outside our volitional control, the result, unavoidably, is a precarious self-esteem that is in chronic jeopardy. But our self-esteem need not be affected or impaired if, in spite of our best efforts, we fail in a particular undertaking, even though we will not experience the same emotion of pride that we would have felt if we had succeeded.

Further, we need to remember that the self is not a static, finished entity, but a continually evolving creation, an unfolding of our potentialities, expressed in our choices, decisions, thoughts, judgments, responses, and actions. To view our self as basically and unalterably good or bad—independent of our present and future manner of functioning—is to negate the facts of freedom, self-determination, and self-responsibility. We always contain within ourselves the possibility of change; we need never be the prisoner of yesterday's choices.

The final issue I wish to introduce here—self-acceptance—is especially pertinent to those of us who are unhappy with the way we experience ourselves and are seeking a change in self-concept.

If we are to grow and change, we must begin by learning self-acceptance. In my experience, self-acceptance is not an easy concept for most people to understand. The tendency is to equate self-acceptance with approval of every aspect of our personality (or physical appearance) and with the denial that any change or improvement might be desirable.

To be self-accepting does not mean to be without a wish to change, improve, evolve. It means not to be at war with ourselves—not to deny the reality of what is true of us right now, at this moment of our existence. We deal once more with the issue of respect for and acceptance of facts—in this case, the facts of our own being.*

To accept ourselves is to accept the fact that what we think, feel, and do are all expressions of the self *at the time they occur.*

So long as we cannot accept the fact of what we are at any given moment of our existence, so long as we cannot permit ourselves fully to be aware of the nature of our choices and actions, cannot admit the truth into our consciousness, we cannot change.[5]

Accepting what I am requires that I approach the contemplation of my own experience with an attitude that makes the concepts of approval or disapproval irrelevant: *the desire to be aware.*

There is still a deeper level on which we need to understand self-acceptance. *Self-acceptance,* in the ultimate sense, refers to an attitude of self-value and self-commitment that derives fundamentally from the fact that I am alive and conscious. It is deeper than self-esteem. It is a prerational, premoral act of self-affirmation—a kind of primitive egoism that is the birthright of every

---

*I explore this issue in some depth in *The Disowned Self.*

conscious organism, and yet that human beings have the power to act against or nullify.

An attitude of self-acceptance is precisely what an effective psychotherapist appeals to or strives to awaken in a person of even the lowest self-esteem.[72] This attitude can inspire a person to face whatever he or she most dreads to encounter within, without collapsing into self-hatred, repudiating the value of his or her person, or surrendering the will to live. Thus, a person might be unhappy about experiencing poor self-esteem yet accept it along with the self-doubts and feelings of guilt—"I accept them as part of how I experience myself right now."

Self-acceptance, at this level, is unconditional. Self-esteem is not, and cannot be.

When I endeavor to communicate the concept of self-acceptance to clients in therapy, I am sometimes met with protests. "But I don't *like* the way I am. I want to be different."

Or: "I don't like to be afraid of what people think of me. I hate that part of myself. I wish I could get rid of it."

Or: "I'm ashamed of the fact that I feel I can't say no to any man who wants to sleep with me. I loathe myself for being that way. Am I supposed to approve of it?"

Or: "I see people I admire—people who are strong, confident, assertive. That's the way I want to be. Why should I accept being a nonentity?"

We can note here the two fallacies already mentioned: the belief that if we accept who and what we are, we must approve of everything about us, and the belief that if we accept who and what we are, we are indifferent to change or improvement.

Even to criticize our own behavior implies that we are competent to make such judgments, however. And the desire to change, to improve ourselves, implies that we are worthy and deserving of such growth. Some people in psychotherapy struggle with this dilemma in the very fact of their treatment. "Do I *deserve* to have this much time and money invested in my problems and struggle for happiness?" Without this most primitive level of self-value and self-acceptance, no further evolution is possible to us. But if we understand self-acceptance in this way, it becomes a powerful lever for change—including growth in self-esteem.

I recall a female client who insisted that she could not possibly feel anything but self-loathing, because of her inability to refuse any man's sexual overtures. I asked her if it was really true that she saw herself as a woman who could not say no. "Yes," she replied tearfully. I asked her if she was willing to accept that fact. "I hate it!" she replied. I said that since it was true that was how she saw herself, was she willing to accept that truth and acknowledge it? After some initial reluctance she said, "I accept the fact that I see myself as a woman who can't say no." When I asked her how saying that made her feel, she replied, "Angry."

Then I asked her if she could accept the fact that she feels very angry when she acknowledges perceiving herself as a woman who can't say no. She said indignantly, "I *refuse* to accept the fact that I am that kind of person!"

I asked her, "Then how can you ever hope to change?"

I guided her through several psychological exercises aimed at facilitating her acceptance of her present state. Essentially they consisted of helping her to experience that this was the way she was *right now*. After a while, she reported a change of feeling; she gave up the sense of fighting herself; she began relaxing into the feeling that "at this time of my life, this is part of who I am."

"This is so strange," she remarked. "Nothing has changed. I still have the problem. But I feel calmer. I've stopped shouting at myself. It's just . . . a fact about me. I don't like it, but it's a fact. I acknowledge it. Not just with words, but, you know, really accepted as true. Nothing has changed, and yet I feel as if I have more self-respect."

Then she made a significant statement. "And as I begin to accept the reality of what I've been doing, how I've been living, it seems as if it would be much harder to go on doing it—I mean, to go on doing things of which I disapprove, that are humiliating. Perhaps that's why I've resisted accepting it. As soon as you stop fighting and accept, something begins to happen."

There is more I will need to say about self-acceptance, but for the moment I will summarize its relation to change and personal evolution as follows: If I can accept that I am who I am, that I feel what I feel, that I have done what I have done—if I can accept it whether I like all of it or not—then I can accept myself. I can accept my shortcomings, my self-doubts, my poor self-esteem.

And when I can accept all that, I have put myself on the side of reality rather than attempting to fight reality. I am no longer twisting my consciousness in knots to maintain delusions about my present condition. And so I clear the road for the first steps of strengthening my self-esteem.

5

The Problem of Guilt

The essence of guilt, whether major or minor, is moral self-reproach: I did wrong when it was possible for me to do otherwise. Guilt always carries the implication of choice and responsibility, whether or not we are consciously aware of it.

We have already seen that, for a child, self-blame and guilt can have short-term survival value if they appear to make the child's world more intelligible and to offer some sense of control over the child's life. A powerful need to believe that the universe is "just" and that terrible things do not happen to innocent people may carry over into adulthood—for example, when victims of political persecution blame themselves, or are encouraged to do so, rather than confronting the fact that they may be powerless pawns in the hands of irresponsible and evil forces.

Certain contemporary consciousness trainings and alleged spiritual disciplines teach people that they are "responsible for everything that they experience" or that they "create everything that happens to them." They appeal to the need to feel in control, the need to feel effective. But this viewpoint can lead to the conclusion that a one-year-old baby in a country at war is responsible for the experience of being napalmed. And, appallingly, there are those who do not shrink from this conclusion.

Some years ago I found myself on a panel with a well-known psychologist who insisted that unborn children are responsible for selecting their parents—which led him to the conclusion that a battered infant has chosen parents as torturers. He had no answer to the obvious question, Did the parents have any choice in the matter, or were they totally at the mercy of the unborn child's will? The point is, if we are not to corrupt the concept of responsibility, we need to keep it within rational bounds.

The failure to do so is a problem I often encounter in my practice. Someone a client loves—a husband, a wife, a child—is killed in an accident, and even though the client knows the thought is irrational, he or she feels, "Somehow I should have prevented it." Sometimes the guilt is in part fed by regrets over actions taken or not taken while the person was still alive. But in the case of deaths that seem senseless, such as when a person is hit by a careless automobile driver or dies during minor surgery, the survivor may experience an unbearable feeling of being out of control, of being helplessly at the mercy of an event that has no rational significance. In such a case self-blame or self-reproach can ameliorate the anguish, can diminish a sense of impotence. The survivor feels, "If only I had done such and such differently, this terrible accident would not have occurred." Thus guilt serves the need for efficacy by providing an *illusion* of efficacy.

Sometimes this same form of unearned guilt follows a divorce or trouble with one's children. In these situations one feels, "*Somehow* I should have known how to prevent this, *somehow* I should have known what to do"—even when one cannot say what one could have done differently, and even when decisive elements quite outside one's personal control may have been present.

It is not uncommon for such guilts to afflict even persons of fairly healthy self-esteem, temporarily lowering their self-esteem. But when one begins with a lower self-esteem, guilts have a naturally fertile soil in which to grow, thereby worsening an already deficient self-regard.

This is why the protection of self-esteem requires a clear understanding of the limits of volitional responsibility. Where there is no power, there can be no responsibility, and where there is no responsibility, there can be no reasonable self-reproach. Regret, yes; guilt, no.

Where there is neither evasion nor irresponsibility nor conscious breach of integrity, there are no rational grounds for the experience of guilt. There may, naturally, be grounds for pain or regret over errors of judgment. From the point of view of self-esteem, this distinction is of life-and-death importance.

The concept of Original Sin—of guilt where there is no possibility of innocence, no freedom of choice, no alternatives available—is anti-self-esteem by its very nature. It is, therefore, antihuman.

The problem of guilt can take many forms. We shall consider some of the most prevalent.

Perhaps the mildest form of guilt is experienced by those persons who, although they may avoid a great deal of thinking in their lives, about their relationships, work, and their values and goals in general, have not knowingly violated their convictions in any major way, have not attempted to cheat reality and get away with what they regard as the irrational. They may operate at a lower level of consciousness than that of which they are capable, but they are more or less honest within that context.

Those who do act against their moral convictions commonly experience a heavier burden of guilt. But here we must make a major distinction.

There are people who, if they violate their own principles, experience guilt as well as anxiety, but do not, in effect, feel guilty "all the way down." They are protected by the fact that they have independent standards to sustain and integrity to uphold. A person may feel, "It was unworthy of me to fail my own standards in this matter," yet still maintain a decent level of self-esteem.

Guilt tends to be more acute and more painful for those whose approach to moral judgments is implicitly authoritarian. There is no healthy core of rational understanding or independent judgment to protect the transgressors from feelings of fundamental worthlessness when they disobey their significant others. Their anxious feelings of guilt are often experienced as fear of the disapproval of those others. Others are perceived as the voice of objective reality calling them to judgment.

In the practice of therapy, so much of the guilt we encounter has to do with the disapproval or condemnation of significant others, such as parents, that it is never advisable to take declarations of guilt at face value. Often, when a person declares, "I feel guilty over such and such," what the person really means but rarely acknowledges is, "I am afraid that if mother or father knew about what I had done, I would be condemned." We frequently find that the person does not actually regard the action as wrong. In these circumstances, the solution to the problem of "guilt" lies in the courage to heed the voice of the self—in other words, increased autonomy.

For example, a man professes to feel guilty over masturbation because his parents taught him it was sinful. Sometimes a therapist "solves" the problem by substituting his authority for that of the client's parents and assuring the man that masturbation is a perfectly acceptable activity. This is the kind of solution one is especially likely to encounter among practitioners whose approach to therapy is heavily didactic. The assumption is that the man's guilt is caused by his mistaken idea about the morality of masturbation. In my experience I would say that this is the smoke screen problem. It conceals the deeper problem of dependency and fear of self-assertiveness, failure to honor one's own judgment, which means a failure to honor the self.

Sometimes professions of guilt are a smoke screen for disowned feelings of resentment. I have failed to live up to someone else's expectations or standards. I am afraid to admit that I am intimidated by those expectations and standards. I am afraid to acknowledge how angry I am over what is expected of me. So instead I tell myself and others that I feel guilty over failing to do what is right, and I do not have to fear that I will communicate my resentment and place my relationship with others in jeopardy.

When an individual with this problem is guided to recognize, experience, and express the resentment, the "guilt" tends to disappear.

In other words, when I become more honest about my own feelings—which is another form of honoring the self—I give up the need to feel "guilty." And when I do, I am freer to think clearly about values and expectations I may need to challenge.

Without denying that there are times when people genuinely do feel guilty because they have not lived up to standards that they themselves respect, an enormous amount of what people call "guilt" proves to be a cover-up for other feelings that have been disowned, as in the above examples. When I suspect the authenticity of the person's declarations of guilt, sometimes I will ask the client to do completions for the sentence "The good thing about feeling guilty is—." Here are typical responses:

The good thing about feeling guilty is—
    It allows me to remain stuck.
    I don't have to do anything.
    People will feel sorry for me.
    It proves I'm a moral person.
    I don't have to change.
    I can feel superior to other people [who don't have the integrity to feel guilty].
    I can feel sorry for myself.
    I can manipulate other people into telling me I am good.
    I can make my parents right.

Most of these endings are self-explanatory. The last one may not be, and it is profoundly important.

Let us suppose that when we are young our parents communicate that we are bad, for reasons that may have little or nothing to do with our actual behavior. A "good" child is one who adapts to the parents' view of things. So if a child wants to be good and is told that he or she is bad, a painful paradox is generated. Thus:

I want to be good.

My parents tell me I'm bad.

A good child does not contradict his or her parents.

So the way to be good is to be bad.

If I were really to be good, that would make me bad, since my parents have told me I am not good, and it is not right to contradict them.

If I am bad, that makes me good, since I am conforming to my parents' view of things.

On the other hand, if I were to be good, that would make me bad—disobedient and noncompliant.

In other words, if I tie my self-esteem to my parents' approval and the cost of approval is compliance, *then I end up pursuing positive self-esteem by accepting negative self-esteem.*

This is one of the most common problems encountered among

people in therapy. The solution, in principle, again lies in increasing autonomy, shifting the sources of self-esteem from external signals to internal signals, from the parents' judgment to the client's judgment—which means, again, learning to honor the self.

The difficulty many people confront when trying to achieve this shift is the fear of aloneness and self-responsibility. They have never transcended the childhood notion that their relationship to their parents is essential for their survival. Nor have they adequately discovered their own resources in meeting the challenges of life. Consciously or subconsciously, they are still children. Never mind that in reality they may be demonstrably more capable of survival than their parents.

The problem thus described may sound almost embarrassing, which is unfortunate, because to confront it and transcend it is an heroic undertaking—if courage and perseverance are essential criteria of heroism.

We do not transcend by denying or repressing our feelings of dependence, but rather by accepting them, experiencing them, and *then* stepping beyond them by learning to listen to and respect our internal signals—to think for ourselves—and to be guided by our own conclusions.

From the point of view of protecting self-esteem, it is essential to distinguish between rational guilt and self-damnation.

Rational guilt means an authentic evaluation of some action of mine as wrong, a genuine feeling of regret or remorse, and the determination to exercise a better choice in the future. *Self-damnation* is a verdict directed at my person as such and contains a contradiction: If I am irredeemably worthless, who is the person who cares enough to pronounce that verdict? Whose is the soul I have offended? If I am the one who is pronouncing the verdict, then I cannot be totally worthless.

Rational guilt is an alarm signal. It would not serve the purposes of our survival and well-being to be devoid of the capacity for self-reproach. Sometimes, in the state of half-focused awareness, we behave blindly, inappropriately, or irresponsibly, and the first signal to reach our conscious attention is an uneasy feeling that pertains to guilt.

But irrational guilt—which subverts the purposes of survival

71

or well-being—is of virtually epidemic proportions. Thus, a person declares: "I feel guilty for desiring my best friend's wife."

Implication: Our sexual desires are under our direct volitional control and should never flow in an inconvenient or inappropriate direction.

Most likely translation: People whose good opinion I care about would condemn me for having such desires.

Or again: "I feel guilty for being so good-looking."

Implication: My good looks are my reprimand to all those who do not possess them.

Most likely translation: I am afraid of other people's jealousy or envy.

Or: "I feel guilty for being so intelligent."

Implication: I was born with a good brain at the expense of all those who do not possess one; furthermore, since everyone chooses to exercise such potential intelligence as he or she is born with, I deserve no credit for what I have done with my endowment.

Most likely translation: I am afraid of the animosity of those who resent intelligence.

Or: "I feel guilty for having been given preferential treatment by my parents over my sisters, because I was an only son."

Implication: I am morally responsible for the behavior of my parents.

Most likely translation: I feel resentment over the burden and expectations that are the other side of the preferential treatment sons receive.

Or: "I feel guilty because I am human—I was born in sin."

Implication: It is meaningful to speak of guilt in a context where innocence does not exist. Furthermore, I must accept a concept that does violence to reason and morality because authorities proclaim it.

Most likely translation: Those authorities hold a monopoly on morality and moral judgments; who am I to set my judgment against theirs?

Or: "I feel guilty because my parents never loved me."

Implication: My parents' response to me could only have been determined by my own moral character, not by any problems of theirs that might have had nothing to do with me. They must have seen that I was worthless from the very beginning.

Most likely translation: The only way to protect my relationship to them, the only way to remain their child and to keep a sense of belonging, is to accept their judgment and allow them to define me.

Or: "I feel guilty over making a success of my life."

Implication: Not only do I deserve no moral credit for my achievements, but they represent an injustice against all those who, for whatever reason, did not achieve equally. Furthermore, I am in the moral debt of all those who have made less of their lives than I have made of mine.

Most likely translation: If I do not give any indication of feeling proud of what I have accomplished, if I conceal my feelings of pride not only from others but from myself, then perhaps people will forgive me and like me.

Perhaps I should acknowledge that in an age in which egalitarianism appears to be running amok and in which there are some people who believe that inequality of any kind—intelligence, character, wealth, physical attractiveness—implies an injustice on the part of someone toward someone else, certain of the instances of guilt listed above may not be regarded as irrational. Perhaps not only will the above examples resonate to some readers, but some may feel that they represent sound thinking. I will point out that when these attitudes are explored in the context of psychotherapy, what surfaces is not a process of moral reasoning but an uncovering of a deep fear of autonomy, a fear of not "belonging."

There is a paradox in the acceptance of unearned guilt. Very often the result is the creation of real guilt. If, for example, I am afraid to assert my right to exist or be happy, if I lack the courage to be honest about my pride in my achievements or my pleasure in whatever benefits I enjoy, then somewhere deep within there is the uneasy sense of self-betrayal, a surrender of integrity, a capitulation to values and standards I do not honestly respect. And when my self-esteem is undermined, I may go on to perform actions that conflict with principles I do respect.

Just as learning to accept and express feelings of resentment can cause the disappearance of that which a person calls "guilt," a similar procedure with feelings of pride and happiness can dispel feelings of self-reproach that have no valid reason for being. Just as courage may be needed in order for a person to be truthful about feelings of resentment, so too may it be needed before he or she can admit to feelings of pride and happiness. In my experience, more courage seems needed for the latter than for the former.

That guilt, rational or irrational, can have a damaging effect on self-esteem is obvious. Before concluding this discussion, therefore, I want to say a little more about the correction of rational, or realistic, guilt.

Let us suppose that I have done something genuinely wrong by my own standards—say, betrayed a secret entrusted to me by a friend, or claimed credit for an achievement not my own, or been financially dishonest with my employer. Allowing for the fact that sometimes there are special circumstances requiring special considerations, there are, generally speaking, fairly specific steps I can take to free myself of the resultant guilt.

The first is to own the fact that it is I who have taken the action.

The second is to acknowledge explicitly to the relevant person or persons the harm I have done and convey my understanding of the consequences of my behavior, assuming that this is possible.

The third is to take any and all actions available to me that might make amends for or minimize the harm I have done.

Finally, as indicated above, I need to make a firm commitment to behave differently in the future.

In the absence of all of these steps, a person may continue to feel guilty over some wrong behavior, even though it happened years ago, even though his or her psychotherapist has offered the assurance that we all make mistakes, and even though the wronged person may have offered forgiveness.

Sometimes we try to make amends without ever really owning and facing what we have done. Or we keep saying, "I'm sorry." Or we go out of our way to be nice to the person we have wronged without ever dealing with the wrong act itself. Or we ignore the fact that there are specific actions we could take that would undo some of the harm we have done. Sometimes, of course, there is no way to undo the harm, and we must accept that; we cannot do more than is possible. But if we do not do that which is possible and appropriate, guilt tends to linger on.

If we attempt to avoid, disown, and repress our negative feelings, rather than deal with them honestly, all we succeed in doing is driving them underground, and then guilt spreads and diffuses through the entire sense of self. Again, then, we are led back to the importance of awareness—awareness and appropriate action that flows from that awareness.

Action is essential. If we take actions that have damaged our self-esteem, then only by taking the appropriate counteractions can we repair our self-esteem.

I am reminded of a scene in Sir Richard Attenborough's film *Gandhi*. A Hindu comes to Gandhi in great despair and announces, in effect, that he is morally irredeemable because in a fit of rage he has murdered a Muslim child. When asked why he did it, he replies that the Muslims murdered his own child. "I am in hell," the man tells Gandhi. Gandhi replies that there is a way out of hell. He instructs the man to find a child whose own parents have been killed and to raise that child as his own. Then Gandhi adds that the man should be certain that the child is a Muslim—and should raise the child as a Muslim. To a devastating problem Gandhi thus provides an exquisite response, a metaphor for the process I have been describing.

We deceive ourselves if we imagine that we can redeem our self-esteem merely by suffering—or by telling ourselves that there is no way to redeem our self-esteem. With relatively rare exceptions, there is always a way, and it is our responsibility to find it. The challenge is not to surrender to passivity. Passivity—the abdication of the responsibility of action—is the ultimate enemy.

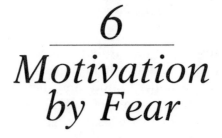

6
Motivation by Fear

To the extent that a person suffers from poor self-esteem, his or her consciousness is ruled by fear: fear of other people, fear of the real or imagined facts about the self that have been evaded or repressed. There is fear of the external world and fear of the internal world.

Feelings of anxiety, insecurity, and self-doubt, the nameless sense of being unfit for reality, inappropriate to the challenges of life, arise inevitably when and if a person fails to attain a reasonably satisfying level of self-confidence and self-respect. Fear thus becomes the central motivating force within the personality.

A man of low self-esteem, for example, becomes a husband and father. He rules his home by evoking fear in his wife and children, using the same fear that motivates him as his chief source of energy and action. He avoids the expressions of pain and unhappiness in their eyes; he avoids their efforts to communicate with him; he becomes sullen and withdrawn when they refuse to obey him. The years go by, and he sees whatever love or respect they once felt for him vanishing. His spirits drop lower and lower. At the age of fifty, he is worn out, depressed, occasionally suicidal in his fantasies. He is the casualty of an uncorrected low self-esteem.

Fear sabotages mind, clarity, efficacy. Fear undermines the sense of personal worth. And actions motivated by fear rather than by confidence are generally the kind of actions that leave an individual feeling diminished in stature.

When a person who suffers from low self-esteem institutes various defenses, or *reality-avoiding strategies*, to escape facing the feeling of deficiency, distortions are inevitably introduced into thinking. The person's mental processes are regulated, not by the goal of apprehending reality clearly, but, at best, by the goal of gaining only such knowledge as is compatible with the maintenance of the defenses.

The individual attempting to counterfeit a healthy self-esteem makes perception of reality conditional; certain considerations supersede reality, facts, and truth in their importance. Thereafter, consciousness is pulled, to a significant and dangerous extent, by the strings of wishes and fears—above all, fears; *they* become the masters; it is to *them*, not to reality, that the individual has to adjust. The individual is thus led to perpetuate and strengthen the same kind of antirational, self-defeating policies that occasioned loss of self-confidence and self-respect in the first place.

Consider, for instance, such a person who possesses the near-delusional image of himself as a daring and shrewd operator who is just one deal away from a fortune. He keeps losing money and suffering defeat in one get-rich-quick scheme after another, always blind to the evidence that his plans are impractical, always brushing aside unpleasant facts, always boasting extravagantly, his eyes on nothing but the hypnotically dazzling image of himself as a brilliantly skillful businessman. He moves from one disaster to another, dreading to discover that the vision of himself that feels like a life belt is, in fact, a noose choking him to death.

Or consider a middle-aged woman whose sense of personal value is crucially dependent on the image of herself as a glamorous, youthful beauty and who therefore perceives every wrinkle on her face as a metaphysical threat to her identity. She plunges into a series of sexual relationships with men more than twenty years her junior, rationalizing each relationship as a grand passion, avoiding the characters and motives of the young men involved, repressing the humiliation she feels in the company of her friends. She constantly seeks the reassurance of fresh admiration, running faster and faster from the haunting, relentless pursuer, which is her own emptiness.

There is no way to preserve the clarity of our thinking so long as there are considerations in our mind, chiefly governed by fear, that take precedence over the knowable facts of reality. There is no way to preserve the uncontaminated power of our intelligence so long as we are implicitly committed to the belief that the maintenance of our positive self-esteem (or our pretense at it) requires that certain facts not be faced.

The misery, the frustration, the terror that characterize the psychological state of so many people testify to two facts: that positive self-esteem is a basic need without which we cannot live the life appropriate to us, and that positive self-esteem is intimately related to honesty and integrity. This is why, in psychotherapy or in life, it is so important to create a context in which a person discovers that it is safe to be truthful—truthful about thoughts, feelings, and behavior. Any time we admit a difficult truth, any time we face that which we have been afraid to face, any time we acknowledge, to ourselves or to others, facts the existence of which we have been evading, any time we are willing to tolerate temporary fear or anxiety on the path to better contact with reality, our self-esteem increases.

Anxiety in general is a psychological alarm signal warning of real or imagined danger to the organism. In varying degrees of intensity, the experience of such anxiety is a human condition.

The anxiety of which I am speaking here, generally described as neurotic or pathological anxiety, is of a very special kind. I prefer to call it *self-esteem anxiety*.

Self-esteem anxiety differs not only from those rationally warranted fears affecting the world at large, such as fear of war or of economic breakdown, but from the ordinary fears of everyday life, such as of standing in the path of an oncoming car. Ordinary fear is a proportionate and localized reaction to a concrete, external, and immediate danger. It differs, also, from objective or normal anxiety in which, like ordinary fear, feelings of apprehension and helplessness are directed toward a specific source, but in which the danger is less immediate and the emotion is more anticipatory, such as the feeling that might overcome a person confronted with signs of some serious illness or might strike parents whose child is in the hands of kidnappers. Fear and objective anxiety vanish when the danger is removed.

On the other hand, self-esteem anxiety is a state of dread experienced in the absence of any actual or impending objectively perceivable threat. Such anxiety does not always appear in an intense or violent form. Many sufferers know it, not as an acute attack of panic or a chronic sense of dread, but only as an occasional uneasiness, a diffuse sense of nervousness and apprehension, coming and going unpredictably, pursuing some incomprehensible pattern of its own—and they are oblivious to how many of their responses are motivated by the desire to escape it.

Whenever a person feels fear, any kind of fear, the response reflects an estimate of some danger, some threat to something valued. In the case of self-esteem anxiety, the thing of value being threatened, ultimately, is the sufferer's *ego*.

By *ego*, to repeat, I mean the unifying center of awareness, the center of consciousness; the ultimate sense of "I"; that which perceives reality, preserves the inner continuity of one's own existence, and generates a sense of personal identity.

Any threat to a human being's ego—anything that he or she experiences as a significant danger to the mind's efficacy and control—is a potential source of self-esteem anxiety. Anything that threatens to collapse the sense of personal worth is a source of self-esteem anxiety.

Certain characteristics link the mildest form of this anxiety to the most extreme. The person feels afraid of nothing in particular and of everything in general. If the fear-struck sufferer tries to offer a rational explanation for the feeling, grasping at some external sign to prove the danger, the resultant explanations are transparently illogical. And the person acts as though reality is the "object" of fear, rather than anything specific or concrete. This is why the anxiety is sometimes described as "free-floating."

This anxiety is a powerful force in the lives of countless millions of human beings. We cannot understand their behavior if we cannot understand how much of their energy they use to defend against a dread they do not understand. They are the ones who cannot bear to be alone; who cannot live without sleeping pills; who jump at every unexpected sound; who drink too much to calm a nervousness that comes too often; who constantly feel a pressing need to be amusing and to entertain; who flee to too many movies they have no desire to see and to too many gatherings they have no desire to attend; who sacrifice any vestige of independent self-confidence to an excessive concern with what others think of them;

who long to be emotional dependents or to be depended upon; who succumb to periodic spells of unaccountable depression; who submerge their existence in the dreary passivity of unchosen routines and unchallenged duties and, as they watch their years slip by, wonder, in occasional spurts of frustrated anguish, what has robbed them of their chance to live; who run from one meaningless sexual affair to another; who seek membership in the kind of collective movements that dissolve personal identity and obviate personal responsibility. This is the vast, anonymous assemblage of men and women who have accepted fear as a built-in, not-to-be-wondered-about fixture of their soul, often dreading even to identify that what they feel is fear or to inquire into the nature of that which they seek to escape.

Such anxiety is a response to an unconsciously perceived threat to self-esteem—to the sense of control, efficacy, and worth. The fear seems to be metaphysical, directed at the universe at large, at existence as such. It implies that "to be" is to be in danger—beyond any ordinary, rational sense in which this may be said to be true. There is a feeling of shapeless but impending disaster, a sense of helplessness. Sometimes there is, in addition, a metaphysical guilt; the person feels wrong *as a person*, wrong in some fundamental way that is wider than any particular defect he or she can identify.

The threat and the danger lie within. The threatening demons are disowned perceptions, thoughts, memories, feelings or emotions against which the individual has barricaded him- or herself in order to preserve psychological equilibrium.

If self-esteem is the conviction that we are competent to grasp and judge the facts of reality and that we are worthy of happiness, then self-esteem anxiety, in its extreme form, is the torment of a person who is crippled or devastated in this realm, who feels cut off from reality, alienated, powerless.

Behind a fear that may be experienced as existential lies a problem that is internal, cognitive: an inappropriateness in the functioning of consciousness itself.

If a person defaults on the responsibility of awareness, the result is self-distrust: the feeling that his or her mind is not a reliable instrument. Refusing to give thought to issues that require attention, we may evade the fact of the evasion, but we cannot escape the contradiction between knowledge and performance nor the issues themselves. Taking actions contrary to what we believe to be right, we may escape the implications of the actions but not their existence. We are left with self-distrust: the implicit knowledge that mind, judgment, convictions are expendable under emotional pressure.

So much has been written, from the time of Freud[23] on, about the relationship between anxiety and defenses against it on the one hand and consequent emotional and behavioral disorders on the other—from phobias to obsessive-compulsive reactions to depression—that I shall not dwell on that aspect of the issue. I am not concerned here with the clinical manifestations of self-esteem anxiety so much as with the consequences for personality, life course, and general level of fulfillment.

The ability to feel anxiety, self-distrust, or guilt is an asset: these are alarm signals warning of danger to our well-being. Such emotions can be painful, even devastating, but if they cause a person to stop, to question his or her policies, perhaps to seek professional help, then they serve a useful purpose in protecting the person's life. If they are ignored, however, they wreak havoc with the person's life.

The experience of self-esteem anxiety always involves and reflects a particular kind of conflict, and the acute anxiety attack is occasioned by the ego's confrontation with this conflict.

Suppose, for example, that a man aspires for years to a position for which he secretly feels inadequate. Shortly after he is promoted to that position, he awakens in the middle of the night with queer sensations in his head and a painful tightness in his chest. He experiences a state of violent anxiety. In the days that follow, he begins to express worry and concern about his children's school grades; then he begins to moan that his house is under-insured; finally he begins to cry that he is going insane. But the fact of his promotion does not enter his conscious mind.

His anxiety is triggered by the collision of two absolutes: a value imperative—"I must know what to do to handle the responsibilities of my new position"—and the feeling that he is inadequate to obey that imperative—"I don't and can't." The conflict is not conscious; it is repressed. But the effect of the conflict is to demolish his pretense of control over his life and thus to precipitate his anxiety.

Observe the nature of the conflict. It is a clash between a value imperative ("I should know what to do; I must know what to do") engaging the man's sense of personal worth and a failure or flaw or inadequacy that the man experiences as a breach of that imperative ("I don't know what to do").

Another example is the woman raised to believe that her personal worth is a function of her role as wife and mother. For years she has repressed any impulse toward self-assertiveness or self-expression that threatens to interfere with her officially designated function. Building within her is enormous rage that she does not allow herself to identify or confront. But more and more frequently, she finds herself having fantasies of her husband and children being killed in an automobile accident. She becomes oversolicitious of her family's well-being, to the point of annoying and burdening everyone. She feels rejected. Rage keeps on building. The fantasies of her family's death increasingly dominate her consciousness.

One day, standing at the kitchen sink and washing dishes, she suddenly finds that she has difficulty distinguishing the colors of objects, everything in her field of vision begins to swim, and terrible pains appear to be coming from her heart. She feels certain she is going to die of a heart attack. But what has hit her is the onset of an anxiety attack.

The collision is between the value imperative of "I must not" and the contradictory emotion of "I did, do, and will continue to wish for my family's death."

The clash is between a value imperative (should, should not; must, must not) engaging her sense of personal worth and an emotion, a desire, a fantasy, that contradicts that imperative.

In every instance of self-esteem anxiety, we will find a conflict in the form of "I must/should have" versus "I cannot/did not," or "I must not" versus "I do/did/will." There is always a conflict between, on the one hand, some value imperative that is tied, in a crucial and profound way, to the person's self-appraisal and inner equilibrium, and, on the other, some failure, inadequacy, action, emotion, desire, or fantasy that the person regards as a breach of that imperative, a breach that the person believes expresses or reflects a basic and unalterable fact of his or her "nature."

Psychologists have understood self-esteem anxiety—which they call *pathological anxiety*—in many different ways. But I am convinced that if one studies the case histories they themselves report, or any of the case histories pertaining to anxiety in the many textbooks available today, one can discern very clearly the basic pattern described above, however the particular cases may differ in details.

One of the most common errors made by theorists in their interpretations of the anxiety process is to mistake a particular instance of pathological anxiety for the abstract prototype of all pathological anxiety.

Freud, for instance, in the final version of his theory of anxiety, maintained that anxiety is triggered by forbidden sexual desires that break through the barrier of repression and cause the ego to feel threatened and overwhelmed.[23] Karen Horney countered with the declaration that this may have been true in the Victorian age, but in our day the source of anxiety is the emergence of hostile impulses.[36]

Both of their explanations will fit into the formula I have outlined, but neither explanation is a universal. The basic principle involved is demonstrably wider than either Freud's or Horney's theory. Pathological anxiety is a crisis of self-esteem, and the possible sources of anxiety are as numerous as the rational or irrational values on which a person's self-appraisal may be based.

The value imperative involved in these anxiety-producing conflicts may be consonant with the facts of reality and appropriate to human nature, or it may be contrary to both, yet the person somehow believes that satisfying the demand of this imperative should be within his or her volitional power. The conflict is typically subconscious; either half of it, however, may be conscious or partially conscious.

There is no object of fear more terrifying to human beings than fear itself and no fear more terrifying than that for which they know no object. Few people consciously experience self-esteem anxiety in the terms in which I am discussing it here. In order to make it more bearable, it is commonly converted into specific, tangible fears, which might seem to have some semblance of plausibility in terms of the circumstances of one's life. Though a person may be beset by a dozen narrower fears, none really rational, all are a smoke screen and defense against an anxiety whose roots lie in the core experience of self.

Since positive self-esteem is a fundamental need, human beings who fail to achieve satisfactory self-esteem are driven by anxiety to counterfeit self-esteem. *Pseudo-self-esteem*, a pretense at self-confidence and self-respect, is a nonrational, self-protective device to diminish anxiety and to fulfill the need for positive self-regard.

In order to generate some semblance of psychological equilibrium, however, it is necessary to avoid or perhaps rationalize and otherwise deny ideas, feelings, memories, and behaviors that could adversely affect self-appraisal. And, further, it becomes necessary to seek a sense of efficacy and worth from something *other than* the appropriate use of consciousness, something *other than* rationality, honesty, responsibility, and integrity. This alternative value or virtue, such as "doing one's duty" or being stoical or altruistic or financially successful or sexually attractive or "tough," is perceived as more easily attainable.

This complex process of self-deception, this misguided attempt at self-healing on which an individual may build his or her life, holds the key to the individual's motivation, values, and goals—to the impulses that drive the individual along a particular path.

Let us establish a point of contrast here. In the psychology of a man or woman of authentic self-value, there is no clash between the recognition of the facts of reality and the preservation of positive self-esteem. Positive self-esteem is based on the determination to know and to act in accordance with the facts of reality as perceived and understood. But to the man or woman of pseudo-self-esteem, reality is often the enemy: reality precludes positive self-esteem, since the pretense at self-confidence and self-respect is purchased at the price of avoidance.

A person may be perfectly rational and lucid in an area that does not touch on or threaten pseudo-self-esteem and be flagrantly irrational, evasive, defensive, and downright stupid in an area that is threatening to self-appraisal. A woman, for example, may operate her business smoothly; she is open to recognizing her mistakes in judgment, when she makes them, and quick to correct them. In this sphere, she has a strong reality orientation. At home, when dealing with her husband or children, she becomes hysterical at the smallest challenge to her authority; her equilibrium is disturbed by any failure of her family to acquiesce to her judgment. Her pseudo-self-esteem is invested in being "the perfect wife," "the perfect mother," and any suggestion of failure activates her anxiety, which activates her defenses, which makes her unable to hear or respond appropriately to what her family is telling her. Her family is left to wonder, How can she be so brilliant in one area of her life and so blind in another?

The process of avoidance and repression is not sufficient to provide a person with the illusion of good self-esteem; that process is only part of the self-deception. The other part consists of the values chosen as the means of achieving the sense of personal worth.

Again, we will develop a point of contrast. An individual who develops healthily derives intense pleasure and pride from the work of his or her mind and from the achievement that that work makes possible. Feeling confident of the ability to deal with the challenges of life, the individual will desire an effortful, stimulating, creative existence. Feeling confident of his or her own value, the individual will be drawn to good self-esteem in others; what he or she will desire most in human relationships is the opportunity to feel admiration. In the spheres of both work and human relationships, the individual acts from a firm base of security, of efficacy—and, as a consequence, a love for the fact of being alive. What he or she seeks are means to express and objectify good self-esteem.

The person with poor self-esteem acts out of fear rather than confidence. Not to live, but to escape the anxiety of living, becomes the fundamental goal. Not creativeness, but safety, becomes the ruling desire. And in human relationships, such a person seeks, not admiration, but, more commonly, an escape from moral values, an escape from standards, a promise to be forgiven, or to be accepted without being respected, or to be admired without being understood—to be comforted and protected or else held in blind awe.

The principle that distinguishes the basic motivations of high self-esteem from that of low self-esteem is the principle of motivation by love versus motivation by fear: the love of self and of existence versus the fear that one is unfit for existence. Motivation by confidence, which places its primary emphasis on the possibility of enjoyment, versus motivation by terror, which places its primary emphasis on the avoidance of pain.

To the extent that a person suffers from poor self-esteem, he or she lives negatively and defensively—that is, out of motivation by fear. When that person chooses particular values and goals, the primary motive is not to realize a positive enjoyment of existence but rather to defend against anxiety, against distressing feelings of inadequacy, self-doubt, guilt, and the possibility of being hurt.

An analogy may prove helpful. If a person's life is in physical danger as a result of having contracted a major disease, the primary concern in such an emergency situation is not the pursuit of enjoyment but the removal of the danger, the regaining of health, the reestablishing of a context in which the pursuit of enjoyment will again be possible and appropriate. But to the person significantly lacking in self-confidence and self-respect, life is, in effect, a *chronic* emergency; that person is *always* in danger—psychologically. He or she never feels free to pursue the enjoyment of life, because the method of combating the danger consists, not of dealing with it rationally, not of working to remove it, but *of seeking to become persuaded that it does not exist.*

I call any value chosen to support pseudo-self-esteem a *defense value.* A defense value is one motivated by fear and aimed at supporting an illusion of psychological equilibrium. It is an antianxiety device.

Such a value may be intrinsically admirable; what is irrational and unhealthy about it is the reason for its selection. Productive work is certainly a value worthy of esteem; but escaping into work as a means of avoiding one's conflicts, shortcomings, anxieties—and the resultant unhappiness caused to self and others—is not admirable. Sometimes, however, defense values are irrational in both respects—as in the case of a person who seeks to escape anxiety and fake a sense of efficacy by acquiring power over other human beings.

The number of different defense values that people can adopt is virtually limitless. Most of these values, however, have one thing in common: they are values held in high regard by the culture or subculture in which a person lives. A number of common defense values of this type appear in the following examples:

The man who is obsessed with being popular, who feels driven to win the approval of every person he meets, who clings to the image of himself as "likable," who, in effect, regards his appealing personality as his sole means of survival and the proof of his personal worth.

The woman who has no sense of personal identity and who seeks to lose her inner emptiness in the role of a martyr for her children, demanding in exchange only that her children adore her so that their adoration fills the vacuum of the ego she can hardly be said to possess.

The man who never forms independent judgments about anything but who seeks to compensate by making himself authoritatively knowledgeable concerning *other* people's opinions about everything.

The man who works at being aggressively "masculine," whose other concerns are largely subordinated to his role of woman chaser, and who derives less pleasure from the act of sex than from the act of reporting his adventures to the men in the locker room.

The woman whose chief standard of self-appraisal is the prestige of her husband and whose pseudo-self-esteem rises or falls according to the number of people who court her husband's favor.

The man who feels guilt over having inherited a fortune, who has no idea of what to do with it and proceeds frantically to give it away, clinging to the "ideal" of altruism and to the vision of himself as a humanitarian, keeping his pseudo-self-esteem afloat by means of the belief that charity is a moral substitute for competence and courage.

The man who has always been afraid of life and who tells himself that the reason is his superior "sensitivity," who chooses his clothes, his furniture, his books, and his bodily posture by the standard of what will make him appear "idealistic."

Sometimes defense values are of a religious nature. Obedience to some religious injunction(s) may be made the basis of pseudo-self-esteem. Faith in God, asceticism, systematic self-abnegation, and adherence to religious rituals are devices commonly employed to allay anxiety and purchase a sense of worthiness.

Still another type of noteworthy defense value may be observed in the person who rationalizes behavior of which he or she feels guilty by insisting that such behavior "does not represent the real me," that "the real me is my *aspirations*, and I am prevented from acting in accordance with my professed ideals only by reasons beyond personal control: the evil of the system, the malevolence of the universe, the tragedy of circumstances, human infirmity, I never got a break, I'm too honest and decent for this world." The concept of a "real me" who bears little relation to anything one says or does in reality is an especially prevalent antianxiety device and often coexists with other defense values.

If an individual took responsibility for every one of his or her actions *in the moment of performing the action*, not only would defense values of this kind be impossible, but a radical elevation of self-esteem would be inevitable. To appreciate the kinds of changes that would be inevitable if we were to take responsibility for our actions in the moment of performing them, consider the following.

"Right now I am choosing not to do the work I promised my boss I would do, and I plan to alibi later—and I take responsibility for that."

"Right now I am choosing not to answer, honestly and directly, my wife's question—and I take responsibility for that."

"Right now I am choosing not to deal with the look of pain in my child's eyes—and I take responsibility for that."

"Right now I am choosing to steal this money from my guest's handbag—and I take responsibility for that."

"Right now I am choosing to stay home and feel sorry for myself rather than go out and look for a job—and I take responsibility for that."

"Right now I am choosing not to correct the job that I know I have done sloppily—and I take responsibility for that."

"Right now I am choosing to procrastinate rather than confront an issue with my friend/spouse/employee/employer/colleague that I know needs to be confronted—and I take responsibility for that."

"Right now I am choosing to pretend a love I do not feel—and I take responsibility for that."

"Right now I am choosing to pretend that I am indifferent when the truth is I am hurting—and I take responsibility for that."

"Right now I am choosing to act tough when the truth is I want to reach out for help—and I take responsibility for that."*

Obviously, it would be nearly impossible to talk to ourselves in this manner and go on performing actions we know to be inappropriate. Therefore, to the extent we learn to talk to ourselves in this manner, we irresistibly generate changes in behavior—and thus we have the power to take a major step toward the rebuilding of damaged self-esteem.

More broadly, to the extent that we are able to step back from any of our defense values and ask ourselves, "Does this really make me good? Why do I think so?" we have the power to move toward placing our self-esteem on a saner and less precarious foundation. Even when we are afraid, this possibility is open to us. We can accept fear and then rise above it by taking unfamiliar but desirable risks in the service of our mind and life; we need not remain trapped at the level of poor self-esteem.

While some defense values are more serviceable than others (or less harmful than others), under the best of circumstances they rob the individual of possibilities for evolution and aliveness. Perhaps the ultimate defense value, at a concrete and specific level, the level of an actual object, is the tranquilizer. The fire alarm is turned off, but (in the subconscious) the fire continues to rage.

I am not denying that tranquilizers have their uses, at times, as short-term emergency measures. But as a way of life they be-

---

*This series of formulations is adapted from a way of talking heavily encouraged in Gestalt therapy, which places strong emphasis on "taking responsibility."[59]

come a denial of life. I pause here on the phenomenon of tranquilizers and other instances of drug abuse, to which I shall turn
in a moment, because they are a metaphor for the entire issue of
defense values and the problem of motivation by fear.

If tranquilizers are a boom industry, it is absurd to blame
pharmaceutical companies, as if they are the cause of the problem.
The "cause," if one wishes to be simplistic, is the human inclination
to follow the path of least resistance, the inclination to accept,
not the right solution, but the one that appears easiest and least
demanding. In tranquilizer abuse (and alcohol abuse and recreational drug abuse) people often find "solutions" that seem appealing when other defense values break down, when the tide of
anxiety fails to be stemmed.

Tranquilizers, alcohol, and recreational drugs share these
common features that tend to make them addictive: they reduce
pain and anxiety; they sometimes create a temporary buoyancy,
a temporary illusion of efficacy, power, and high self-esteem; and
they tend to perpetuate just those behaviors that created the need
for their use in the first place. Thus, the problem of such abuse is
intimately connected to problems of self-esteem and cannot be
understood outside that context.

Just as (inappropriately used) Valium is a defense value, so
is an obsessive preoccupation with approval and popularity, or
mindless material acquisitiveness, or role-playing the "good boy"
or "good girl," or compulsive pursuit of sexual "conquests," or
sexual asceticism and renunciation, which reflect the other side
of the same madness, or selfless obedience to a leader, which is
aimed at escape from the burden of identity and responsibility.
These are all antianxiety devices. They are all engaged for the
purpose of coping with the problem of the human need for self-
esteem, but in self-destructive ways.

When we see an addict withdraw from the object of his or
her particular addiction, we ask the individual to confront the
question, Who am I without this particular crutch? We might ask
the same of any defense values. Who am I without my popularity?
Who am I without my possessions? Who am I without my leader,
my movement, the cause in which I lose myself? Who am I when
there is no one to tell me what to do, no one to obey or rebel

against, no one to surpass or be subordinate to, no one to impress or control or manipulate or serve? Who am I, facing myself in the mirror?

This, perhaps, is the ultimate question all of us must face: Who am I, naked and alone, with only my mind and my being and with none of the external supports or trappings by which I may seek to sustain my self-concept?

One of the core meanings of *enlightenment* is liberation from false and spurious value attachments that blind the individual to his or her true essence. When and if I learn that ultimately I am my mind and my manner of using it—when and if I understand that ego is only the internal experience of consciousness, the ultimate center of awareness—I am free.

But for those who are trapped in a maze of false notions of self, an elaborate structure of social "roles" and "images," and barricaded behind a network of defense values, such a concept of ego as I am propounding is almost ungraspable. At best, it is likely to be only a distant vision. But the path of our evolution is the path we follow toward the actualization of that vision.

We cannot, however, complete our discussion of the dynamics of self-esteem without considering the impact of self-esteem on the two cardinal issues of our existence: work and love.

7

Self-Esteem, Work,
and Love

While self-esteem touches virtually every aspect of our existence, there are two aspects to which it is related in very distinct and powerful ways: work and love. Through work and through love, we act out the level of our confidence and our sense of personal worth. The drama of our life is the external reflection of our internal vision of ourselves. The higher the level of our self-esteem, the more likely it is that we will find a work and a love through which we can express ourselves in satisfying and enriching ways. And, conversely, the lower the level of our self-esteem, the more likely it is that our experiences with work and love will be such as to cause our self-esteem to remain on an unsatisfying plane.

Let us first examine the relationship between self-esteem and productive work. By *productive work* I mean any purposeful activity involving mind and labor and serving the purposes of life, from digging a ditch, driving a tractor, designing a building, and operating a business to engaging in scientific research.

Earlier, when I introduced the concept of efficacy as one of the two essential elements of self-esteem, I was speaking of *fundamental efficacy*. We may call this *metaphysical efficacy*. But the concept of efficacy is also applicable to our effectiveness in specific areas of endeavor, resulting from particular knowledge and skills we have acquired. This is expressed in the domain ˙ ´ productive work (although not only there). I shall call this latter type *particularized efficacy*.

As I discussed in chapter one, a person may exhibit a degree of particularized efficacy and yet be profoundly lacking in that sense of fundamental efficacy essential to healthy self-esteem. For example, a man or woman may be skilled and confident on the job but terrified by any wider need for independent thinking in the moral, ethical, or intellectual sphere, fearing to step outside a familiar frame of reference established by the particular group to which he or she belongs. Thinking about the essentials of life is left to others. Others determine the context in which this individual operates—the moral context, the value context, the intellectual context. A highly efficient "organization man" is an example of this type.

On the other hand, a person may possess a healthy self-esteem, a profound sense of fundamental or metaphysical efficacy, but, being highly specialized in his or her interests, may lack many of the practical skills that most people take for granted, such as how to drive an automobile, cook a meal, or perform some simple task of home repair. Rather than fearing such tasks, however, he or she normally feels confident of the ability to acquire the requisite skills should the need arise. A sense of metaphysical efficacy imparts a confidence in the ability *in principle* to learn whatever is necessary.

Metaphysical efficacy is necessarily expressed through *some* form of particularized efficacy. But metaphysical efficacy is not confined, in its expression, to any particular form of activity; it is applicable to, and expressible in, every form of constructive endeavor. It would be impossible, of course, to acquire or sustain a sense of metaphysical efficacy without also acquiring some forms of particularized efficacy—in other words, without engaging in some form of productive work. We maintain our metaphysical efficacy by continuing to expand our particularized efficacy; that is the meaning of growth as a way of life.

The position I take here obviously stands in sharp contrast to that taken by contemporary writers who speak disparagingly of work and achievement, as if such values were merely a diabolical invention of capitalism. We have to wonder, for example, at the following statement of Irvin D. Yalom in *Existential Psychotherapy*: "The belief that life is incomplete without goal fulfillment is not so much a tragic existential fact of life as it is a Western myth, a cultural artifact." If there is anything we know for a biological certainty, it is that life is *impossible* without "goal fulfillment"—impossible on every level of evolution, from the

93

amoeba to the human being. It is neither "a tragic existential fact" nor "a Western myth," but rather the simple nature of life—and often exhilarating. (It is particularly disappointing to encounter such a statement in a book that is, in so many ways, a brilliant accomplishment.)

Every achievement is a value in itself, but every step upward also opens to us a wider range of action and achievement and creates the *need* for that action and achievement. Survival demands continuing growth and creativeness. There is no final, permanent plateau.

In stressing the importance of growth and achievement to a uniquely human existence, I do not intend to imply that the meaning of life is simply work and that there are no other values of supreme importance. Love, friendship, leisure, recreation are vital elements in a fulfilled existence. But if we do not discover the necessity and joy of using our productive and creative powers, we have missed one of the highest rewards available to our species; we have deprived ourselves of one of the great, distinctively human experiences.

I have often been struck by the fact that the earliest self-generated pleasure of a person's life is the pleasure of a sense of control. As a child learns to move his or her body, to crawl, to walk, to bang with a spoon against a table and produce a sound, to build a structure of blocks, to pronounce words, the enjoyment he or she exhibits is that of a living organism gaining power over its own existence. It is profoundly significant, psychologically and morally, that a child begins his or her life experiencing the sense of virtue and the sense of efficacy as a single, indivisible emotion; pride is inextricably tied to achievement. It is as if nature, at the start of life, points us in the right direction.

Whereas some of us subsequently lose this awareness, forget what a child is gifted to know, it is just this knowledge that a psychologically well-functioning human being does not lose: it remains a central motive in life. This attitude accounts for the phenomenon of the mentally active person who is young at ninety, just as the absence of this attitude accounts for the phenomenon of the mentally passive person who is old at thirty.

Many factors—such as intelligence, energy level, and available opportunities—influence the scope of a person's productive ambition, but certainly one of the most powerful determining factors is the degree of self-esteem. On any level of intelligence or ability, one of the characteristics of high self-esteem is an eagerness for the new and the challenging, for that which will allow an individual to use his or her capacities to the fullest extent—just as a fondness for the familiar, the routine, and the unexacting coupled with a fear of the new and the difficult is a virtually unmistakable indication of low self-esteem.

I want to stress once again that productive achievement is a consequence and expression of high self-esteem, *not* its primary cause. A person who is brilliantly talented and successful at work but irrational and irresponsible in his or her private life may desperately *want* to believe that the sole criterion of virtue is productive performance, that no other sphere of action has moral or self-esteem significance. Such a person may hide behind work in order to evade feelings of shame and guilt stemming from other areas of life, so that productive accomplishment becomes, not a healthy passion, but a defense value, an avoidance strategy, a refuge from reality and from the judgment of one's own ego. Furthermore, if a person makes the error of identifying self with his or her work, with accomplishments, success, income, or being a good family provider, economic circumstances beyond the individual's control that lead to the failure of a business or the loss of a job may also lead to depression or acute demoralization.

Some years ago, lecturing on this subject in Detroit, with members of the automobile industry in the audience, I made the following observation: "Right now Washington is trying to decide whether or not to bail out Chrysler. Never mind for the moment whether or not you think that's an appropriate government function; I don't think it is, but that's irrelevant. The point is, if you work for Chrysler and your self-esteem is tied to being a high achiever in that company, or to earning a good income this year, then what that means practically is that you are willing for some persons in Washington literally to hold your soul in their hands, to have total control over your sense of worth. Does that idea offend you? I hope so. It offends me."

It is bad enough, during economic hard times, to have to worry about money and our family's welfare and future, but it is still worse if we allow our self-esteem to become undermined in the process—by telling ourselves, in effect, that our efficacy and worth are a function of our earnings.

On occasion I have had the opportunity to counsel older men and women who found themselves unemployed, passed over in favor of people a good deal younger who were in no way better equipped, or even as well equipped, for the particular job. We are living during a time when there tends to be a strong prejudice in favor of youth against age. I have also worked with highly talented young people who suffered from the reverse form of the same prejudice, a discrimination against youth in favor of age—where, again, objective competence and ability were not the standard. In such circumstances, there is tragically often the sense of the loss of personal effectiveness. Such a feeling is a hairline away from the sense of diminished self-esteem—and often turns into a feeling of diminished self-esteem. It takes an unusual kind of person to avoid falling into the trap of this error: it takes a person who is already well centered within him- or herself and who understands that some of the forces operating are beyond personal control and that, strictly speaking, these do not have (or should not have) significance for self-esteem at all.

Whenever we are weighing whether or not a matter bears on our self-esteem (or should bear on our self-esteem), the question to ask is, Is this issue within my direct, volitional control? Or is it at least linked, by a direct line of causality, to matters within my volitional control?

If we are willing to take responsibility for that which is within our power, I think that frees us to see clearly that which is not, and to understand, therefore, the limits of our accountability. But if we too often fail to take such responsibility and feel vaguely guilty over our avoidance, the paradox is that in our confusion we often end up blaming ourselves for events beyond our control. Further, one of the most common forms of evading appropriate responsibility is to clutter up one's thinking with notions of utterly inappropriate and absurd responsibility—like the person who is unwilling to assume responsibility for his or her own existence but who professes to feel "responsible for the whole world."

We can never judge positive self-esteem on the basis of a single trait or characteristic, taken out of context. Just as we cannot deduce it simply on the basis of an erect, relaxed, well-balanced posture, so we cannot deduce it simply on the basis of a high level of ambition—although both can be expressions of good self-esteem, and often are.

Many an individual, feeling he or she is not "enough," may be driven to more and more demanding levels of performance and accomplishment, in order to "prove" him- or herself—and if the person has intelligence and energy, he or she may succeed in achieving a great deal. What this individual will not achieve, of course, is high self-esteem.

One of the most common errors made by people of poor self-esteem about people of high self-esteem is the assumption that the latter always feel cheerful, confident, and secure, never feel anxious or demoralized, never know anguish or despair, always are certain about what they are doing. Not all anxiety is self-esteem anxiety, and not all despair pertains to doubt of personal worth. To possess healthy self-esteem is not to be immune to the vicissitudes of life or to the pain of struggle.

One of the forms of psychological heroism is the willingness to tolerate anxiety and uncertainty in the pursuit of our values— whether those values be work goals, the love of another human being, the raising of a family, or personal growth.

To stay with the arena of productive work, for example, an artist, a scientist, or an industrialist of high self-esteem may set extraordinarily difficult goals that may generate times of anxiety, doubt about choices made, uncertainty about the possibility of success, and periods of depression. This person is likely to feel, "If this, sometimes, is the price I have to pay for the attainment of my goals, I am willing to pay it"—an attitude that a person of lower self-esteem would not be likely to adopt.

The person of high self-esteem may even revel in the struggle, in spite of all the painful feelings that sometimes occur; people of high self-esteem tend to preserve a spiritual point that remains untouched, even by their own suffering.

To accept the process of struggle as part of life, to accept all of it, even the darkest moments of anguish (which is motivation by love rather than motivation by fear, motivation by confidence rather than motivation by insecurity)—that is one of the most important attitudes that differentiates individuals with high self-esteem from individuals with low self-esteem. The wish to avoid fear and pain is not the motive that drives the lives of highly evolved men and women. Rather it is the life-force within them thrusting toward its unique form of expression—the actualization of personal values.

Like work, love too can be sought, not as an expression of self-esteem and of esteem for another, but rather as a means of raising a self-esteem that is painfully low. The quest to find someone who will love me and thereby make me love myself does not succeed. Nonetheless, millions attempt it every day. When the quest fails, we often move on to another relationship, which also fails, and then perhaps we move on to another relationship—or else we give up and decide that "there's no such thing as love."

I am reminded of a famous actress-singer I once saw being interviewed on television. The interviewer commented on the astonishing number of projects and engagements in which she had been involved during the past several years. "I like to keep busy," she smiled. The interviewer sighed gravely, "I'm the same way—always running from one project to another, always juggling twelve balls in the air. Why do we do it?" Her smile vanished, and she said slowly, thoughtfully, a little sadly, "For myself . . . I'm afraid that if I ever stop running, if I ever stop doing things all the time, if I ever get off the treadmill and allow myself to look inside . . . I'll find out there's nothing there." Nodding in silent, eloquent understanding, the interviewer responded, "Yeah." What made the interview significant was the subject's willingness to articulate explicitly what millions feel but do not name.

Just as many people run from one work project to another, so they may run from one relationship to another, for the same purpose: dread of finding out that if they ever stop and look inside, they may discover "there's nothing there."

Love is our emotional response to that which we value highly. It is the experience of joy in the existence of the loved object, joy in proximity, and joy in interaction or involvement. To love is to delight in the being whom one loves, to experience pleasure in that being's presence, to find gratification or fulfillment in contact with that being. We experience the loved person as a source of fulfillment for profoundly important needs.

To provide a formal definition, I would say that love represents a disposition to experience the loved being as the embodiment of profoundly important personal values—and, as a consequence, a real or potential source of joy. The full reasons for this definition are offered in *The Psychology of Romantic Love*. Here I will simply say that while I believe this definition names the essence of love, it is generally recognized that "love" can be confused with loneliness, neediness, transitory physical attraction, fantasy, wish fulfillment, affection, gratitude, and even the comradeship of mutual contempt.

One of the characteristics of people with healthy self-esteem is that they tend to recognize the difference between authentic love and these other conditions—in contrast to individuals with low self-esteem, who often do not make such distinctions. Not that a person on any level of self-esteem cannot be honestly confused about his or her feelings; but people with high self-esteem are relatively less prone to self-alienation and consequently enjoy a more intimate acquaintance with their inner life.

We know, from clinical observation and from a number of studies, that people of high self-esteem tend to fall in love with people of high self-esteem; people of average self-esteem tend to fall in love with people of average self-esteem; people of low self-esteem tend to fall in love with people of low self-esteem. In the area of self-esteem and love, there is a powerful tendency for like to be attracted to like. This is hardly surprising. Love may require the excitement of complementary differences, but it also requires a foundation of basic affinities.

Many people can "fall" in love, but to sustain love across time requires self-confidence and self-respect. If I enjoy a fundamental sense of efficacy and worth, and if, as a consequence, I feel lovable as a human being, I have an emotional wealth within me that I can channel into loving. Without respect for and enjoyment in who I am, however, I have very little to give. I see other people essentially as sources of approval or disapproval, not as people in their own right.

Further, if I do not feel that I am lovable, it is very difficult to believe that anyone else loves me. Your profession of love conflicts with my self-concept. Even if I consciously disown my feelings of being unlovable, my poor self-concept remains, operating beneath the surface of awareness to undermine my attempts at relationships. In my insecurity, I may subvert love in any number of ways: by demanding excessive reassurances, by venting irrational possessiveness, by making catastrophes of small frictions, by seeking to control through subservience or domination, by finding ways to reject my partner before my partner can reject me.

A former client, a man with poor self-esteem, married a woman who cared for him deeply. But nothing she could ever do was enough to make him feel loved. Whatever she offered, he wanted more. Whatever she said, he wondered if she meant it. But she loved him, and she persevered. Finally, the day came when he no longer could escape knowing how much he meant to her. His response was to begin wondering whether he had set his own standards too low. More and more he questioned whether she was good enough for him. "How can I love this woman who is inferior even to me, who has been so easily duped into loving me?"

The marriage did not survive his problem. But the pain of losing his wife was not an unqualified negative; it became the catalyst activating him to search for a solution. Later, as his self-esteem was rising, he fell in love again. I encouraged him to maintain a daily diary of his interactions with his lover, to keep note of the behaviors that nurtured the relationship and the behaviors that frustrated it, and to share his fears with his lover when they arose. Over time he learned to relinquish self-sabotaging thoughts and behaviors, and in so doing, he saw the quality of his self-esteem and of the relationship continue to rise together.

I recall another client, a woman with low self-esteem, who felt she had to tell the man who cared for her all the ways in which other women were superior; they were more attractive, more intelligent, more feminine, and so forth. When he did not concur in her judgment and said he preferred her, she became frustrated and sometimes very angry. Her irritability became chronic, as did her tendency to ridicule him for his poor judgment. Eventually she exhausted him; worn out, bewildered, and disenchanted, he left her. She was deeply hurt, shocked, and dismayed. She wondered how she could have been so misguided in her assessment of him. She spoke of feeling like an abandoned child. "I always knew no one could love me."

In therapy she became sensitive to the countless ways in which her love life was operating by negative self-fulfilling prophecies. *By making that which she most feared happen, she had retained a sense of being in control.* In order to solve her problems, she had to relinquish that control by finding out what would happen in a relationship if she gave her best rather than her worst. It was not an easy struggle. Afterward she wrote to me, "What a strange kind of triumph. What an odd notion of bravery. And yet God knows it was hard, just to learn to have a man say, 'I love you' and for me to answer, very simply, 'I love you, too.'"

If self-esteem is confidence in one's appropriateness to life, then we can readily understand why men and women of high self-esteem tend to expect success and happiness and why, as a consequence, they are likely to create these conditions for themselves. Men and women of low self-esteem tend to expect defeat and suffering, and their lives are shaped accordingly.

No one can understand the course of his or her life who does not understand the power of self-fulfilling prophecies. They are the central dynamic of our existence.

In understanding the relationship of self-esteem to love, there is another aspect of the process we need to consider: whether or not, or to what extent, we feel worthy of happiness.

If I do not not feel deserving of happiness, consciously or subconsciously, or if I have accepted the belief that happiness is somehow wrong or cannot last, that attitude will inevitably subvert my attempts at love. If I do not feel it is appropriate for me to be happy, then the presence of happiness triggers anxiety. Joy does violence to my self-concept because pain (my pain) is my lot in life. I must not allow myself to be "set up" by transitory flickers of joy for the devastating pain that inevitably must follow.

In other words, happiness makes me feel anxious. When we feel anxious, we do something very natural: we attempt to reduce our anxiety by ridding ourselves of its cause.

Not that poor self-esteem forbids me to dream of happiness, aspire to happiness, yearn for happiness. Not necessarily. As long as joy remains out of reach, as long as it remains a distant longing, I can allow myself to believe I am reaching for it.

People can "work on" their relationships for years. They can read books on psychology. They can consult marriage counselors. They can participate in an endless stream of workshops and seminars. And yet their underlying problem is one they are very unlikely to confront. I call it *happiness anxiety*. Here again we encounter the principle of motivation by fear.

I have had the opportunity to work with many thousands of people in a variety of professional contexts and settings, at the seminars and workshops I conduct in addition to my psychotherapy practice. And I am absolutely persuaded that happiness anxiety is one of our most widespread and least understood problems. Many people feel they do not deserve happiness, are not entitled to happiness, have no right to the fulfillment of their emotional needs and wants. Often they feel that if they are happy, either their happiness will be taken away from them, or something terrible will happen to counterbalance it, some unspeakable punishment or tragedy. That is why happiness for such people is a potential source of anxiety. While they may long for it on one level of consciousness, they dread it on another.

A person may be quite unaware of the problem consciously. He or she may insist, "Of course I am entitled to happiness!" But when the person is in a relationship that is working, for example, often the response to happiness is a feeling of anxiety or disorientation.

Many an individual, particularly if raised in a religious home, has been taught that suffering represents a passport to salvation, whereas enjoyment is almost certainly proof that one has strayed from the proper path. Psychotherapy clients have spoken to me of times when, as children, they were ill, and a parent told them, "Don't regret that you are in pain. Every day you suffer, you are piling up credits in heaven." Then what are they piling up on the days when they are happy?

We all know how often children are told, in effect, "Don't be so excited. Happiness doesn't last. When you grow up, you'll realize how grim life is."

If a man and woman who are infected by this attitude fall in love, and the attitude itself will not prevent them from falling in love, they will find a way to bring their experience back into alignment with their self-concept, with their view of "the way things really are": for example, facing one another across a dinner table, feeling joyful and contented, one of them suddenly can't stand it and starts a quarrel over nothing or withdraws and becomes mysteriously depressed. At this moment of their existence, happiness is not a dream but a reality. Joy is not a fantasy or an aspiration but a fact. That is unbearable. First of all, they don't deserve it. Second, it can't last. Third, if it does last, something else terrible will happen. They feel: "Let me out of here, I can't stand this!"

After an ecstatic experience of lovemaking, one partner may crack an inappropriate joke, or leap out of bed without any emotional transition, or say something gratuitously critical and estranging, or withdraw and become depressed, or escape into sleep when he or she is not tired—as if the strain of joy and intimacy has become too much to endure.

Here we can note an analogy to work. I once went to observe a meeting of Alcoholics Anonymous. What made this particular group interesting to me was that almost all of them were high achievers. One after the other they stood up and described the circumstances under which they resumed drinking after months or years of abstinence. The most common story I heard that day concerned the progression of striving toward success in a career, then reaching (or being on the verge of reaching) an important goal, then feeling excited and happy, then experiencing an overwhelming desire to drink—which, more often than not, led to behaviors that sabotaged the success. Happiness anxiety and success anxiety are very intimately related; both have their roots in deficient self-esteem.

I will have more to say about the origins of this problem when we discuss separation and individuation, the process by which an infant evolves into an independent human being— and some of the ways in which that evolution often fails to take place.[49,50] Separation pertains to discovering one's own boundaries, understanding where self ends and the world begins. Individuation has to do with the discovery of one's own center, one's own resources, the process of evolving toward a more and more comprehensive recognition, understanding, and integration of the self.

For the moment, I will simply observe that poor self-esteem and inadequate separation and individuation are intrinsically linked; and happiness anxiety is often a consequence of the failure to achieve adequate separation and individuation. Without successful separation and individuation, I do not sufficiently discover my own internal resources; I can very easily persist in the belief that my survival depends on protecting my relationship with my mother and father, at the expense of enjoying the rest of my life.

Suppose that a woman has witnessed the unhappy marriage of her parents. It is not uncommon for a child to internalize subtle messages from mother or father to the effect that "you are not to be any happier in your marriage than I was in mine." A woman with poor self-esteem who wants to be a "good girl," who feels the need to retain mother's or father's love at all costs, often proceeds very obediently either to select a husband with whom happiness is clearly impossible or to manufacture unhappiness in a marriage where happiness might have been possible. "I couldn't bear to let mother see that I was happy in my relationship with a man. She would feel betrayed, she would feel humiliated. I might cause her to feel overwhelmed by her own sense of inadequacy and failure. And I couldn't do that to her." Translation: "Mother might become angry at me, mother might repudiate me, I might lose mother's love—and without mother's love, how can I survive?"

This pattern is not uniquely feminine. "If father saw me making a success of my marriage/my career, he would feel hurt. It would be my way of saying to him, 'You're a failure.' I would be saying, 'I succeeded where you didn't.' I would lose father's love. I want to remain my father's son." Translation: "Without father's love, I cannot conceive of having acceptable self-esteem."

It is often futile to treat romantic problems by teaching communication skills, improved sexual techniques, or methods of "fair fighting." This is what is wrong with so much marriage counseling. While all such teachings are valuable, and there is good reason to learn them, they rest on the assumption that the persons involved are *willing* to be happy, *want* to be happy, feel *entitled* to be happy. What if they don't? The success of love relationships requires an appreciation of the fact that happiness is our human birthright.

How, then, are men and women to proceed? What are they

to do if happiness triggers anxiety? Their desire to reduce anxiety is clearly normal. And if happiness ignites anxiety, then the impulse to reduce or sabotage happiness is understandable. Self-sabotage has its own logic; understood in context, it is a survival strategy.

When we begin to understand the model of reality with which we are operating, we become open to the possibility of finding better solutions, strategies that support our life rather than impoverish it.

The first step is to cultivate in ourselves an awareness of when we are feeling anxious, rather than simply allowing ourselves to be manipulated by an anxiety of which we are unconscious. We need to pay attention to the moments and situations in which apprehension in relation to happiness or success or any other value arises. Then we need to study (and perhaps make lists) of our particular style of self-sabotage—specific behaviors we have learned to undermine our joy and thereby reduce our anxiety. If possible, this is information to communicate to our partner. One of the very best things we can do when we are feeling happiness anxiety or success anxiety is to talk about it. To describe the experience is to begin to drain it of its power. And the honesty and responsibility of responding in this way itself contributes to the strengthening of self-esteem.

Sometimes when we feel happy and the happiness triggers anxiety and disorientation, we must learn to do *nothing*—beyond, perhaps, feeling, describing, and sharing the experience, without being manipulated into behaving self-destructively. We can slowly build a tolerance for happiness, we can increase our ability to handle joy without panicking. We can eventually discover that being happy is far less complicated than we had believed and that joy is our natural state.

And in keeping the presence of mind not to surrender to fear, in generating the consciousness needed to function at this level, in practicing the emotional honesty that may be required between us and our partner, we are at the same time causing self-esteem to increase—and thereby deepening our sense of our right to happiness.

I wish to permit myself a small digression concerning the relationship of two earlier books of mine to this discussion. *The*

105

Psychology of Romantic Love was written to develop a new vision of man-woman relationships (a departure, in some respects, from the historical notion of romantic love and the development of a new paradigm); to define the psychological needs that romantic love, rationally understood, can fulfill; and to indicate in a general way the conditions for the growth or death of romantic love. In its sequel, *The Romantic Love Question & Answer Book*, my co-author, E. Devers Branden, and I had a purpose that bears more directly on this immediate discussion: to outline many of the basic, day-by-day steps and strategies by which people in love can nurture their relationship. We did not assume, in the latter book, that everyone who read it already had a well-developed self-esteem. We wrote from the conviction that if there was a genuine desire to understand the nature of love, and the conditions of successful love, then a willingness to practice the ideas presented would have two results: an increase in the quality of one's relationships and an increase in the level of one's self-esteem.

If we learn to behave appropriately in relationships, even when it is difficult to do so, even when we are not initially supported by a high level of self-esteem, the courage and willingness to persevere tend to raise self-esteem—as well as raise effectiveness at love.

So, in its own way, *The Romantic Love Question & Answer Book* is not only a book about making relationships work but also a book about raising self-esteem. Of course, it deals only with certain aspects of the process—there is far more to be said than was covered in that volume—but every one of the policies and strategies it recommends represents an application of the principles discussed in the present book.

High self-esteem is not all that is needed for success in love, just as it is not all that is needed for success at work. Many other factors are relevant, some of which will be discussed in the chapters that follow. But no single factor is *more* important than self-esteem; and I do not think that any other single factor is *as* important as self-esteem.

In discussions of self-esteem and romantic love, I sometimes hear the question asked: If an individual loses the person he or she loves to someone else, will not self-esteem suffer a severe blow?

While the individual will almost certainly experience pain, it is not really reasonable to give another person total power over our self-appraisal. Pain and damaged self-esteem are not synonymous. Not all pain is the pain of diminished self-regard; that is a very particular kind of pain.

The more insecure or self-doubting we are, the more likely we are to turn any disappointment, any defeat, any failure to get what we want into evidence of our incompetence, inadequacy, and unworthiness. But that is a correctable problem, not a built-in one.

A person of healthy self-esteem who loses a loved one to someone else may respond in any number of ways: by questioning objectively the appropriateness of the initial choice, by examining what errors might have precipitated rejection and loss, by determining what can be learned from the experience, and by resolving not to allow pain to turn into bitterness and into an inability to be open to love in the future.

A period of painful self-examination may follow. Have I failed to perceive my assets and shortcomings realistically? As a romantic partner, do I have liabilities of which I may be unaware? Are there things I need to learn? Or is it simply the case that the romantic needs of the person I love are much better fulfilled by an individual who is different from me, different in ways that do not reflect on the worth of either one of us?

But to decide that if I am not loved by a particular person I am devoid of worth is not to suffer a loss of self-esteem so much as to discover that my self-esteem is lower than I had realized.

I want to offer one last example of how the level of self-esteem can affect our experience of love.

One evening I was having dinner with a man in his mid-fifties who had been married nearly thirty years and who, for some years past, had become more and more unhappy and frustrated in his relationship with his wife. They had grown progressively apart in their values, interests, and preferred lifestyle. But throughout the marriage the man had been scrupulously faithful—until, two years earlier, he had met and fallen in love with another woman and proceeded to plunge into an ecstatic and tormented affair. The ecstasy came from the sense that in some important ways he had

107

found that which he had been searching for in a woman for many years; the torment came from his guilt and indecision as to what to do concerning his marriage.

He had three children, two of them married and the youngest in college. He did not seem terribly concerned by the impact of a possible divorce on his children; he seemed very concerned about the impact on his wife. "She's never done anything really *wrong*," he explained miserably. "I really don't have much to reproach her for. I'm just not in love with her anymore. Do I have the right to make her suffer?"

I pointed out, gently, that his wife was suffering *now*, as was the woman he was in love with. In fact, all three of them were suffering.

"But she wants to remain married to me," he lamented. "She knows our marriage isn't right, she says she wants to work on it, and I don't know what to tell her. The spark just isn't there. With this other woman I feel alive as I've never felt alive before. I feel on fire. There are no words to describe the experience. It's almost like rebirth. I feel I can share myself with her as I never could with my wife. But do I have the right to place my own happiness first? Do I have the right?"

When I asked if his wife knew about the other woman, he replied, "She suspects. And one of these days I'll have to tell her the truth. This can't go on. I dread hurting her. She's such a good person. And I do love her—in a way. I really do. And she's always been so loyal. She's always stuck by me. I feel she always will."

I asked him if he felt equally secure with the other woman. "Not quite," he sighed. "She's more of a free spirit. She says she loves and adores me, but how can I be sure it will last? How can I be sure she'll always be there? I'm positive my wife will always be there."

"You feel your wife will always love you?" I asked.

"Yes," he agreed. "And I don't have to live with the fear that if she really got to know me she might fall out of love with me. We're long past that. But the main thing is, with the other woman, the woman I *really love*, I'm happier than I've ever been. I walk around in a state of rapture. I feel like a schoolboy. I don't know if I can trust this much happiness."

"You're uncertain as to whether or not it will last."

"Uncertain . . . yes. It scares me. And yet, I tell myself the fear is ridiculous. It's not as if it's a one-month infatuation. We spend a great deal of time together. The relationship has already been tested in many ways—and we've come through successfully. I feel this woman understands me in ways no one has ever understood me before. And yet, the fear is there, the haunting question, Will she always love me? With my wife, that question doesn't arise."

"I wonder whether, in addition to what you're saying, any part of your consideration has to do with being a good boy. You know what I mean. A good boy doesn't leave his wife for another woman."

"Oh, of course. Sometimes the guilt is overwhelming."

Hoping to help him clarify his feelings at a deeper level, I asked, "If your physician told you you only had six months to live, what would you do?"

Without a moment's hesitation, he replied, "I'd be out of the house today, and I'd spend those six months with the woman I love."

"And if the woman you love came to you and said that her physician had told her she had only six months to live? In that case, if you left your wife, you couldn't even look forward to a lifetime with the other woman. What then?"

"I'd want to spend every possible moment with her. To tell you the truth, with or without the other woman, the thought of spending the rest of my life with my wife makes me feel unbearably sad."

"Then I have only one thing to ask you," I said. "What makes you think you have six months?"

It seemed a logical question. We forget that we are mortal, and that those we care for are mortal. It is very easy to be reckless with life—and with love. We always imagine we will have time later to correct our mistakes. But what if we won't?

He looked at me and did not answer. He merely sighed and sank deeper into his chair.

A year later, he and his wife were still together. He and the woman he loved were no longer romantically involved; he had broken off with her, as his wife had insisted when he told her of the affair.

I have never been able to escape the conviction that had he a higher level of self-esteem, a greater conviction of his own lovability and of his right to be happy, the story would have ended differently. I do not know how it would have ended; I merely think it would have ended differently.

Multiply this story by many unknown thousands, and you begin to see the kind of quiet tragedy that shaky self-esteem can generate in personal relationships.

Do I mean to imply that no other factor but poor self-esteem is fundamental to this story? I do not; countless many other considerations were operative that my friend had not conveyed to me. I hardly wish to deny the complexities and ambiguities that often attend our choices. But having made this acknowledgment, I cannot help but see the specter of poor self-esteem hanging predominant over this story and its outcome.

Why should honoring the self be so difficult? Why should self-alienation be almost the universal condition of humanity? And what is the road back to self and to self-esteem?

Some of the answers to these questions are contained in the ground we have already covered. But there is more. We need, in a sense, to go back to the beginning—to the moment of birth—then trace some of the steps in the thrust toward selfhood and individuation.

PART TWO

THE STRUGGLE FOR INDIVIDUATION

8
Evolving Toward Autonomy

At birth, the self does not exist. What exists is, in effect, the raw material from which a self can develop. A newborn infant does not yet have a sense of personal identity; there is no awareness of separateness, not, at any rate, as we who are adults experience such awareness.

To evolve into selfhood is the primary human task. It is also the primary human challenge, because success is not guaranteed. At any step of the way, the process can be interrupted, frustrated, blocked, or sidetracked, so that the human individual is fragmented, split, alienated, stuck at one level or another of mental or emotional immaturity. To a tragic extent, most people are stranded along this path of development.

Nonetheless, the central goal of the maturational process is *evolution toward autonomy*. This is the essence of the separation-individuation process.

Discovering boundaries, discovering where self ends and the external world (and in particular the mothering figure) begins—grasping and assimilating the facts of *separateness*—is the foremost task of early infancy, upon which normal development depends. The second and overlapping part of the maturational process is *individuation*: the acquisition of those basic motor and cognitive skills, combined with a beginning sense of physical and personal identity, that represent the foundation of the child's autonomy—that is, the child's capacity for inner direction, self-regulation, and self-responsibility. Separation and individuation mark the child's birth as a human being.[49, 50] They are the necessary precursors of well-developed self-esteem.

Margaret Mahler, the pioneer researcher into the separation-individuation process, became interested in the stages by which a sense of identity is formed as a consequence of observing that "the psychotic child never attains a feeling of wholeness, or individual identity, let alone 'a sense of human identity,'" as she writes in *The Psychological Birth of the Human Infant*. She traces any number of psychological disorders to some partial failure or incompletion of the separation-individuation process. My usage of the term, however, departs from hers—becomes broader—at this point.

In Mahler's context, the separation-individuation process is meant to pertain exclusively to early childhood. I speak of separation and individuation as a process that has meaning at every stage of human development and manifests itself through the entire span of the life cycle. The process is inseparable from the development and maintenance of healthy self-esteem.

We can thus think of separation as emergence and differentiation from any fundamental supporting matrix—be it mother, family, a given stage of development, identification with a particular job or career, an outmoded or unnecessarily limiting belief system. We can think of individuation in a sense perhaps closer to that intended by Jung, as the striving of the human organism toward wholeness, toward completion—an internal thrust toward self-realization or self-actualization reminiscent of Aristotle's concept of entelechy. During the process of individuation, we become more and more completely that which we are potentially—expanding the boundaries of the self to embrace all of our potentialities, as well as those parts that have been denied, disowned, repressed.

On a purely biological level, the birth process itself is the first instance of separation and individuation, a paradigm of the pattern that will later be manifest psychologically. The fetus initially exists as part, literally, of the mother's body; then, at birth, it separates—*differentiates*—and comes into the world as a distinct individual entity. Until the fetus separates from the womb, leaving its first matrix, its first support system, it cannot exist as a (physically) separate being. It must, in effect, say good-bye to one level of existence before it can say hello to a more advanced level. In

114

much the same way, we say good-bye to the "womb" of the family when we go out into the world on our own.

The task of emergence confronts us continually in the course of our existence. We can see the basic pattern in a child's successful growth to adulthood, from learning to walk to selecting a career and establishing a home and a life. But we can see the same process at work in the struggle of a woman who has overidentified with the role of mother and who, when her child is grown, confronts the challenging question of who she is now that her child no longer is dependent on her. When a marriage ends in divorce or when a life partner of many years dies and a person must encounter the question of his or her identity outside the context of the former relationship, once again what is involved is a process of emergence, of separation and individuation.

Each stage of development in the life cycle contains its own hazards and challenges. The more appropriately our needs are met at a particular stage, the more prepared we are for the next stage.[17, 18, 19, 45] Again, let us consider the paradigm of the womb: If the experience of the fetus is positive, if its needs are met as nature requires, it is ready for separation and entrance into the world as a human being. If not, it brings the consequences of its unmet needs with it—for example, frailty or a predisposition to illness.[43]

An appropriately nurtured infant is appropriately prepared for childhood; a child whose needs are appropriately met is well prepared for adolescence; successful negotiation of the transitions through adolescence paves the way for the beginning of adulthood; and so on.

We can think of major stages of development, as self evolves, as a series of matrix shifts, a series of deaths and births, of good-byes and hellos, so that the maturational, intellectual, and psychological attainments at a given stage of development provide the energy, the thrusting power, for evolution to the next stage. We *use* these attainments to *transcend* them.

As we have seen, the first matrix shift is birth itself; the next major shift is from mother to the world, occurring at about age seven. A growing knowledge of self and of the world, through a wide variety of interactions with persons and things, prepares the child for the possibility of independent physical survival. By adolescence, assuming development has proceeded successfully, the individual (mind/body) has become his or her own matrix. The next shift is from concrete thinking to increasingly abstract thinking, with mind itself as the highest matrix in this biological hierarchy.*

There are those who would argue that there is a still further matrix shift—from mind to the Ultimate Ground of Being, or cosmic consciousness, or, to use Aldous Huxley's phrase, "mind-at-large."[38] This viewpoint will be discussed later in the book.

If we think biologically—and the "biocentric" perspective is essential to my approach—then we can see that each matrix shift, each stage of development, entails movement toward greater autonomy. Autonomy does not mean self-sufficiency in the absolute sense. Autonomy pertains to a human being's capacity for independent survival, independent thinking, independent judgment; it pertains to the extent to which the source of self-approval lies within rather than without—that is, within self rather than social environment. Autonomy consists of living by one's own mind.

To live by one's own mind does not mean that we do not learn from others. It means that we do not attempt to live by unthinking conformity and the suspension of independent critical judgment. We take responsibility for the ideas we accept and the values by which we guide our actions.

But this characterization of autonomy is still very abstract. While this is not a treatise on developmental psychology, and there is no need in this context to spell out the stages of development in detail, we do need to grasp, in a more concrete and specific way, some of the essentials of successful self-emergence.

We shall touch on aspects of individuation from four perspectives: sexual, emotional, cognitive, and moral.

In considering the sexual realm, I offer two brief psychotherapy vignettes by way of illustration.

John was a thirty-one-year-old engineer who had come to therapy because of feelings of anxiety, confusion, and incompetence in relationships with women. He was a virgin. He professed

---

*An excellent discussion of this process may be found in Joseph Chilton Pearce's *Magical Child*, although there is much of a speculative nature in this book that needs to be read with more than a little skepticism.

a desire to be married and to have a family of his own and at the same time complained that women might as well be members of a different species, utterly incomprehensible to him.

After we had gone through his history and had developed a rapport, we started on sentence-completion work. I explained that I would give him a number of sentence stems and that he was to keep repeating each stem, finishing the sentence in any way he wished, until I signaled him to stop, at which point we would move on to a new stem. We began with "Mother was always—."

Mother was always—
> Beautiful.
> Remote.
> Walking around the house in a negligee.
> Mysterious.
> Seductive.
> Telling me I was her "little man."
> A little overwhelming.

With mother I felt—
> Confused.
> Fascinated.
> Sometimes excited.
> I loved the smell of her.
> I wanted to be close.
> Good.
> I was special.
> I was her favorite.
> I was more important than father.

Father was always—
> Quiet.
> Looking at me strangely.
> Scaring me without saying a word.
> Off somewhere.
> Looking at me as if he were just about to say something,
>   but he never did.
> Passive and yet ominous.

With father I felt—
   Frightened.
   Uneasy.
   Watchful.
   Sometimes defiant.
   I wanted us to be closer.
   I wanted us to be friends.
   I would have like him to talk to me more.
   I wanted him to help me understand what a man was.

This was enough to suggest that my client was in some sense stuck at a childhood phase of development that, in the Freudian system, is identified as the Oedipal stage. According to the Freudian theory of psychosexual development, to which I do not subscribe, every male and female child is destined to pass through what psychoanalysis describes as the oral, anal, phallic (or Oedipal), latency, and genital phases.[24] Freud's theory of psychosexual development was intended to trace the vicissitudes of the sexual energy that he posited and called *libido* and that he believed to be a prime force in all human behavior. In the Oedipal period, according to Freud, it is the universal fate of every male and female child to desire sexually the parent of the opposite sex and to wish for the death of the parent of the same sex. As a theory of development, it represents an unwarranted generalization; nonetheless, sometimes the problem does occur, and when it does, sentence-completion work as a means of establishing that fact is simpler and more rapid, reliable, and effective than any other approach of which I have knowledge—certainly more so than the techniques of free association and dream interpretation.*

Wanting to explore this line of inquiry further with the present client, I shifted to a new sentence stem.

If I could have had mother all to myself—
   It would have been wonderful.
   We could have been closer.

---

*For more on the uses of the sentence completion technique in therapy, see my *If You Could Hear What I Cannot Say*.

I would have felt loved.
I would have felt like a man.
I wonder how my brothers and sisters would have felt.
Father would have been hurt.
I don't think Mother would have missed father.

In a purposely relaxed and easygoing manner, I gave him a new stem to explore. "Just keep repeating, 'If I could have had sex with mother—,' and let's see what occurs to you." (He gave no evidence of being taken aback by this stem, as my clients almost never do—sometimes to the astonishment of psychoanalyst observers at my group therapy sessions.)

If I could have had sex with mother—
I would have liked it.
I would have known she loved me.
I would have been scared.
It would have been overwhelming.
It would have been exciting.
Father would have hated me; he might have killed me.
Father would have felt I betrayed him.
I might have been able to let go of mother.
Perhaps I would be free to fall in love today.
I wouldn't still feel I want something from mother.

In discussing his reaction to what he had been saying, he seemed surprised and yet unsurprised, as if at one level it was all new and unfamiliar and at another level it was already known— which was precisely the case. We continued with another stem.

If mother thought I was in a happy sexual relationship—
She'd be jealous.
She wouldn't understand.
She'd tell me that no one will ever love me as she does.
She'd feel abandoned.
She'd say, "How can you do this to me?"
She'd try to break us up.
She'd tell me the girl isn't good enough.
She'd say, "I hope you're not planning to get married."

119

She'd warn me about feminine wiles.
She'd want to know what the girl wants from me.
She might suggest that a doctor check me for venereal
    disease.

The scary thing about women is—
    I don't know what they want.
    They're overwhelming.
    They have needs I don't understand.
    They give conflicting messages.
    I'll be swallowed up.
    I won't know what to do.
    I might have trouble having an erection.
    They'll want more from me than I can give.
    I'll be dominated.

Women to me are—
    Overwhelming.
    Powerful.
    Insatiable.
    Frightening.
    Exciting.
    Seductive.
    Controlling.
    Too much like mother.

If it turns out that other women are not my mother—
    Mother would have a fit.
    I might be able to fall in love.
    I could be a man.
    I could grow up.
    I wouldn't have to be so frightened of being controlled.
    Mother would feel I had abandoned her.
    I might be able to let go of mother.

If mother had seen that I was only a little boy—
    I wouldn't be so screwed up today.
    She wouldn't have tried to seduce me.
    Maybe she would have loved me as a little boy.

Maybe I could have loved her as a mother.
Maybe she wouldn't have looked to me for what she
    didn't get from father.
Maybe I wouldn't be so afraid of women.
Maybe I would have gotten the support I needed.
Maybe I wouldn't feel like I'm still four years old.
Maybe I wouldn't still be longing for a mother.
Maybe I wouldn't put mother's face on every woman I
    meet.

In subsequent therapy sessions he engaged in imaginary dialogue with his mother and father in which he played all the roles, the purpose of which was to allow him further to own, experience, and integrate feelings and reactions from long ago that were obstructing his development to normal adulthood. I shall not linger on the therapeutic process here, since my purpose is only to illustrate a failure of adequate separation and individuation as it affects sexual development.

Before going on to the emotional realm, I want to offer another illustration of a sexual problem, this time involving a disposition to masochism.

"It's frightening," Sally said to me during one of our early therapy sessions, "because I'm afraid one day I'll let things go too far. It's been more like playacting so far: me the helpless victim, my lover free to do whatever he wants with me. Me playing the little girl, him playing the punishing daddy. It's exciting. I don't know why ordinary sex doesn't do anything for me. When a man is kind or tender, I can't feel anything. Sometimes I feel repulsed. When I'm tied up, given orders, when I feel like someone else has taken over my will, it's rapture beyond words. I guess this sounds awfully sick, doesn't it?"

"How powerful you must feel!" I said.

She looked astonished and uncomprehending. "Powerful? What do you mean? Haven't you understood? Power is the last thing I feel. The whole point is, I become excited through feeling weak and helpless."

"Yes, exactly, weak and helpless. And the man has made you so."

"Yes!"

121

"And the man is doing just what you want him to do."

"Yes."

"He makes you feel part child, part slave."

"Yes."

"And that's how you want to feel."

She looked at me, puzzled. "So what are you saying?"

"I would say that a woman who is so effective in getting a man to do just exactly what she wants is powerful. Not every woman knows how to do that."

She began to laugh. "Oh, I see. Yes, to tell you the truth, it is rather a lovely feeling. Weakness is its own kind of strength."

"Precisely."

"But it's humiliating."

"And isn't that delicious?"

"But what's it all about? What does it all mean?"

"You mean you don't know?"

"Of course I don't know! If I knew, I wouldn't be here, probably."

"It's a complete mystery."

"Yes!" she said, with some exasperation.

"Let's do some sentence completion. 'When my lover ties me up—'"

When my lover ties me up—
    I feel helpless.
    I feel controlled.
    I feel taken care of.
    I feel someone else is in charge.
    I feel safe.
    I feel loved.
    I feel free of responsibility.
    I feel my life is in his hands.
    I feel he really cares for me.
    I feel I'm really important to him.
    I'm the center of attention.
    Everything revolves around me.

When my lover orders me around—
    I feel submissive.

I feel feminine.
I feel loved.
I become sexually excited.
I feel I really matter.
I feel I have my own god to look after me.
I feel intoxicated.
I remember the one time when daddy lost his temper and spanked me and I thought, Maybe he does love me after all.

Daddy was always—
Not there.
Remote.
Distant.
Leaving me alone.

Mother was always—
Busy.
Flying around.
Playing bridge.
Ignoring me.
Letting me get away with murder.
Telling me I was her good, sweet girl.

What I wanted from father and didn't get was—
To be taught things.
To be cared for.
To be loved.
To be noticed.
To tell me what was right and what was wrong.
To let me know when I've gone too far.
To give me attention rather than money.

What I wanted from mother and didn't get was—
Time.
Love.
To help me understand about life and things.
Guidance.
A role model I could respect.

123

When my father finally spanked me—
   I felt he loved me.
   I felt I mattered to him.
   I thought I had found a way to get his attention.
   I thought, At last I have a father; but it never happened
      again.
   It felt wonderful being overpowered.
   Everything inside me felt like it was swimming.
   I got dizzy, and I wanted the dizziness to get worse.

The bad thing about a man who treats me well is—
   There's no excitement.
   He wouldn't react to my provocations.
   He'd let me get away with things.
   I'd feel alone.
   I'd feel abandoned and unprotected.
   There'd be no ground underneath my feet.
   I'd just be floating.
   There'd be no foundation to my life.
   I'd hate him for not understanding me.

The hard thing about growing up is—
   I don't want to!
   I'm not ready.
   It's boring.
   It means I'll grow old and eventually die.

Building on the foundation of these sentence completions, we were able to see that her masochistic longings reflected the unmet safety and support needs of childhood and the fear of self-responsibility and, in addition, the fear of growing up, growing old, and dying. Once again, I shall not concern myself with the subsequent phases of therapy, which would take us away from the immediate subject.

   These two stories have in common a failure to negotiate successfully a stage of childhood development, which obstructed evolution toward adult sexuality. Sexuality was arrested at the level of preautonomy. A necessary process of separation and individuation had failed to take place.

An individual who appears to fulfill conventional criteria of adult sexuality—say, someone who is heterosexual, orgasmic, and with no bizarre predilections or fetishes—may still be emotionally immature.

Sheila, a married mother, age twenty-seven, displayed symptoms of agitated depression when her forty-four-year-old mother announced her intention to remarry after many years of being single.

"You've always been available to me whenever I needed you," Sheila protested. "Now you'll be traveling, flying around the country with your husband, busy, busy, busy—where will you be when I need you?"

When I suggested that surely, at the age of twenty-seven, she was competent to take care of herself, she gave an astonishing answer. "I didn't ask to be born. Mother owes me. Her obligation doesn't end just because the law says I'm grown up."

She had no friends. When I asked her about this, she answered, "My daughter is my friend." Her daughter was one year old at the time.

In terms of emotional age, I would have put her at a pre-teenage level. She was unable to relate to men and women of her own age. Her voice was that of a child, and so were most of her observations about life.

And yet in school she had been a brilliant student. Her thinking ability was above average, when she and her own life were not involved. But since the time that she left school, she had thought about nothing but herself and her daughter. Her marriage was suffering, in part because of her husband's feelings of neglect, in part because her husband seemed almost as immature as she was.

Her mother had been widowed at an early age and had raised her with help from no one. Because her mother had had to go to work, Sheila had been placed in a nursery school. "You weren't there when I needed you," she told her mother.

"I've spent a lot of years trying to make it up to you," her mother replied sadly.

"You can't make it up," said Sheila. "I feel abandoned."

Her mother, who had requested that our next meeting take place without Sheila, asked what I thought she should do.

"Get married and be happy. Thinking you should be doing

something is playing into her problem. I suspect that you've already overprotected her too much, to make up for your absence during those early years. Let her suffer, let her make mistakes, let her find out she can survive without you. Apologizing or feeling guilty serves only to confirm her in her feelings of helplessness and dependency."

"If only she would agree to come to therapy," her mother said.

"But she won't. You've offered, and she's refused. Besides, your cutting the umbilical cord is part of the therapy she needs. Letting go is the most helpful thing you can do."

After Sheila's husband left her, she moved to Canada and subsequently remarried. The man was homosexual, which Sheila knew, and they agreed to a sexless relationship in which Sheila would be supported in exchange for looking after his home as well as performing social duties.

"This is just temporary," Sheila wrote her mother. "I don't expect the marriage to last. But for the time being it's very convenient. My daughter and I are treated very well. That's all I care about now. I wish you could be more understanding. You supported yourself ever since you were young, so you can't understand my choosing not to work. But I'm not going to treat my daughter the way you treated me. I'm not going to go off to work and leave her alone. So someone has to take care of me. That's just the way it is. In my own way, I'm a very independent person. Didn't I come to Canada on my own? And I'm not immoral, either, because my husband doesn't even want any sex. So why should you be disappointed in me? Why can't anyone understand that my daughter means everything in the world to me and I must be with her twenty-four hours a day? And later, I'll be wanting to be there for her when she comes home from school. It'll be a long time before she's ready to go off on her own. I'll think about my life then."

In the event that Sheila does not change, the likelihood seems high that one day her daughter will have to undergo her own struggle for separation and individuation, and the struggle will probably be unnecessarily difficult, because it is not easy to visualize Sheila supporting her daughter's impulses toward independence. Like many mothers who invest their whole sense of identity and worth in their relationship to their children, she is unlikely to recognize that she has made of her love a choke-hold.

126

Consider some of the differences between emotionally mature and immature people in the conduct of their relationships.

Emotionally mature, autonomous individuals understand that other people do not exist merely to satisfy their needs. Maturity entails accepting the fact that no matter how much love and caring exist between two persons, each of us is ultimately responsible for our happiness and our self-esteem. An autonomous individual does not experience his or her self-esteem as continually in question or in jeopardy. The source of approval resides within the self. It is not at the mercy of every encounter with another person. One of the characteristics of the emotionally mature is that they have grown beyond the need to prove to anyone that they are a good boy or a good girl—or, for that matter, a rebelliously bad boy or bad girl. The essence of their relationship to their spouse or romantic partner is not that of daughter or son, although they may experience moments when they would like their partner to function as mother or father; such moments, experienced occasionally, can be quite normal, but they do not form the essence of the relationship.

In the best of relationships, there are occasional frictions and unavoidable hurts. The tendency of poorly individuated, immature individuals is to translate such minor incidents into major evidence of rejection.

Emotionally mature men and women have a greater capacity to see the normal frictions of everyday life in realistic perspective; even if they are hurt occasionally, they tend not to make such moments into catastrophes. Further, such men and women respect their partner's occasional needs to be alone, to be preoccupied, to think about vital matters other than the relationship. Well-individuated people also give this freedom to themselves.

Men and women who have reached an adult level of individuation and maturity have assimilated and integrated the ultimate fact of human aloneness. They understand that it is the fact of aloneness that gives love its unique intensity.

With emotionally immature men and women, the story is entirely different. Many such persons face life with the attitude that "when I was five years old, important needs of mine were not met—and until they are, I'm not moving on to six!" On a basic level, these people are very passive, even though on more superficial levels they may appear active and even aggressive. They are waiting to be rescued, waiting to be told they are good boys or good girls, waiting to be validated or confirmed by some outside source.

They did not discover their possibilities for strength and self-support in the normal course of their development through childhood and adolescent years; now they may have organized their lives around their sense of deficiency, trying either to please, to be taken care of, or, alternately, to control and dominate, to manipulate and *coerce* the satisfaction of their needs and wants, because they don't trust the authenticity of anyone's professed love or caring. They have no confidence that what they are, without their facades and manipulations, is *enough*.

Whether they seek completion and fulfillment through domination or through submission, controlling or being controlled, ordering or obeying, there is always the fundamental sense of emptiness, a void in the center of their being.

An immature woman looks at her lover and, deep in her psyche, there is the thought "My father made me feel rejected; you will take his place and give me what he failed to give me. I will create a house for you and cook your meals and bear your children—I will be your good little girl."

A man looks at his bride and there is the thought "Now I am a married man; I am grown up; I have responsibilities—just like father. I will work hard, I will be your protector, I will take care of you—just as father did with mother. Then he—and you, and everyone—will see that I am a good boy."

Symbiotic dependency is not a foundation for powerful, passionate love between a man and a woman. When such children marry and fantasy collapses to reality, disillusionment and mutual blame are commonly the result. Passionate love, on the other hand, ignites in a context of separation and individuation.

We now turn to the cognitive realm.

Maturity, in its broadest sense, is the state of being fully grown or developed. Cognitive or intellectual maturity is successful development of a human consciousness. The most famous and influential student of cognitive development is Jean Piaget.[61] No brief summary can do justice to the richness of his observations and researches in this area. Here I offer only the briefest of sketches.

Piaget divides cognitive development into four major periods; these are subdivided into a number of stages and substages. Lasting from birth through the first eighteen to twenty months, the *sensorimotor* stage basically concerns preverbal intellectual development. This is the very period in which the infant is making the early stages of transition from submergent consciousness to explicit consciousness, from nonego to ego, from nonself to self. Here Piaget's studies track the child's way of interacting with the world, from primitive reflex sucking, hand movements, and the random eye movements of the neonate to the stage when the child is using internalized visual and motor symbols to invent new means of solving problems at a still fairly primitive level.

During the *preoperational* period, which extends approximately until the child enters school, children acquire the ability to use symbols and language. They are not yet able to construct chains of reasoning, note contradictions, or adapt what they say in ways appropriate to the needs of the listener.

The years between the start of schooling and the onset of puberty are the period of *concrete operations*, during which children acquire a coherent cognitive system with which they are able to understand their world and effectively interact with it, and into which they can fit unfamiliar experiences.

Adolescence marks the start of the period of *formal operations*, when boys and girls become capable of thinking propositionally, of conceptualizing, and of using hypotheses. Full mastery of the level of formal operations entails the ability not only to conceptualize but *to think about thinking*, to reflect on one's own reasoning processes, which, according to Piaget, represents the highest level of intellectual development. It is also the level that is least often mastered completely. Rarely do individuals reach it on their own; in most cases a good deal of training and education is needed for the cultivation of the cognitive self-examining and self-critical faculty.

Once again we can note a theme mentioned earlier: progressive movement to higher and higher levels of abstraction, culminating in the stage in which abstract thought becomes its own matrix.

In the early stages of development, then, a child knows only perceptual concretes; he or she does not know abstractions or principles. A child's world is only the immediate now; the ability to think, plan, or act on a long-range basis is not yet developed; the future is largely unreal. At this stage, a high level of dependency is naturally inevitable, even though great differences are already observable among children with regard to independence and self-assertiveness.

As the child grows, the intellectual field widens. The child learns language, begins to grasp abstractions, begins to generalize, learns to make increasingly subtle discriminations, learns to look for principles, progressively acquires the ability to project a more and more distant future; the child rises from the sensory-perceptual level of consciousness to the conceptual level. Entailed in this progression is a growing capacity for *objectivity*—an ability to perceive persons, situations, and facts apart from the individual's own desires, fears, and needs. This capacity for objectivity is an essential of independence, of autonomy.

Intellectual maturity is the ability to think in principles; it presupposes both the conceptual function and the capacity for objectivity. Of course, cognitive or intellectual development is not entirely separable from moral and emotional development. There are persons who are brilliant at conceptualizing principles in higher mathematics or the stock market but who become helplessly blind to abstractions and principles when their focus is on personal problems with their spouses, children, friends, or associates at work. Perhaps I should say that an ultimate manifestation of maturity is evidenced by the ability to think in principles *about oneself*.

I need hardly stress how rare is the ability to have the same perspective on one's own behavior that one has on the behavior of another person.

In the absence of this level of maturity, there is always some dependency, no matter how responsible the person may be in other aspects of his or her life. It is our spouses, our children, our friends, our work associates who are left to absorb the consequences of our underdeveloped consciousness.

Maturity entails the ability to perceive the fairness or unfairness, the right or wrong, the justice or injustice, of our own behavior and the behavior of others *with equal clarity*. This is one of the meanings of objectivity. It is also one of the manifestations of well-realized autonomy. It is not "unselfishness" but a triumph of selfhood—a triumph of individuation.

This leads us directly to the fourth aspect of self-development that I would like to consider: the progression toward moral autonomy.

While the ability to make appropriate moral or ethical discriminations is obviously tied in the most intimate way to the ability to make cognitive discriminations, it does not follow that a high level of cognitive development automatically guarantees a correspondingly high level of moral development. Moral development is a separate track in an individual's evolution.

Contrary to the teachings of behaviorists and social-learning theorists, whose accounts of morality and moral behavior are put forth exclusively in terms of social conditioning, positive and negative reinforcement, and the like, there exists within the growing human organism the need to generate moral choices, decisions, and discriminations; this is intrinsic to the developmental process. And it is easy enough to perceive why it would have to be. Reality continually confronts us with a wide variety of alternatives; we require a code of values to guide our actions. Moral values are not an arbitrary invention of society or of religion; they are biological, in that they are requirements of survival and effective functioning. I shall elaborate on this point when I discuss the relationship of morality and self-esteem.

Just as a newborn infant has no sense of ego or self, so it has no awareness of morality. A capacity for ethical judgment slowly evolves and goes through various stages in the course of an individual's growth. While psychologists specializing in the process of development are by no means in full agreement concerning how the self as moral agent evolves, there is fairly strong agreement that successful culmination of this process is a condition of moral autonomy, in which the individual behaves in ways he or she judges to be moral, not because of fear or punishment or social disapproval, and not because of blind, conformist rule following, but rather because of an authentic, firsthand assessment of the right and wrong of given situations.[41, 46]

I am not concerned, in the immediate context, with the important question of *how* we justify our assessments; that will have to await the discussion of ethics in a later chapter. Here I am concerned only to observe that autonomy in the field of ethics represents a very advanced level in the maturational process and is not widely attained.

We have already seen, in our discussion of guilt, how commonly people reproach themselves for violating standards not of their own choosing: the values and expectations of significant others, of parents and other authority figures. Often, when persons are wrestling with moral dilemmas, they are unaware of the different voices debating within them, the voice of mother pointing to one path, the voice of father to another, the voice of a teacher, spiritual guru, or psychotherapist to a third—and underneath all of this, the often faint voice of the individual involved, weakly struggling to have a say in the decision-making process.

One of the characteristics of a high level of autonomy is respect for inner signals, the voice of the authentic self, which often contradicts the teachings of conventional morality. This self might tell one to be compassionate when conventional morality says to be stern, or to be angry when conventional morality says to be humble, or to be proud when conventional morality says to be self-disparaging, or to be challenging when conventional morality says to be compliant.

While psychologists generally agree that imitative rule following represents a fairly early stage of a child's moral development, a stage to be outgrown and transcended with subsequent knowledge and maturity, it is difficult to escape the conclusion that imitativeness and conformity to authority are more the norm than the exception among most adults. Lest this judgment seem too severe, let us shift our perspective from the intimately personal to the sociological.

Every twenty seconds on this planet, one human being kills another human being.

To interpret the above statistic as evidence of humanity's innate cruelty or "selfishness" is to miss the point of the horror completely. Viewed globally, the overwhelming majority of these killings were not committed for personal gain. They do not fall into the category of individual crime. Most of the persons who did the killing were obeying authority, fighting for a cause, submerging self and personal judgment in the service of something allegedly greater than themselves, more important than their "private egos" or "individual consciences."

Recall, in this context, the famous experiment conducted at Yale University by Stanley Milgrim and reported in his book *Obedience to Authority*. Since the experiment is so well known, my summary will be brief.

In a brilliantly executed research study, Milgrim arranged that a group of experimental subjects, drawn from the general population, would be led to believe that they were serving the goals of science by administering increasingly severe and painful electric shocks to other volunteer subjects who failed to answer certain questions correctly. They were told that they were taking part in a study of the effects of punishment on learning.

Unaware that this latter group of subjects were, in effect, playacting, that the screams and cries to be released were merely a performance, and that the electric shocks were not real, the "aggressor" subjects were being tested, in a daringly imaginative way, on the limits of their willingness to surrender moral autonomy to the voice of authority.

Numerous controls were built into the design of the experiment to rule out any element of personal aggressiveness. The presiding experimenter had absolutely no power over the volunteer subjects and no financial reward to offer for compliance. Every factor was effectively eliminated except one: the disposition to obey perceived authority.

In advance of conducting the experiment, Milgrim invited a group of psychiatrists to predict the outcome. "With remarkable similarity they predicted that virtually all the subjects would refuse to obey the experimenter," he reports. The thirty-nine psychiatrists who answered Milgrim's questionnaire shared the view that "most people would not go beyond 150 volts (i.e., when the victim asked the first time to be released). They expected that only 4 percent would reach 300 volts, and that only a pathological fringe of about one in a thousand would administer the highest shock on the board."[53]

Under the instructions of the presiding scientist/authority figure, ignoring the cries and screams of the "victims," *more than 60 percent of the Yale subjects* kept pressing the dummy buttons up to the limit of 450 volts, even though this voltage was clearly marked "Danger—severe shock."

This experiment has been repeated in a number of universities throughout the world, with essentially the same results. In other countries, the percentage of persons who obeyed to the upper limit of voltage was generally higher than at Yale. In Munich it was 85 percent.

Milgrim writes:

> For a man to feel responsible for his actions, he must sense that the behavior has flowed from "the self." In the situation we have studied, subjects have precisely the opposite view of their actions—namely, they see them as originating in the motives of some other person. Subjects in the experiment frequently said, "If it were up to me, I would not have administered shocks to the learner."[53]

As suggested by the psychiatrists' predictions, most people are astonished when they learn the results of this experiment. They are certain that in the same circumstances they would act differently. They profess not to understand how such cruelty is possible among civilized human beings, especially fellow Americans.

The experiment is well known; I submit that its meaning is not. One of the theses of this book is that most of us have been trained to push those buttons since the day we were born. This training is not the result of some person's or group's malevolence but is inherent in our methods of child-rearing and education. We deal here with the whole process by which a new human being is prepared for life in society, a process that throws countless obstacles in the path of developing moral autonomy.

We are taught very early to respect external signals about internal signals, to respect the voice of others above the voice of self. A "good" child is one who "minds" his or her elders, who "behaves." We are taught to identify virtue with compliance with the wants and expectations of others. We are taught conformity as the ultimate civic good. We are taught obedience as the price of love and acceptance. We are taught, sometimes explicitly, sometimes implicitly, and from the widest possible variety of sources, that the self is evil!, or unimportant, or petty, or something to be tamed and suppressed, or negligible in the vast scheme of things, or merely an illusion—and that to honor the self in the sense I have been developing is to alienate the individual from family or community or society or God or the Universe or the Whole.

Very few forces within our culture actively encourage intellectual or moral autonomy. The more common goal of parents and teachers is social adaptation.

Generally, schools are places where children learn not to think, but to follow the rules. That favorite word of psychologists and sociologists, *socialization*, which describes this process of learning the rules, is also used in a political context to signify "given over to public ownership."

I vividly recall my own experiences in grade school and high school. I quickly learned the two most important values in that world: the ability to remain silent and motionless for long periods of time and the ability to march with my fellow students in a neat row from one classroom to another. In other words, don't cause the teacher trouble. School was not a place to learn independent thinking, to have one's self-assertiveness encouraged, to have one's autonomy nourished; it was a place to learn how to fit into some nameless system created by some nameless others and called "the world" or "society" or "the way life is." And "the way life is" was not to be questioned.

Many brilliant minds have commented on their dismal experiences in school, their boredom, their lack of appropriate intellectual stimulation and nourishment, their sense that the last thing the educational system was designed for was the cultivation of minds. Schools are interested, not in autonomy, but in the manufacture of someone's notion of "good citizens."

"In education," writes Carl Rogers in *On Becoming a Person*, "we tend to turn out conformists, stereotypes, individuals whose education is 'completed,' rather than freely creative and original thinkers."

What makes this state of affairs particularly unfortunate is that schools represent priceless opportunities to undo or at least counteract a child's negative experiences at home. Teachers have a unique opportunity to offer the child an alternative view of self and the world, to give a child the experience of having his or her feelings, dignity, and mind respected, and thereby to provide a powerfully healing transition to adolescence and adulthood. And this sometimes does happen—but when it does it is the exception, not the norm.

Commenting on the disposition of parents and teachers to demand obedience and conformity as primary values, to discourage normal and healthy progress toward autonomy, Piaget writes in *The Moral Judgment of the Child,* "If one thinks of the systematic resistance offered by people to the authoritarian method, and the admirable ingenuity employed by children the world over to evade disciplinarian constraint, one cannot help regarding as defective a system which allows so much effort to be wasted instead of using it in cooperation."

None of the foregoing is offered as an argument for giving a child unrestricted freedom. Children need limits. They need guidelines. They need them for their security, and they need them for their survival. Teachers and parents who refuse to take a stand on anything with children, refuse to uphold any values, or who convey the notion that all moral principles are old-fashioned or irrelevant, do not do their children a service. Adults do possess greater knowledge than children. The question is, How is this knowledge to be transmitted? One can teach with respect, or one can teach with intimidation. One can speak to a child's intelligence or to his or her fear of punishment. One can offer a child reasonable choices within sane and comprehensible ground rules, or one can lay down the law, as is done in the army. One can accept a child's making mistakes as a natural part of the growth process, or one can inculcate a terror of mistakes by reacting with ridicule or harsh punitiveness.

Let us pause for a moment on this issue of the right to make mistakes, because it is of supreme importance to the art of teaching and to the art of parenting. Many a client in therapy, when given the sentence stem "If I had been given permission to make mistakes—," has responded with such ends as:

I wouldn't be such a procrastinator.

I'd be willing to tell people what I think.

I wouldn't be afraid to commit to a goal.

I'd trust myself more.

I'd be more ambitious.

I'd take more risks.

I'd care more about what I thought and less about what others think.

I'd make fewer mistakes.

I'd have more confidence in my mind.

One of the most important ways in which teachers and parents can lay a valuable foundation for the growth of healthy self-esteem in children is by accepting as natural and normal the process of making mistakes. With or without adult support, when an individual of any age acquires a rational perspective on mistakes—allows him- or herself to err without punitive self-reproach—then self-esteem is nourished and fostered. And fewer mistakes are perpetrated, because the individual's consciousness is not controlled by fear.

No one who is terrified of making mistakes can attain moral autonomy.

The process of successful growth to psychological maturity—to intellectual and moral autonomy—depends on a person's accepting intellectual responsibility for his or her own existence. As a human being grows to adulthood, reality presents increasingly more complex challenges in thought, knowledge, judgment, and decision making. At each stage, the responsibility involves both cognition and evaluation; the individual has to acquire knowledge of facts and has to pass value judgments and choose goals. The consequence of accepting responsibility is the self-confident state of a sovereign consciousness. The consequence of responding negatively is a state of intellectual, or cognitive, dependency.

Apart from the environmental factors we have already discussed, there are at least four factors that can motivate—*not* necessitate—a person's default on the responsibility of independence and cognitive self-reliance:

1. Thinking requires mental work.

2. A policy of responsibility toward truth and facts, practiced

consistently as a way of life, forbids one the possibility of indulging antithetical desires or emotions.

3. If a person makes an error at any step of the thinking process and acts on that error, he or she may suffer pain, defeat, or destruction.

4. Independent thinking often brings a person into conflict with the opinions and judgments of others, thus provoking disapproval or animosity.

While intellectual and moral autonomy are obviously related, the fact is that there are persons who have the courage to challenge the *cognitive* judgments of world figures, but lack the courage to challenge the *value* judgments of the folks next door. Why is this so?

As I discuss in *The Psychology of Self-Esteem*, normative abstractions, such as "justice," for instance, stand on a higher, more advanced level of the hierarchy of our concepts than do many of our cognitive abstractions, such as "green" or "industry." For many, the distance of moral abstractions from direct perceptual experience is fearsome and discomfiting; it demands a stronger commitment to the efficacy of their own mind than they possess.

Furthermore, the fear of relying on the judgment of our own mind is felt most acutely in the realm of values because of the direct consequences of our judgments for our life and well-being. The evaluative errors that we make affect us personally far more often—and often far more devastatingly—than do most of our cognitive errors. To assume responsibility for choosing our values, principles, and goals, relying solely upon our own reason and understanding—to honor our internal signals to that extent—is to practice the ultimate form of intellectual independence, the one most difficult for the overwhelming majority of human beings and for which their upbringing has least prepared them.

Still another reason that the fear of independence is most intense in the sphere of value judgments is the fact that independence in this area is most likely to bring a person into conflict with other people. Cognitive differences do not necessarily generate personal animosity among people; value differences commonly do, particularly when basic issues are involved. Therefore, independence in the sphere of value judgments is more demanding psychologically.

Since a social form of existence is natural and appropriate to us, and since we derive many survival benefits from living among and dealing with others, the desire to have harmonious and benevolent relationships with others is not a breach of proper independence. It becomes such a breach only if a person places that desire above his or her own perception of reality. When the price of harmony with others becomes the surrender of our mind, an autonomous individual chooses not to pay it.

In understanding the barriers to autonomy, still another motive needs consideration. We can learn from one another, but we cannot share the act of being conscious or of thinking. We can share the results—namely, our thoughts and perceptions—but consciousness, awareness, thinking, reasoning is, ultimately, an individual, solitary process, not a social one. And many people dread independent thought and judgment precisely because of this factor of inescapable aloneness; it makes them aware of their own separateness as living entities; it makes them aware of the responsibility they must bear for their own existence.

Finally, to think for oneself is to face the fact of one's own being and thus to confront the possibility—perhaps the terror—of *non*being.

To think, to judge, to choose our values is to be *individuated*, to create a distinct, personal identity. But thus to affirm that I exist is to open myself to the realization that I am finite, that my life is limited, that I am mortal, that one day I will die.

The rebellion against the inevitability of death results in a rebellion against the challenges and opportunities of life. If I refuse to live fully, I cannot die.

So: fear of autonomy entails fear of self-responsibility entails fear of identity entails fear of aloneness entails fear of death.

That which does not exist cannot perish.

This issue is of such profound importance that I shall need to return to it after we have explored further and from other perspectives the nature and challenges of the individuation process.

9

The Problem of Self-Alienation

Today, there appears to be growing recognition that philosophically, culturally, and educationally, we require a psychology of balance, of integration. Awareness of the world and awareness of the self are understood increasingly as equal necessities for optimal human existence.

An excessively external focus commonly results in self-estrangement, spiritual impoverishment, and the compulsive pursuit of activity for its own sake. An excessively internal focus leads to passivity, helplessness to cope with many of the basic problems of existence, and resignation to avoidable human suffering—which results, once again, in self-alienation.

In this chapter I am chiefly concerned with showing that the repression of emotion and the disowning of experience, the precursors of self-alienation, inevitably sabotage clarity of thinking and the integrity of consciousness—with disastrous consequences for autonomy, most particularly with regard to value judgments.

Let me begin with the general observation that in order to function successfully a person needs to be in contact with the universe in which he or she acts—and with his or her own needs, feelings, desires, frustration, capabilities, and goals. To the extent that awareness is blocked in either direction, life and well-being are impaired.

It is particularly important to understand that a blindness concerning important aspects of self leads to a blindness concerning important aspects of the environment. A person who denies a need for companionship and nurturing, for instance, may be oblivious to opportunities to satisfy that need, such as signs of interest and friendship from people who care. A person who denies the reality of his or her pain will be blind to the source of the pain, such as the wrong kind of friends, and be hurt again and again by these friends. A person who disowns feelings of anger may falsely attribute them to others—the process of *projection*—and see anger where it does not exist. We deal here with a profoundly important law of psychological functioning: *Awareness moves freely in both directions—or it moves freely in neither.*

But how do self-blindness, self-fragmentation, and self-alienation come into being? That is the issue we shall proceed to consider.

The phenomenon of self-alienation, or self-fragmentation, may refer to one or more of a number of interrelated problems: dissociation from the body as part of self; being out of touch with our needs; emotional blockage; the severance from explicit awareness of thoughts, attitudes, inclinations, yearnings; the denial of important capacities that lie dormant or unrecognized. Taken as a whole, with all of these overlapping meanings included, this is the condition I described in an earlier book as the problem of the *disowned self*.

To disown means to cease to recognize as our own—to cease to recognize our body, our emotions, our thoughts, our attitudes, our aspirations, our abilities as ours. We thus radically restrict and impoverish our sense of self. We have less access to our inner signals, and consequently we become more dependent on signals from others. We need others to tell us what to think, how to live, when to express which emotion, what is appropriate and what is inappropriate, and so forth. By ourselves, we barely exist; our sense of self is often reduced to little more than a sense of anxiety. In such a state of self-alienation, we are prone to becoming approval addicts, love addicts, group-membership addicts, system and structure addicts, belief-system addicts, guru and leader addicts, escape from pain/inner emptiness/anxiety addicts.

Self-alienation precludes autonomy. Although, granted, we are dealing with matters of degree, and most people exist on a continuum, this principle is an underlying theme of the discussion that follows.

Let us begin with alienation from the body.

The infant child's first sense of self is almost entirely as a body self: self as physical organism. This was what Freud meant when he said that our first ego is a body ego.[22] Later, as the mind develops, the child learns to relocate the sense of self "upward": ego and self find their primary location in mind.

When growth proceeds appropriately, the body is recognized as part of self but not the totality. Consciousness differentiates from body—or, as some would say, *transcends* body—and a more complex and comprehensive sense of self evolves.

But inherent in this process is the potential for *dissociation* from body. Where there is dissociation, body is neither all of self or even an aspect of self but, rather, *non*self. In our culture the overwhelming majority of people exist in varying degrees of estrangement from their own bodies—and often the voice of parents joins the voice of nuns joins the voice of athletic coaches in encouraging that split.*

The child can see the body as a source of parental irritation and even revulsion if, for example, the mother conveys disgust in the way that she bathes or touches it. Perhaps the child becomes ill and then begins to hate the body as a source of suffering and betrayal. Or the child sees a loved one sicken and die, and again the body is perceived as the traitor. It is the body that allows not only pain but death to enter. In childhood or adolescence the body may be perceived as the sinful source or repository of sexual longings and therefore of guilt. In school, a child's mind/body split may be exacerbated through physical education teachers who see the body as an object to be beaten into performing, to be controlled and manipulated. The child may be taught to override bodily signals of pain or to become unconscious of them. There is growing evidence that any number of unnecessary accidents and injuries among professional and amateur athletes and dancers are the

---

*Partly as a response to this split, there have developed any number of innovative body therapies that aim, in different ways, at reintegration. Some of the most outstanding include the Alexander technique, the revolutionary work of Wilhelm Reich, Alexander Lowen's Bioenergetics, Ida Rolf's Structural Integration, Charles Kelley's Radix program, the body work of Stanley Keleman, the discoveries of Moshe Feldenkrais. An excellent introduction to this subject may be found in *Listening to the Body* by Robert Masters and Jean Houston.

consequences of inappropriate practice and training methods that reflect a perspective of body-as-adversary.

The end of the road of bodily dissociation is the privilege of dying of a heart attack at the age of fifty. It is worth contemplating the fact that any number of major illnesses are preceded by long periods of ignored exhaustion.

By way of illustrating the relationship between autonomy and the body, I want to mention an incident that took place some years ago in a weekly personal growth group I was conducting. One of the participants was a twenty-five-year-old, rather attractive Catholic woman who complained of social insecurity, fear of self-assertiveness, and the inability to recognize her own desires. During the first few sessions, she sat for three and a half hours with a perfectly upright posture, her hands at her sides, her legs pressed tightly together from thighs to ankles, while others in the group, in a perfectly natural manner, adusted their body movements from time to time.

One evening, when she began to speak of her problems, I pointed out how she was sitting and asked her how she felt about it. She smiled pleasantly and responded, "I've always been taught to sit this way. Ever since I was a little girl. Mother taught me that's how a lady sits."

"But how does it feel to you?" I asked.

She looked thoughtful for a moment, as if this was a question she had never considered. Then she replied. "Actually, it's very uncomfortable. Quite painful, really."

"Can you sense what your body might like to do right now?"

Again she remained thoughtful for a moment, then wriggled in her chair, then grinned shyly and crossed her legs.

"How does that feel?" I asked.

"Much better," she said, sighing.

"So your body gives you one kind of signal, and your mother gives you another."

"Yes."

"Now you're confronted with a choice. To which signal will you listen?"

"Listening to my body feels better than listening to my mother," she said, as if she had just made an extraordinary discovery—which she had.

143

Autonomy begins with the body. The first voice of the authentic self is the voice of the body. The body is not all there is to autonomy, by any means, but it is the root, the foundation. Without the data the body provides, thinking cannot proceed effectively.

Indeed, human beings are often ignorant of their own bodies, dangerously out of touch with them, and this attitude is encouraged in all spheres. In the medical realm, for example, numerous reports have shown that a chief cause of damage to patients, including death, is the physician's failure to listen to the patient—out of a conviction that the body is a foreign object about which a patient is presumed not to have knowledge, even when the body in question is the patient's own. The solution lies, not in unthinking obedience to the dictates of authorities, but in a philosophical and cultural reorientation, beginning with the ability to hold two thoughts in our heads simultaneously: "On the one hand, I am more than my body; on the other, my body is me, a part of me, a manifestation and expression of me. Therefore, getting to know myself includes getting to know my body. If I allow my body to remain a stranger, 'the other', then in an important way I remain a stranger to myself."

One of the areas in which alienation from the body is most glaringly evident is the sexual. Studies demonstrate that a woman can have an orgasm while denying that she is sexually experiencing anything in particular, so blocked is she from her own pelvic sensations. If this particular problem is found more commonly in women that in men it is because women, in our culture, receive more messages aimed at inhibiting sexuality. The consequence is that many women do not know what gives them pleasure. They have been taught not to know—or not to find out.

Sometimes, working with a woman who is dissociated from her own body, and, more specifically, blocked in the pelvic area, I will ask her to perform bump-and-grind movements while saying aloud, over and over again, "I am a good girl." This exercise is a multilevel assault on the problem. Physically, the movements induce some relaxation of the pelvic musculature, increase blood circulation, and thereby raise the level of feeling. Psychologically, the physical movements are a complete repudiation of her childhood training, while the ironic humor of "I'm a good girl" interrupts her routine thought patterns and releases in her a fresh perspective. Sometimes, as the client begins to feel an increase of sensation in the pelvic area, anxiety arises, and she makes direct experiential contact with the fear of disapproval that inspired the blocking in the first place. As she is encouraged to accept the anxiety, it tends to disappear, and what she progressively experiences is a sense of liberation and excitement—*the sense of waking up*. Further work needs to be done on the voices within telling her that she is not to be a sexual being, but the first step is almost always to give the *body* a voice, to allow the life-force within her an opportunity to be felt and heard. Unblocking the body—unblocking feelings—is unblocking consciousness.[47]

Alienated and estranged from our bodies and our bodies' feelings, we sometimes experience our own impulses as something foreign. This is often the case with sexual desires. As a child, a man may have been starved for intimate physical closeness with his parents. To survive the pain of his unmet needs, he has learned to shut down, ceasing to feel his body's longings, armoring himself against it. Now, as an adult, he is compulsively sexual. He cannot understand why he feels driven to seduce almost every woman he encounters. At times he feels humiliated by his own sexual urges. Where do they come from? Why is he thus afflicted?

Once, working with such a man in therapy, I guided him into a hypnotic trance in order to explore his thoughts and feelings during the first moments of making love to a new woman. In the voice of a young boy, he said, "Why do I have to do this? Why can't I just ask you to hold me? Why do we have to have sex? Why can't we just cuddle?" He began to weep a child's tears.

Subsequent therapy consisted of allowing him to feel the pain of his unmet childhood needs—touch and body contact needs, in particular—with the consequent waking up of his emotional life in general. The more integrated he became with his body, the more connected with his feelings, the freer he became of the impulse toward undiscriminating sexual encounters. He began to experience sex as an expression of self, not as an embarrassment to self.

No matter how much we may value autonomy intellectually, the degree to which we can achieve it is intimately related to the degree of integration among our mind, emotions, and body. Autonomy is more than cerebral. It involves our entire being.

This principle is clearly evident when we consider the problem of alienation from our needs, feelings, and emotions.

We live in a psychological age—or at the beginning of one. It is doubtful if at any other time in history there has been so much awareness on the part of so many people that often they do not know what they feel, what they long for, or where they are going. The source of this emotional self-alienation—or, as it might better be described, this *unconsciousness*—resides in several factors.

To recapitulate the simplest and most obvious: most parents teach children to repress their feelings and emotions. They teach unconsciousness as a positive value, as one of the costs of being loved, found acceptable, regarded as "grown-up." Furthermore, emotionally remote and inhibited parents tend to produce emotionally remote and inhibited children, not only through their overt communications but also by their own behavior, which signals to the child what is "proper," "appropriate," "socially acceptable." Parents who accept certain teachings of religion are likely to infect their children with the disastrous notion that there are such things as "evil thoughts" or "evil emotions." The child may be filled with moral terror of his or her own inner life.

Let us pause to consider what, precisely, an emotion is. An emotion is both a mental and a physical event. It may be defined as an automatic psychological response, involving both mental and physiological features, to our subconscious appraisal of what we perceive as the beneficial or harmful relationship of some aspect of reality to ourselves. Emotions reflect the perceiver's value response to different aspects of reality: "for me or against me," "good for me or harmful," "to be pursued or to be avoided," and so forth.*

To cease to know what we feel is to cease to experience what things mean to us, *which is to be cut off from our own context*. And it is just this state that most of us, as children, were educated to regard as normal. Let me emphasize that I am speaking here and

---

*For a detailed discussion of the psychology of emotion, see *The Disowned Self*.

146

throughout about *feelings* and *emotions*, not about *actions*. I am not suggesting that we should act on or express everything we feel, not even in our most intimate relationships. We cannot avoid the responsibility of discrimination and judgment. But here we are concerned with the issue of consciousness itself. What are we allowed to be conscious of? What are we forbidden to be conscious of?

A child is typically encouraged by parents to conclude that emotions are potentially dangerous, that sometimes it is advisable to deny them, that they must be "controlled." What the effort at such control amounts to practically is that the child learns to disown the emotions and ceases to experience them. Just as emotions are a psychophysical experience, a mental and a physiological state, so the assault on emotions occurs on two levels. On the psychological level, a child deflects awareness, thereby ceasing to recognize or acknowledge undesired feelings. On the physical level, a child inhibits breathing, tenses his or her body, induces muscular tensions, and blocks the free flow of feelings, thereby inducing a partial state of numbness.*

Not only parents but also teachers communicate many messages concerning which feelings and emotions are acceptable and which are not. The child's peers also contribute to the process of self-estrangement, since children pass on to one another the messages they receive from their elders. It is a child of rare independence who manages to withstand this onslaught.

In the process of individuation, the individual encounters obstacles virtually from the beginning of life. In being encouraged to deny certain of his or her feelings, to nullify certain judgments and evaluations, to repudiate certain experiences, the child is

---

*While there have been many areas of disagreement concerning various aspects of Wilhelm Reich's work, one of his great achievements was to make us aware that the repression of emotions is not merely an intellectual act but is ultimately achieved at a bodily level. Interrupted breathing lowers the amount of oxygen available to the organism and diminishes its capacity to feel. By repeatedly tensing the various muscles that would ordinarily be mobilized were the emotions to be allowed free expression, we make our muscular contractions chronic, part of our structure, and thus our body becomes more and more "armored." The essence of growth, in Reich's view, is the process of dissolving our psychological and physical armoring, thus becoming a more free and open human being.[68, 69, 70]

taught that certain feelings or emotions are unacceptable; none-theless they are felt. Eventually, the child arrives at a solution: *unconsciousness.*

While self-alienation is clearly encouraged by others, this is by no means the only source of the problem. A child can actively employ the strategy of repression and disowning to defend against any feelings experienced as threatening or overwhelming: pain, fear, anger, sexuality, excitement, and so forth.

We have already noted that for the majority of children, the early years of life contain many frightening and painful experiences. Perhaps a child has parents who never respond warmly to physical needs; who continually scream at the child or at each other; who deliberately invoke fear and guilt as a means of exercising control; who swing between oversolicitude and callous remoteness; who subject the child to lies and mockery; who are neglectful and indifferent; who continually criticize and rebuke; who overwhelm with bewildering and contradictory injunctions; who present the child with expectations and demands that take no cognizance of the child's knowledge, needs, or interests; who subject the child to physical violence; or who consistently discourage and oppose efforts at spontaneity and self-assertiveness.

A child does not have a conceptual knowledge of his or her own needs, nor does the child possess sufficient knowledge to comprehend the behavior of the parents. At times, fear and pain may be experienced as incapacitating, or rage seems terrifying to reveal or express. And so in order to remain able to function, the child decides, wordlessly and helplessly, that the inner world of feelings must be escaped, that contact with emotions is sometimes intolerable. The fear, pain, and anger are not permitted to be experienced, expressed, and thus discharged; they are frozen into the body, barricaded behind walls of muscular and physiological tension. The child inaugurates a pattern of reaction that will tend to recur whenever feelings he or she does not wish to experience threaten to emerge. And just as fear, pain, and anger tend to be blocked, so do sexuality, excitement, and joy—any powerful response that threatens to disrupt equilibrium, bring down parental disapproval, evoke guilt, endanger self-esteem.

To varying degrees, then, the child learns to play dead in

order to survive. In order to protect self-esteem, the child learns to surrender more and more of the self. The average child becomes an expert at self-sacrifice at the most profound psychological level: the level of mind and spirit, the level of the life-force itself.

This problem, which originates in childhood, becomes built into the personality, built into an individual's manner of being and coping with life—becomes what Reich[70] calls the "character armor"—so that by the time a person is an adult, the condition of self-alienation feels natural.

The point is not that the individual loses the ability to experience emotion but that emotion often tends to become muted, diluted, trivialized. Emotional life tends to be distorted; surface feelings defend against and conceal deep feelings, misleading both self and others. Thus, deep pain may be concealed behind surface anger. Anger may be concealed behind a surface indifference that becomes "unconscious" cruelty. A deep longing for love and companionship may be buried beneath a facade of cheerful, happy-go-lucky self-sufficiency. Powerful, denied sexual feelings may emerge disguised as a ruthlessly intolerant asceticism.

I can recall my often acutely painful teenage feelings of loneliness and of longing for someone with whom I could share my thoughts, interests, and feelings. But by then I had accepted the view that loneliness was a weakness, and longing for human intimacy represented a failure of independence. I clung to self-alienation as a virtue. I convinced myself I did not care. I told myself I had my thoughts and my books and that that was enough—or that it should be, if I were properly self-reliant. I did not begin to understand until my twenties that, had I known, accepted, and experienced from the beginning my desire for human contact and interaction, my emotional development and subsequent relationships would have been more natural and satisfying.

It is extraordinarily difficult to communicate about emotional self-alienation to a person who has not confronted the issue at the level of personal experience. Many years ago I gave a copy of *The Disowned Self* to a friend who was one of the most emotionally repressed persons I knew. After reading it he said to me, "I'm sorry if I disappoint you, but I absolutely cannot relate to this book. In the past, when I've heard you lecture on philosophy or theoretical psychology, I think I could follow you completely and very easily. This time, I have no real sense that I understand you."

Sometimes, in order to awaken a person to this issue, I will simply ask him or her to become absolutely still, breathe into the abdomen, and be available to any feelings or emotions that may spontaneously begin to arise. Within a few minutes, a person may report feelings of sadness or anxiety or anger that seem to have sprung out of nowhere. Not uncommonly, a person will begin to weep.

Opening the breathing is generally the first step to opening the feelings.[47, 70] It creates a condition of stillness, a condition in which we stop running, so that our emotions have a chance to catch up with us, to enter conscious experience.

This is the reason why meditation can be, among its many other functions, a powerful tool for the releasing of blocked feelings and emotions. Its emphasis on breathing and on stillness leads a novice at meditation often to violent and sometimes to frightening emotional eruptions. Serenity may not occur until later stages of meditative practice. Patricia Carrington writes about this phenomenon in *Freedom in Meditation*.

There are any number of processes by which a person can be led to an awareness of the problem of blocked emotions—from the strategies employed by the various body therapists, to guided fantasy, to psychodramatic exercises, to the use of the "awareness continuum" in Fritz Perls's Gestalt therapy, to hypnosis, to sentence-completion exercises. I will illustrate some of these procedures in the course of our discussion.

We cannot adequately understand the problem of emotional repression if we do not appreciate that the average person carries within his or her being the burden of an enormous quantity of unacknowledged and undischarged pain—not only pain originating in the present, but pain originating in the early years of life.

One evening more than a decade and a half ago, discussing this phenomenon with some colleagues, I was challenged by a psychiatrist who felt I was exaggerating the magnitude of the problem in the general population. Since I sensed debate would be futile, I asked him if he would participate in a demonstration.

He said he would be glad to but warned me that if I was proposing to explore his childhood I might defeat my purpose, even if my general thesis was correct. He had had an exceptionally happy childhood. His parents, he said, had always been marvelously responsive to his needs. It might be better to ask for another volunteer, as he had no desire to embarrass me. I replied that I would like to work with him; he laughed and invited me to proceed.

I asked him to do an exercise that I sometimes use with my clients in therapy. He sat back in his chair, relaxed his body, let his arms rest at his sides, and closed his eyes.

"Now," I said, "I want you to accept the following situation. You are lying on a bed in a hospital, and you are dying. You are your present age. You are not in physical pain, but you are aware of the fact that in a few hours your life will end. Now, in your imagination, look up and see your mother standing at the side of the bed. Look at her face. There is so much unsaid between you. Feel the presence of all the unsaid between you—all the things you have never told her, all the thoughts and feelings you have never expressed. If ever you would be able to reach your mother, it is now. If ever she would hear you, it is now. Talk to her. Tell her."

As I talked, his hands clenched into fists, blood rushed to his face, and one could see around his eyes and forehead the muscular tension that was aimed at suppressing fears. When he spoke, it was in a younger and much more intense voice, one that rose in a moan as he said, "*When I spoke to you, why didn't you ever listen to me? Why didn't you ever listen?*"

It was obvious that this man had been speaking sincerely when he had referred to his childhood as a happy one, but in repressing his early pain, he was disowning certain of his own legitimate needs, disowning important feelings, therefore disowning a part of himself. The consequence for him as an adult was not only an emotional impairment *but also a thinking impairment*. His distorted judgments necessarily would affect his present effectiveness in human relationships.

It is productive to do this exercise with both parents, and you can also adapt it to an encounter with any important person in your life. You can do the whole exercise in reverse as well, imagining that the other person is dying.

When the exercise is done as I have described, with mother,

father, or any other important person entering the hospital room—or with the roles reversed and the other person on the deathbed—the emotion tapped into more often than any other is disowned pain, often combined with anger. Reconnecting with and experiencing disowned pain enables us to gain a new perspective on old experiences. It allows us the possibility of integrating that which previously had been driven underground and sealed off from conscious awareness. The past thus begins to lose its hold over the present.

Otherwise, we remain prisoners of that which we do not confront.

Jerry entered therapy because, he said, he was unable to fall in love. "I've never cared deeply for anyone," he explained, "and that feels wrong. Something inside me seems numb or dead. It is as if other people have something I'm lacking."

In an early session we began to explore the problem, using sentence completion.

If I were to fall in love—
>   It couldn't happen.
>   I'd be frightened.
>   I'd be overwhelmed.
>   I wouldn't know what to do.
>   I'd feel helpless.

Love to me is—
>   Death.
>   Loss.
>   Abandonment.
>   Unspeakable pain.
>   It ends in loneliness.
>   Being unprotected.
>   Being vulnerable.
>   Losing.

I learned never to love when—
>   My little sister died.
>   No one would explain what was happening.
>   Father told me not to cry.

Father told me I must be strong for mother.
No one ever talked to me about it.
I saw mother and father at the dinner table talking to
each other like zombies.
I wanted to scream but couldn't.

Jerry was now weeping. Several moments passed before it was possible for him to continue. Then:

If I had been allowed to mourn my sister's death—
I wouldn't still carry this dead weight inside of me.
I wouldn't hate my father.
I could feel.
I would have cried for a long time.
I would feel whole today.
I wouldn't be so afraid.
Love wouldn't mean pain.
I could have let go.
I could have gotten on with my life.
I wouldn't still be waiting to say good-bye to her.
I wouldn't feel so dead myself.
I wouldn't be so afraid that if I loved someone, they'd
leave me.

The sentence-completion work had to stop at this point because of the depth of his sobbing.

Over the next several sessions, our work was concerned chiefly with facilitating the mourning process. We did a series of different exercises to allow him to experience the loss fully. I also encouraged him to visit his sister's grave, to spend some time talking to her, and to say good-bye.

At a subsequent session, his first words were, "I feel as if I've been asleep for twenty-five years. And three days ago, at the cemetery, I finally woke up."

No amount of "thinking" about his relationships with women as an adult could possibly be effective so long as he remained unaware of a disowned pain that, never having been assimilated, had arrested and distorted his development in ways that inevitably contaminated the higher levels of consciousness—specifically, the level of adult thinking about interpersonal relationships and the arena of emotions in general.

Whenever there is loss, at any age, there is a psychological need for mourning, a period during which we allow ourselves to feel our pain, reflecting on what is gone from our life and how we are affected by the absence. This is an essential step in the healing process. We may need to mourn a death, a divorce, the breakup of a love affair, the loss of a friend, the failure of a career aspiration, the defeat of a dream.

To face our painful emotions—to allow them to be felt, to acknowledge them, to listen to the messages they contain, and perhaps to describe in words what we are feeling—requires courage and honesty; it is not an exercise in self-pity. To say, "*Right now* I am feeling forlorn, miserable, hopeless" is not self-pity; to say, "My situation is hopeless" is (usually) self-pity. In the first instance, we are describing a feeling; in the second, we are making a statement of alleged fact. This is a distinction of the highest importance.

Descriptions of feelings, however painful, can be therapeutic; statements of alleged facts about the cruelty of life or the futility of struggle, motivated solely by our painful emotions of the moment, are often self-destructive. In the first case, we try for awareness; in the second, we make no effort to deal with our suffering or understand it.

Unfortunately, few of us were educated in this distinction, and few of us appreciate its importance to our lives—not only with regard to the mourning process but with regard to any painful experience we may need to confront in order to transcend it. We cannot liberate ourselves from that which we have never experienced; we cannot leave a place we have never been.

Fritz Perls coined the expression *unfinished business* to describe unresolved life experiences that distort and subvert our responses in the present. Unfinished business represents a blockage of the maturational process. It is through the repression of feeling that such blockage chiefly occurs. That is why opening the feelings is a central goal in so many of the newer therapies.

Psychotherapy entails the pursuit of a great many goals, but a good portion of the work centers around the client's dealing with the consequences of unmet needs in an earlier stage of his or her development. Indeed, psychotherapy can be conceptualized as a discipline that aims at redressing failures in development. No single task in this effort is more important than liberating the client's ability to feel.

A child rarely feels free to express feelings of anger and rage, for example. More often there is the thought "If mother or father knew what I was feeling, I would be killed—or abandoned." Too often, an internal injunction is laid down: "It is dangerous to express anger." And years later the adult is still operating on the basis of that injunction, still unable to protest wrongs done against him or her, and the injunction forbidding anger is commonly facilitated by a prohibition against knowing what there might be to be angry about, which of course entails cognitive sabotage. Or again, the anxiety of some children's early years is too much to bear; it feels utterly incapacitating; it is repressed (perhaps to surface in nightmares). But to be repressed is not to go out of existence. That which is denied by the mind is trapped within the body. Let a therapist work the appropriate muscles in the neck or face or throat or chest or diaphragm or thighs—wherever the block may appear to be located—and the long-denied feelings will erupt. The fear will be experienced, expressed, discharged. The adult will understand and feel organismically why he or she has retreated from so many of the challenges of life, why the avoidance of fear-evoking situations has taken priority over almost all other considerations, why life has had to be so circumscribed and restricted. A new and wider vision of life's options then becomes available. *As feelings are experienced, the mind clears.* Autonomy becomes a more realistic possibility.

As I observed earlier, psychotherapists of different schools have developed numerous techniques and methods aimed specifically at bringing people into touch with themselves and guiding them to experience a meaningful sense of their own identity. Unfortunately, however, just as the ordinary layperson tends to dichotomize thinking and feeling, reason and emotion—often regarding them as antagonists—so do many psychotherapists. The result is that in their enthusiasm to help people become recon-

155

nected with their denied selves, psychotherapists sometimes imply or explicitly state that people cannot feel because they think too much.

Any normal human faculty is susceptible to a perversion of its proper function by a wish to avoid confrontation with some frightening or painful aspect of reality. This applies to thoughts, feelings, and actions.

In the area of thought, there is the intellectual who discusses his or her personal problems as though they belong to someone else. In a state of total dissociation, this individual does not experience the emotional meaning of anything he or she says or hears; such an individual prefers to talk about psychology in general rather than his or her agony in particular. This person, in the context of his or her personal life, engages in mental activity, not for the purpose of expanding awareness, but for the purpose of avoiding it.

In the area of feeling, there is the emotionalist who dwells on, say, the emotion of sadness, but refuses to confront the rage beneath it; or who blindly surrenders to anger while refusing to confront the pain that motivates it; or who talks endlessly about emotions as a means of avoiding knowing what he or she feels.

In the area of action, there is the man or woman who, impatient with thought and scornful of emotions, runs compulsively from one activity to another, dreading to face the question of what these actions are adding up to, what benefits they bring or fail to bring to his or her life—the person who uses action as a means to avoid facing the meaning and significance of action.

As I have already mentioned and want to stress again, flight from inner experience is by no means confined to feelings and emotions that we characterize as negative. Often we repress and disown our excitement, our enthusiasm, our happiness—perhaps because in the past we have been ridiculed for such feelings, because no one seems to understand or share them, or because experiencing them increases our painful sense of aloneness.

Avoidance always has its reasons. The organism is trying to protect itself, ensure its well-being, and preserve self-esteem—but in the wrong way.

Since emotions, negative and positive, express our assessment of the significance of different aspects of reality for ourselves, when we bury feelings and emotion we also bury ourselves. This is what it means to exist in a state of alienation. We rarely know it, *but we are lonely for ourselves.*

If we are able to experience our feelings, then in any given situation, we have a choice: to express them or to contain them. Sometimes one option is desirable, sometimes the other. But so long as we are blocked, we do not have that choice.

To be unable ever to contain our emotions is obviously unhealthy and subversive to effective functioning. But to tell ourselves that we do not *wish* to let anyone know what we feel, when the truth is that we are blocked and semiunconscious, is to practice self-deception.

Just as we evolve through interaction with the environment at the level of behavior, so we evolve through interaction at the level of feeling and emotion. If we do not allow ourselves to experience the normal emotions of a child, we impede unobstructed growth into adolescence. If we do not allow ourselves to have the normal emotions of an adolescent, we do not evolve into well-integrated adults.

Sometimes, when we are older, we fling ourselves into the feelings, emotions, and behavior appropriate to a far earlier stage of development, in an unconscious attempt at self-healing—to give ourselves the childhood or adolescence we never had. Our behavior may bewilder and appall our family and friends who do not understand the nature of the process in which we are engaged. We ourselves are unlikely to understand it. A man of forty-five may find himself carrying on like a teenager. He may feel awkward and embarrassed yet unable to stop. In all likelihood, unless he becomes conscious of his actions and their underlying intention, he will at some point reinstitute inhibition and repression, aborting his own attempt at growth, so that nothing ever gets solved, the pain is never relieved, the joy is never expressed, and he helplessly settles into what he has been taught to call the realism and practicality of middle age.

As to what a person should do in such circumstances, it is obviously far preferable to permit the mind free play in fantasy, to avoid self-condemnation and self-censorship, and to search for realistic, nondestructive opportunities to satisfy pent-up longing, if and to the extent that this is possible, than it is to seek escape in repression and unconsciousness.

Sometimes we may have longings and fantasies that we have no way of fulfilling. It may simply be too late to do so, or to fulfill them may clash with other important values. Undeniably, we sometimes need to make hard choices.

But often people dismiss their longings, telling themselves that fulfillment is impossible, when in fact nothing stands in the way except the rigidity of their own thinking or their fear of family or social disapproval. If we do not learn to listen to ourselves, to respect our inner signals, if we are too quick to assume self-sacrifice as a necessity, we miss opportunities for growth and enrichment.

Sometimes that which we label as childish longings are nothing of the kind; we call them that only because we have learned to call *any* personal longing "childish" if its sole purpose is our own pleasure.

At the age of fifty-three, a physician who had had to work hard ever since he was a small boy shocked his wife by announcing that he wanted to close his practice for a year—"Perhaps longer; who knows?"—and take a trip around the world. The more his family opposed him, the more flippant, jocular, and defiant he became—almost to the point of being manic.

He had read one of my books and decided to consult me. "What do you think?" he asked. I answered, "I think that a man of fifty-three is competent to know what he wants to do with his life."

This seemed to disorient him; evidently he had expected another lecture on his responsibilities.

"Should I take my wife with me?" he asked.

"Sure. If she wants to. If she can get into the spirit of it. Otherwise, no."

When he saw that someone took him seriously, accepted and respected his feelings, he became calm. He needed to take himself seriously, the part of him that had never lived.

When his wife came to see me, she said, "But I don't *want* to take a trip around the world!"

"Well, then, I guess you won't go."

"But if I let him go without me, how do I know he'll ever come back to me?"

"Well, then, I guess you have to make a choice."

"But I want our life to go on as before!"

"You mean, what you want matters and what your husband wants doesn't?"

"But he's behaving like a child!"

"You mean, grown men aren't supposed to have fun? Personally, I think that it's wonderful for grown men to have fun, and I also think it's wonderful for grown women to have fun. And I especially think it's wonderful when they find a way to have fun together. But I am talking about fun, not self-sacrifice—not for either one of them."

As they are still traveling, I do not know the outcome of the story.

Feelings are often the first form in which we become aware that something is wrong with our life. We need thought in order to know what to do, but feelings often alert us to the existence of a problem. If our response to feelings that seem to challenge our ordinary routine is to ignore or repress them, then we condemn ourselves to living mechanically, at a level of consciousness, or unconsciousness, that forbids authenticity or autonomy.

In the area of our personal life, *if we cannot feel deeply, it is very difficult to think clearly.* This is contrary to the notion that thinking and feeling are opposed functions and that each entails the denial of the other.

We can avoid perceptions and thoughts, just as we can avoid feelings and emotions. A child, for instance, may observe behaviors in parents that are terrifying—mother is a liar, father is a brute, and so forth—and the child can twist consciousness to deny this, to forget it, to wipe out an awareness that seems to make daily existence intolerable.

A grown daughter may suddenly grasp, "Mother does not want me to be happily married; she is jealous," or a grown son may suddenly grasp, "Father does not want me to rise higher in life than he did"—and the next moment brings the reprimand "What a terrible, ridiculous thing to think!"

A student in college, listening to a lecture, may have the flash "What this professor is saying is nonsense," and the next moment the fearful thought "Who am I to know?" buries the insight.

A woman may be happily married, in love with her husband, proud of her children, fulfilled in her own work, and yet one day be troubled by the thought "There's something more. What have I missed? What is there that still feels unsatisfied?" Committed to the belief "I have everything I could possibly want," she reproaches herself for her foolishness.

In the middle of a speech, a politician may suddenly think, "What I am now telling my constituents—the position I have been representing all my adult life—is ridiculous." The next moment, the thought is gone.

We may have been raised in a particular religion, philosophy, or belief system that we have accepted for many years. Then, one day, something within us begins to challenge it. We find ourselves wondering, "How do I know any of this is true?" Or we find ourselves thinking, "This makes no sense to me." But we are afraid—afraid that our thinking may alienate us from the people to whom we have been close for so many years. So we alienate ourselves from ourselves.

Sometimes the thoughts and feelings we repress are those beckoning us toward a higher level of development. Just as we may disown our depths of terror or rage, so we may disown our glimpses of the heights of peace or ecstasy waiting for us at the next level of growth. As we disown the child within us, so we disown the sage—the wisest part of us, the most daring, the most intelligent, the most intuitive about our ultimate needs.

Certainly the positive force we are often most prone to disown is our intelligence. We fear the turbulence that too much awareness can generate. Of all our attachments, the one we cling to most tenaciously is the one that binds us to the present level of development, the one that says, "Stop. Go no further." I often find myself speculating about the millions of times new ideas die stillborn, new possibilities are left unexplored, creative and spiritual yearnings are ignored or repressed, either because we are afraid of the unknown into which we may be drawn or simply because we have become accustomed to tuning out unfamiliar inner signals. Creativity and psychological-spiritual growth have this in common: both require times of aloneness, of silence, of meditation or contemplation, so that inner signals can be heard and allowed to reach explicit awareness, so that the subconscious can become conscious, the bodily become mental, the disowned become owned, so that the life-force can continue propelling us toward higher levels of self-actualization.

For many people, estrangement from others feels more frightening than estrangement from self. Not uncommonly a person will enter therapy complaining of an excessive preoccupation with gaining the approval and avoiding the disapproval of other people. Telling such individuals that the opinions of others needn't matter all that much or that they must learn to think for themselves is rarely therapeutic.

What I sometimes do is give sentence-completion work beginning with such stems as "If I were willing to be more honest about my needs and wants—"; "If I were willing to be more honest about expressing my emotions—"; "If I were willing to be more straightforward about expressing my thoughts and opinions—." Almost invariably the client will spontaneously produce endings such as "I wouldn't be so preoccupied with other people's reactions"; "I wouldn't always be so busy trying to get people to like me"; "I wouldn't care so much what others think"; "I'd belong to myself"; "I'd have more self-respect"; "I'd be my own person"; "I'd feel like a tremendous weight had been lifted"; "I'd realize how foolishly I've been living my life"; "I'd be free."

Understanding arrived at in this manner tends to be not merely cognitive but also emotional, organismic as well as intellectual, an insight of the whole being and not merely of the cerebral cortex. Any such process that facilitates reowning disowned elements of the personality provides a foundation for the growth of autonomy.

The essence of the disowning process is that the self is at war with the self—or, more precisely, that the ego sets inappropriate boundaries concerning where self ends and the not-self begins. The correction of this process is the central subject of the following chapter.

10
The Art of Being

The art of being is the art of knowing ourselves, of accepting and existing in harmony with ourselves, and of living out, in action, the highest possibilities of our nature. It includes three basic concepts: self-awareness, self-acceptance, and self-assertion.

Self-awareness, in this context, concerns our ongoing needs, desires, emotions, values, aspirations, capabilities, mental states, and behavior. As we continually extend the boundaries of what we experience as the self, we encompass more and more of what we had previously overlooked or repressed. Self-awareness is not obsessive. Cultivating access to the self does not mean taking our mental or emotional temperature every ten minutes or dissociating ourselves from our own life.

Perhaps the single most important step in moving toward self-awareness is the realization that such a goal is necessary and desirable, after a lifetime of being taught to respond to the signals of others.

With self-acceptance comes our willingness to experience rather than to disown whatever may be the facts of our being at a particular moment. This carries no implication that feelings are always to have the last word on what we do. I may not be in the mood to work today; I can acknowledge my feelings, experience them, accept them—and then proceed to work. I will work with a clearer mind, because I have not begun the day with self-deception. Self-acceptance is my refusal to be in an adversary relationship to myself.

Self-assertion brings us further into reality as we express our inner life in words and actions. Self-assertion means that I honor my own needs, that I honor my own judgment, as I honor my own values, as I recognize that a successful life requires that I translate my self into action. It does not mean that only I exist or have needs or rights. Sometimes I may defer to others, giving their feelings priority, or recognizing that their rights in a particular situation may supersede my own. When I do, I am practicing, not self-sacrifice, but *objectivity*.

Self-awareness begins with learning to be more conscious of our feelings and emotions, since—as we have already seen—this is the area where we learn to shut down from our earliest years. During this process we inevitably experience a series of varied emotions. The art of awareness consists of observing without interfering, but initially this can be a very frightening experience. We may not know why we are feeling what we do or what feelings may arise in the next moment. We may experience the panic of being out of control. But panic is only another emotion.

As we become more and more conscious of the flow of our feelings, we become more and more conscious of the impulses behind our actions. We learn to notice, for example, when we are being propelled by a fear or anger we may have disowned or not even recognized. We begin to discover our own projections, such as a repressed hostility within ourselves that we falsely attribute to others. We can become more conscious of how our relationships affect us and more sensitive to which activities we should and should not pursue.

In terms of expanding self-awareness, there is a difference between *experiencing* an emotion and merely *naming* it to ourselves—and this difference is profound. Suppose I am in a rush, agitated over something connected with my work, and barely aware of my state of mind. My wife asks, "How are you feeling?" I answer, a little abruptly, "Fine"—and then, when I see the way she is holding my glance, I add, in an attempt at greater truthfulness, "Irritated." My wife says sympathetically, "It looks like you're really feeling distressed about something." I sigh, and the tension begins to flow from my body. In an altogether different tone of voice, I respond, "Yes, I'm upset about my writing today. I can't seem to get anything right. Everything I put down on paper is choppy and out of focus. I feel worried and miserable." Now I am no longer trying to outrun my emotions; I am no longer tensed against them; nor am I trying to dismiss them by labeling them "irritated." I am allowing myself to *experience* what I feel.

In this example even my initial labeling of my emotion is incorrect. I may be irritated, but I am a good deal more: I am worried, agitated, troubled. I might have answered my wife's original inquiry more correctly by saying, "Worried, agitated, troubled"—but in a tense, abrupt tone of voice, that would have signaled, "Don't ask me to feel what I am feeling!" I could have named my emotional state correctly without actually experiencing it in any meaningful sense. My self-awareness would have remained at a superficial level. In allowing myself to experience my feelings, I deepened my awareness.

Experiencing our emotions rather than merely naming them is necessary for self-healing. A professional singer preparing for his first important role in an opera came for therapy, complaining of extreme stage fright. Even as he described the problem, I could see him tensing his body against his feelings, producing still greater tension, even panic. I suggested to him that instead of hiding his anxiety, he try to experience it more intensely. He looked at me with horror. It took considerable urging to persuade him to make the attempt. I asked him to describe his feelings, both his emotions and his bodily sensations.

After much faltering, he came out with "I can feel my heart pounding in my chest, going a mile a minute. My chest is tight, it feels like it's being pulled in two opposite directions. My breathing is shallow, my breath keeps jerking in and out in little spurts. My throat feels tight, feels constricted, I feel like I'm choking. I'm aware of tension in my legs, my thigh muscles feel strained. My arms are shaking. . . . I just had a flash of myself on the stage, and now I feel myself beginning to perspire. At the thought of all those people looking at me, I feel terrified." I asked him, "Would you say, very loudly, 'I feel terrified'?" He gasped and shouted, "I feel terrified!" I asked him to shout it again; he did so. I had him do this a few more times, then inquired, "How are you feeling now?" He paused for a moment and then brightened. "Better," he said. "I'm beginning to feel relaxed."

When we are aware of and experience our unwanted feelings, they diminish. The opposite happens with wanted feelings: they grow stronger. Thus, in allowing myself to surrender to my feelings of love for another human being, the love intensifies and inspires behaviors that deepen the love. In pausing to experience fully the joy I take in my work, my passion for my work is augmented, my excitement rises, and I am inspired to give my best, which nurtures my love for my work.

I often recommend the following exercise for opening oneself to emotional awareness. Simply sit quietly, eyes closed, and breathe deeply and gently through the mouth into the stomach, while paying attention to the smallest details of what you experience within, just noting, just observing, without analysis, without self-criticism, without speculation as to meaning. The apparent simplicity of this exercise belies its power to awaken feeling. People may find themselves weeping, angry, sexually excited, euphoric, depressed, or ecstatic—and in awe of the richness of the emotional life to which they had previously been oblivious.

Another exercise I sometimes recommend can be done standing up or lying down. Tighten successively all the muscles of the body, moving upwards from the feet, holding the contractions as long as possible, then releasing explosively, letting everything relax at once, allowing the body to breathe as it needs to breathe, without interference. Go through the entire procedure five or six times, then stand or lie down quietly and mentally observe yourself, breathing into the feelings that arise within, not fighting back by tensing muscles against the emergence of whatever emotions and memories arise. Do not distract yourself with such questions as, Should I be feeling this? or What does this feeling mean? or, worse still, What does it imply about me that I am feeling this?

If our purpose is simple perception, psychologizing and moralizing are deadly.

In cultivating self-awareness, we want to remember that we know far more than we are aware of knowing. The mind does not have a sharp division between the conscious and the unconscious; rather, it has (or consists of) a *continuum of awareness*. The degrees of awareness range from focused awareness to peripheral awareness to total unawareness or unconsciousness. The points on this continuum blur into one another as adjoining colors on the spectrum do. The barrier between focused awareness and the unconscious is nowhere as formidable as Freud supposed. The sentence-completion technique presented throughout this book offers a stunning illustration of that fact; more than one psychoanalyst has expressed surprise at seeing clients through sentence completion bring up the kind of material, in minutes, that is presumed to require months or years of excavation to uncover. But any number of psychological processes apart from sentence completion, such as guided fantasy or psychodramatic exercises, similarly demonstrate the potential accessibility of "the unconscious."

Given the appropriate circumstances and approach, that which is apparently unknown to a person or only implicit in his or her understanding can be brought into consciousness. Here are some simple examples.

We will begin with hypnosis, because it clearly demonstrates that by altering our state of mind we can gain access to material not normally available. An adult professes to have little or no memory for his early years. When he is hypnotized and age regressed, guided back in time to the first years of life, we see his posture and facial expression changing, as if he were becoming younger before our eyes, and forgotten or repressed experiences are awakened within him. And, usually with considerable emotional involvement, he reexperiences and/or reconnects with events that had been submerged and inaccessible to his conscious mind. The altered state of consciousness does not create the memories but allows them to emerge.

Another well-known technique for connecting with what we know but are not aware of is used today by psychotherapists of many different orientations. Originated early in this century by Joseph Moreno, founder of psychodrama, and later adopted by Fritz Perls, founder of Gestalt therapy, the technique involves talking in fantasy to a significant person in our life, one with whom we have unfinished business. In the Moreno version someone plays the part of the significant person; in the Perls version there is only an empty chair. The principle is the same in both, however: if we truly move into the spirit of the exercise, we cannot avoid shifting to an altered state of consciousness, a state in which it becomes possible to express thoughts, verbalize feelings, and experience attitudes that have been denied explicit awareness.

For instance, a woman in therapy speaks with apparent apathy about the death of her husband. Her eyes are dull, her voice is muted, her manner is dejected. She claims to feel nothing. The therapist asks her to imagine her husband sitting in the chair opposite her and talk to him out of her direct and immediate experience. As she begins the exercise, she says, "Looking at you, I feel nothing. You are gone. I don't care. I knew you would leave me. Everyone leaves me." She begins to cry. "Mommy and daddy died and left me. Why did they do that? I always knew I would end up alone. When you came home from the doctor and told me you had cancer, that was it. I was finished right then. In that moment, it was over. I am angry. I am so angry at you. *Why did you have to leave me, too?*"

An example of a different technique may be found in my version of a well-known fantasy exercise. We imagine an encounter with a wise old person in a cave or on top of a mountain or in some other remote place. This wise being knows the answers we desperately need after our long journey. In fantasy we ask questions such as, Who am I that I do not yet know I am? or How am I standing in the way of my own growth? or What do I need to do to let go of the pain of the past? We listen very carefully to the answers; sometimes they come in words, sometimes in images. And then we meditate on, or discuss with our therapist, the marvelous and illuminating things we learn from this wise old person who resides within the self.

The simplest technique (if *technique* is not too grand a word here) is a strategy that I unearthed one time late at night. I was feeling a little tired and asked my client a question I was sure he could answer. When he looked at me blankly and said he didn't know, I said jokingly, "OK, you don't know. But *if* you knew, what *might* the answer be?" He proceeded to answer the question I had originally asked. After he left the office, I remained in my chair, mildly stunned and convinced that something important had happened. It was as if the original version of my question had evoked some kind of pressure—perhaps the obligation to be "right"—that caused him to lose contact with what he knew. When I conceded that he did not know, the pressure disappeared, and when I shifted from reality into the realm of "if" and "might," he felt a freedom that gave him access to the appropriate answer. Sometimes when

I am stuck on some question or problem I think I should have an answer for, I tell myself, "OK, you don't know. But *if* you knew, what *might* the answer be?" Surprisingly often, the answer appears.

Let me introduce a distinction implicit in the preceding discussion, the distinction between an *absolute* "I don't know" and a *contextual* "I don't know." Again I will refer to hypnosis. If a person does not know what she received for her fifteenth birthday and is then assisted to know through a hypnotic trance, it is clear that her "I don't know" is contextual. That is, in the context of her ordinary state of awareness, she truly does not remember what she received for her fifteenth birthday. A change in her state of consciousness makes it possible for her to know. On the other hand, if we ask her for the population of a small town in Africa of which she has never heard, she would say, "I don't know," and no hypnotic technique could draw the correct answer from her because the correct answer does not exist in her. It is not buried on some deeper level of mind; it is not forgotten or repressed; she is ignorant of the answer in the absolute sense.

When a client says, "I don't know"—"I don't know what I feel," "I don't know whether I want to remain married," "I don't know what I was trying to accomplish by doing that," "I don't know what I see in her," "I don't know whether I was molested as a child"—I assume, until it is shown otherwise, that I am being confronted with a contextual "I don't know" rather than an absolute "I don't know."

The sentence-completion technique makes it possible to achieve just that shift in consciousness necessary for us to gain access to material that may not be readily available in awareness. We can use this technique in a group, or working with another person, face to face, or talking to ourself in a mirror or into a tape recorder, or writing in a notebook; in any case, the important thing is to say or write whatever comes to mind, freely and spontaneously, without worrying for the moment about the literal truth or falsehood of any particular ending.

Here is a sentence-completion exercise you can use to begin to explore aspects of your emotional life. Write each of the following stems at the top of a blank page, then do a minimum of ten endings as rapidly as possible.

For exploring feelings of pain or hurt: "I can remember feeling hurt when—"; "When I was hurt, I told myself—"; "Sometimes I feel hurt when—"; "Sometimes when I am hurt, I—"; "One of the ways I sometimes hide my hurt is—"; "One of the ways my hurt comes out is—"; "If I ever fully admitted when I feel hurt—"; "A better way to deal with my hurt might be—." (The purpose of the last stem in the sequence is, of course, to allow us access to a deeper wisdom concerning ways we might deal with our pain.)

For exploring fear: "I can remember feeling afraid when—"; "When I was afraid, I told myself—"; "One of the ways I sometimes hide my fear is—"; "One of the ways my fear comes out is—"; "If I ever fully admitted when I feel afraid—"; "A better way to deal with my fear might be—."

For exploring anger: "I can remember feeling angry when—"; "When I felt angry, I told myself—"; "Sometimes I feel angry when—"; "Sometimes when I'm angry I—"; "One of the ways I hide my anger is—"; "One of the ways my anger comes out is—"; "If I ever fully admitted when I'm angry—"; "A better way to deal with my anger might be—."

For exploring sexuality: "Sometimes I feel sexually excited when—"; "Sometimes when I am sexually excited I—"; "One of the ways I sometimes hide my sexual excitement is—"; "One of the ways my sexual excitement comes out is—"; "If I ever fully admitted when I feel sexually excited—"; "A better way to deal with my sexual excitement might be—."

For exploring feelings of joy or happiness: "Sometimes I feel happy when—"; "Sometimes when I am happy I—"; "One of the ways I sometimes hide my happiness is—"; "One of the ways my happiness comes out is—"; "If I ever fully admitted when I feel happy—"; "A better way to deal with my happiness might be—."*

We can readily understand the fear that may accompany the prospect of encountering painful emotions. But sometimes joy, too, can be threatening. A woman who had not worked outside her home for many years took a job to augment the family income.

---

*Detailed instructions for the use of the sentence-completion technique and a wide variety of sentence stems for self-exploration may be found in *If You Could Hear What I Cannot Say*.

Being highly competent, she was rapidly promoted. But she concealed from herself the extent of her pride and happiness at what she was doing, because she intuitively felt it would disturb the equilibrium of her marriage; she sensed that her husband would feel threatened. Participating in one of my Intensive Workshops, "Self-Esteem and Romantic Relationships," and introduced to the technique of sentence completion and, specifically, to the sentence stem "Sometimes I feel happy when—," she was brought face to face with the sudden realization that many of her greatest moments of joy took place in the office where she worked.

In the course of talking about her reaction to this exercise, she became aware of why she had been blocking and disowning. She began to confront tensions in her relationship with her husband that she had chosen largely to overlook. Like a string of exploding firecrackers, one burst of awareness led to another, from a recognition of the kind of programming she had received from her mother about "a woman's place," to the amount of boredom she had endured while doing what she regarded as her duty, to her previously unadmitted contempt for religious teachings about self-sacrifice, and on and on and on. She reported an enormous increase in self-assurance and internal freedom, even though she felt some trepidation concerning what her husband's reactions might be when she shared her feelings with him. She declared herself willing to face whatever might need to be faced. Her husband was present at the workshop, and from observing him, my guess was that they would be able to negotiate successfully this transition in her development—but I do not know the ultimate outcome.

I think it is clear by now why we are far better off knowing our needs, feelings, and wants than by being oblivious to them. Where there is knowledge, there is the possibility of action. But why, for example, might it be desirable to know about an unmet need from our past, from our childhood, a deep-seated frustration of long ago, where it would seem that action is no longer possible?

Very often we resist knowing about a need or a want we see no possibility of fulfilling. Our father may have died when we were young. He may have been impossibly distant and remote, unloving and rejecting, or nonsupportive. And to diminish our pain, long ago we buried the knowledge of how much we would like to have had a different kind of father. We tell ourselves, "I am an adult now—why do I have to think about it?" But only when I am prepared to experience how much the child in me wanted and needed a father, only when I am prepared to feel the pain of his absence, only when I can give comfort and understanding to the child within for what he or she never had, only then can I complete the unfinished business of my past and move into a freer, more harmonious adulthood. This may entail a kind of mourning, a period of allowing myself to feel the pain I never acknowledged before, a time of talking in fantasy to the child within, leading to the point when the past is finally laid to rest—*really* laid to rest. To grow up is to assume responsibility for parenting the child within.

By way of further illuminating this point, I offer the following example, an experience I myself have lived. Although I loved my father and our relationship was cordial, we were never close except during the first few years of my life and, to a lesser extent, during the last years of his. He was a shy, withdrawn man, completely unable to relate to any of my interests. Nor was I close to my mother. I never felt comfortable in school; I was bored and restless a good deal of the time. And yet I longed for an older person to teach me things, to offer some kind of guidance. After a while, I repressed the longing. I decided it was impractical and turned more and more to my own resources. My sole form of intellectual nurturing from the environment was through books.

A month before I turned twenty, I met and became friendly with novelist-philosopher Ayn Rand, whose book *The Fountainhead* I had greatly admired. Our association spanned eighteen years. I benefited greatly from it and was harmed greatly by it. It came to an end in 1968, when I was thirty-eight years old. As with many relationships that begin in the student-mentor mold, our parting of the ways was rather violent. Our differences were both philosophical and personal. I used to wonder why I had remained in the relationship so long, past the time when it had obviously become detrimental to my development.

Only when I was forty years old, when I finally reconnected with my frustrated childhood longing for a father—for a teacher and a guide—did I grasp at least one of the powerful forces that had influenced my choices. I recalled that at the age of twenty, when my first article was published, I had brought her a copy; because my visit coincided with Father's Day, I had autographed the article, as a joke, "To my father, Ayn Rand." It took me twenty years to realize it was not a joke.

When I allowed myself not only to recognize my childhood need for a teacher and guide but to feel it, it very rapidly began to fade; the young boy who had wanted a mentor found him— in me.

Just as self-awareness can be directed at our needs, emotions, and mental states, so it can be directed at our actions.

I can learn to notice the kinds of actions that enhance my life and the kinds that produce frustration or disappointment. I can learn to pay attention to what works and what does not work. Or, in the absence of self-awareness, I can proceed to act blindly and obliviously, not bothering myself with such questions, blaming others and feeling sorry for myself when my life does not develop as I had hoped.

Suppose, for example, I feel frustrated in my relationships with other people. Let us say that I am vaguely unhappy and do not know why. In order to clarify my frustrations, I might complete such sentence stems as "One of the things I want from people and don't know how to get is—," saying or writing as many endings as I possibly can, as rapidly as I can. But then I follow with the stem "One of the ways I make it difficult for people to give me what I want is—" and "One of the ways I keep people at a distance is—." Here my attention is directed toward those behaviors by which I contribute to my own disappointment. Thus:

> *One of the ways I make it difficult for people to give me what I want is—*
>> I don't tell them what I want.
>> I act as if I don't need anything.
>> I act as if I am totally self-sufficient.
>> When they attempt to reach out to me, I don't acknowledge them.
>> I always find fault with whatever they offer me.
>> I keep myself remote and detached.

> *One of the ways I keep people at a distance is—*

I don't meet their eyes.
I stay detached.
I get sarcastic.
I act superior.
I look indifferent.
I never show interest.
I don't listen.
I pretend I don't notice when they are reaching out.

The essence of self-awareness is *learning to notice, learning to pay attention.*

And self-awareness can include a good deal more than I have discussed thus far: the pattern of our breathing and the moments when we interrupt its natural rhythm; the tone of our voice and the messages our tone conveys; the ways we stand or move and the silent statement contained in our stance and posture; the signals we emit through the expression in our eyes and on our face.

And beyond that: our dreams and the secrets often encoded within them; our fantasies and the longings they contain; the music within us we may never fully share, out of the fear that we may not be understood or approved of—or may not approve ourselves.

The self is a vast continent whose exploration we can never complete.

I do not want to conclude this discussion of self-awareness without touching briefly on the subject of subselves or subpersonalities, although this is an issue that properly deserves a book in itself. I merely wish to acknowledge it here because it adds another dimension to our understanding of what self-awareness can entail.

In addition to the adult self that most of us are familiar with, there is within the psyche a child self—the living presence of the child we once were. As a potential of our consciousness, that child's frame of reference and way of responding is an enduring component of our psyche. But we may have disowned that child long ago, repressing his or her feelings, perceptions, responses, out of the belief that "murder" was necessary in order that we grow to adulthood.

By way of introducing clients or students to this concept, I sometimes ask them to enter a fantasy, to imagine themselves walking along a country road and, in the distance, to see a small child sitting by a tree and, as they draw near, to see that the child is the self they once were. Then I ask them to sit down by the tree and enter into dialogue with the child. What do they want and need to say to each other? Not uncommonly there are tears; sometimes there is rapture. But there is almost always the realization that in some form that child still exists within the psyche (as a mind state) and has a contribution to make to the life of the adult—and a richer, fuller self emerges from the discovery. Another way to facilitate contact with the child self is to do sentence-completion exercises, utilizing the stem "If the child in me could speak, he/she might say—."

Another self (subpersonality), as Jungian psychologists have long proclaimed, is the female self in each male and the male self in each female. This self is usually unconscious, usually disowned, but when brought to consciousness, accepted, and integrated, it is an invaluable source for the total personality—a source of growth, expansion, energy, higher awareness, and higher efficacy. Jung suggested decades back, and subsequent studies bear him out, that creative men and women in general exhibit a much higher level of integration of the male and female within their personalities than do average people; they are less willing to disown those aspects of the self that do not conform to cultural sex-role stereotypes; they are more open to the totality of their inner being.*

I have already mentioned, earlier in the book, that which I call the sage self—the wisest, most daring, and most intuitive part of us, that within us which is often most aware of our deepest needs and highest possibilities. The sage self may be the voice of evolution within us—the voice that whispers to us in our dreams, or in moments when we are alone, or when listening to great music, or when making passionate love, that our journey is not finished, that it is never finished, that higher possibilities of creativity, joy, consciousness lie beyond the next mountain range in

---

*An excellent introduction to the Jungian concept of male-female subpersonalities may be found in *The Invisible Partners* by John A. Sanford.

our awareness. Because it is a voice that speaks only in whispers, it is easy to ignore; it does not scream as the child self sometimes screams. If, in reading these words, you are aware of some resonance within you, a vaguely familiar trembling, that is the voice of the sage self signaling for your attention.

This passing introduction to the issue of subselves or subpersonalities represents, necessarily, a simplification of an extraordinarily complex subject. The various subselves or subpersonalities (the potential for different mind states, different frames of reference) that exist within us—and there are many more than I have mentioned—generate emotional tensions and problems if disowned and repudiated, but, if recognized and integrated, can enrich and enliven enormously that which we call our "self."

So: Internal signals can be organic sensations, desires, emotions, memories, thoughts, images, fantasies. Any can be allowed into awareness, and any can be shut out of awareness. Some signals go unheeded simply because they are so faint they remain unnoticed. Some signals disappear from awareness because we have no frame of reference within which to understand them or because they seem to conflict with what we think we know. And some signals are avoided because they threaten our equilibrium, disturb the precarious structure of our security or self-esteem. This is what makes the attainment of self-awareness a continual challenge.

Which leads us, once again, to the subject of self-acceptance.

Without self-acceptance, there is a limit to how far self-awareness can proceed.

Sometimes we become aware of a feeling, a thought, or a memory, and then involuntarily we begin to tense against it, feeling powerless to control our response. Self-acceptance in that moment seems impossible to us. The solution is not to try to resist our resistance; if we cannot accept a feeling (or a thought or a memory), we should *accept our resistance*. If we stay with the resistance at a conscious level, it will begin to melt.

We become off-center when we try to fight ourselves; when we flow with what is, we regain balance and control. This is the essence of the art of self-acceptance.

When we fight ourselves—when we refuse to practice self-acceptance with regard to our experience—we obstruct the integrative function of mind. We keep ourselves in a state of conflict and tension. We produce a sense of self-alienation. If we permit ourselves to experience that which we are denying, we reestablish contact with ourselves, we make it possible for unwanted feelings to be discharged, and we unblock the integrative process that maintains our internal equilibrium and well-being.

One of my favorite ways to demonstrate this is when someone in therapy or in one of my seminars complains of being unable to speak freely because of an overeagerness to win my approval. I typically will ask the person to tell me several times, clearly and firmly, of the desire for my approval. After seven or eight repetitions the person is usually relaxed and smiling and proceeds to say something like, "I feel calm and clearheaded. I don't care what you think of me. There are certain things I want to say, and now I am going to say them. I feel free and good."

The difficulty in speaking openly is caused, not by the desire for approval as such, but by resistance to that desire. By expressing the desire either aloud to the person concerned or internally, we increase the sense of self-respect and autonomy. We also free the mind to be aware that there is a wider context, other needs, and that the most important need in this particular situation is to say what we want to say rather than to gain approval.

We can better practice self-acceptance when we understand that it is not unwanted feelings that impair healthy functioning but the denial and disowning of those feelings. It is the act of blocking that gives rise to a different set of responses than would occur were we in solid contact with our inner experience.

A woman who does not permit herself to know when she feels assaulted and mistreated, for example, condemns herself to feeling helpless and impotent, a state in which self-assertiveness is impossible. A man who does not permit himself to know when he is afraid cannot be aware of the defenses restricting his growth, and thus he cannot take action to correct the situation.

Unfortunately, many persons desiring to change begin by repudiating what they are, looking toward what they seek to become. Even when these ideals are valid, we cannot move toward them successfully by pronouncing the self a *nonvalue* in its present state and disowning what we are now.

Another example, a personal one, may help clarify further the relationship between self-acceptance and the self-healing, integrative function of mind. Some years ago, while I was writing *The Disowned Self*, a young man came to my office to discuss entering therapy with me. He did not have a great deal of money, and coming to Los Angeles had not been easy for him. I liked him and found him interesting, but I saw that he needed far more personal attention than I was in a position to give. This was during a period when I was confining my work as a therapist exclusively to groups; I had ceased practicing individual therapy because I needed time for writing.* I explained why I was unable to accept him as a client and recommended him to a colleague. Although he handled himself with great dignity and composure, I could see that he was sadly disappointed. When he left my office, I felt troubled, depressed, and guilty. I felt that I had somehow been cruel. Then I told myself that my feelings were nonsense; I returned to my desk to resume writing *The Disowned Self* and to explain to future readers the importance of accepting one's feelings. My feeling of distress continued, despite my impatient efforts at dismissal. Then I appreciated the contradiction between what I was doing and what I was writing.

I got up from my desk and went to sit in a chair. I closed my eyes, began to breathe deeply, and whispered to myself, "I'm really feeling bad right now. I feel troubled. I feel miserable. I feel depressed. I'm wondering if I am not lacking in compassion because I did not find a way to stretch my time. I see the look of sadness in his eyes as he departed, and I feel low, terribly low." Within a few moments, the troubled feelings were gone; my head cleared, my spirits lifted, I saw the whole situation in realistic perspective, and I calmly returned to work.

I didn't need to give myself a sermon; I needed to allow myself to feel regretful for a moment—even to feel self-reproachful—without reproaching myself for feeling self-reproachful. Then my wider context returned of its own accord, restoring harmony.

Integration is central to every aspect of the life process. An organism is a complex integrate of hierarchically organized struc-

---

*Later I resumed doing individual therapy.

tures and functions. It sustains itself physically by taking materials from the environment, reorganizing them and converting these materials into its means of survival, achieving a new integration. We can observe an analogous phenomenon in the process by which the mind apprehends reality—from the integration of sensations into perceptions, the integration of perceptions into concepts, the integration of concepts into still wider concepts, the integration of new experiences into conceptual knowledge. Just as integration is the cardinal principle of life, so it is the cardinal principle of mind.

To integrate is to bring together into a nonconflicting, noncontradictory unity those elements that are being integrated, in accordance with a goal, need, or standard that operates as the organizing principle. The ultimate *biological* principle of integration is, of course, that which is required for the life of the organism. All self-healing, at the psychological level, entails the principle of integration: for example, the integration of traumatic experiences, so that they lose their negative charge; or the integration of a single troublesome situation into the wider context of our knowledge, as in the incident concerning the young man who came to me for therapy; or the integration of new skills into our repertoire of behavior so as to facilitate a higher level of effectiveness.

Evasion and repression are, by their very nature, anti-integrative processes. When evasion and repression have obstructed the integrative process, the task of reason, self-awareness, and self-acceptance is to remove those obstructions. Ultimately, of course, most integrations take place beneath the level of conscious awareness, at deeper levels of the psyche, but the stimulation for the process of integration is provided by the means I am describing. Even when, in the context of psychotherapy, explicit awareness may seem to be bypassed almost entirely—as in hypnosis, for instance—this merely means that the acceptance required for integration is triggered elsewhere along the continuum of consciousness.

In the course of their work, many psychotherapists have been impressed by the frequency with which self-healing and growth-inducing integrations occur when previously avoided material is brought into conscious awareness and is appropriately experienced—experienced organismically, one might say, rather than merely grasped cerebrally. The self-repairing process observable on the physical level of our being clearly has an analogous process on the psychological level, evidenced by this phenomenon of spontaneous integrations. The self-repairing tendency is not infallible, neither in body nor in mind, but its existence on the psychological level is indisputable—and the challenge for those involved in psychotherapy is how to use it creatively. For example, after a long string of sentence completions in which significant material is brought to the surface, I might give a client the stem "As I begin to understand what I am saying—," and that stem activates the integrative process. Individuals who learn to work with sentence completion on their own may employ such a stem for just the same purpose. Other such integrative stems include: "I'm beginning to see—"; "It is slowly and reluctantly dawning on me—" and "Right now it seems obvious—."

Since so much of denied and avoided material consists of repressed emotions, and since their release often leads to dramatically successful results, there has been an understandable emphasis, for some decades past, on the liberation of feeling as a cardinal therapeutic goal. If it becomes our primary concern, however, anti-intellectualism, indifference to reason, and self-indulgent subjectivism may result. Contact with feelings may often be the beginning of the process of self-healing, but it is hardly the end. It does not automatically generate the thinking, honesty, integrity, and attitude of self-responsibility our well-being requires.

Successful functioning entails the ability to be aware of the facts and requirements of external reality and of inner experience *without* sacrificing one awareness to the other.

Suppose, for example, that a man is ill and knows that a surgical operation is necessary. He experiences considerable fear at the prospect of this operation. It would obviously be self-destructive for him either to capitulate to the fear and avoid the needed surgery or to be aware only of the need for the surgery and to be oblivious of the fact of his fear. A fear that is experienced and acknowledged can be dealt with; a fear that is denied, in a case such as this, can actually precipitate shock.

Or again, suppose that a woman feels enraged at her husband. It is important for her well-being—and for the well-being of the relationship—that she be able to accept her rage. Her right to accept it is not dependent on whether or not it is "justified." At the same time she accepts and experiences her rage, it is possible— and necessary—for her to be aware that her rage may or may not be an authentic response to her husband's behavior, that it may be the result of unresolved conflicts within herself having little relevance to her husband's behavior. So two different issues are involved, both of which deserve awareness and acknowledgment. One is the fact of her emotional state. The other is the matter of objectivity: What has happened *in reality* between her husband and herself? It would obviously be a mistake for her to assume, before examining the objective reality of the situation, that her rage is entirely "justified." But it is equally a mistake to forbid herself to know that she feels rage until and unless she can "prove" that it is justified. In either case, the mistake involved is essentially the same: *avoiding reality*. She can accept her feeling without being obligated to act on it.

If a person believes that objectivity consists of accepting and experiencing only "justifiable" emotions, the person ends up by corrupting the ability to be objective. It happens when one feels uncomfortable simply experiencing an emotion and perhaps expressing it. Ignoring the feeling, the person sets out to "prove" that the object of the emotional response is "immoral" or "wonderful" or "vile" or "brilliant" or whatever. Now, sometimes it happens that the qualities he or she projects *are* justifiable, but that is not the point. The point is that the person is incapable of knowing it.

Self-acceptance is, quite simply, realism. That which is, is. That which I feel, I feel. That which I think, I think. That which I have done, I have done.

Reason and emotion need not be adversaries. If the essence of rationality is respect for the facts of reality, that includes the facts of our own psychological state.

Reason is the conceptual instrument of awareness; reason is the power of integration made explicit and self-conscious; it is the faculty by means of which we apprehend logical relationships and organize the contents of our awareness.

Clearly the appropriate exercise of reason does not entail the conceptual analysis of every experience, an undertaking neither possible nor desirable. Often, however, we sense the presence of significant relationships we cannot grasp, or the presence of some dissonance among the signals we are receiving from the external world or from ourselves. In such instances it becomes the task of reason to guide the process of integration on a (relatively) explicit and self-conscious plane.

In seeking to dissolve conflicts within ourselves, we sometimes need to reflect conceptually on the meaning of our feelings, responses, and actions, to engage in a sustained process of reasoning. But sometimes we merely need to bring some aspect of our experience into awareness. In any case, reason remains the ultimate arbiter, since only reason can determine which course of mental action is appropriate to a given set of circumstances.

If we understand this concept of reason and rationality, we can appreciate that self-acceptance is the application of the principle of reason to the world of inner experience.

The essence of self-assertion is to respect our own values and live by our own judgment, so that we experience integrity: what we do in the world is the appropriate expression of what we are.

When self-assertion is thus defined, the ability to be angry, to meet challenges to our dignity with appropriate aggressiveness, or to "stick up for our rights" plays a very small part. Important as these responses may sometimes be, they are far from the entirety of what self-assertion entails.

There is a sense in which everything I have been discussing in this book pertains to self-assertion. The choice to be conscious is the ultimate act of self-assertion. The decision to be true to the judgments of our own mind is an act of self-assertion.

The choice to see is an act of self-assertion. Humility and insecurity are associated with downcast eyes. The training of Carmelite nuns, who are taught that their ego is the single most formidable barrier between themselves and God, contains the specific admonition to see as little as posssible.

This issue of sight is both literally applicable and a metaphor that illuminates the deepest meaning of self-assertion. Therefore I will allow myself a momentary historical digression.

THE STRUGGLE FOR INDIVIDUATION

There is an extraordinary passage in Augustine's *Confessions* in which, after denouncing all the pleasures of the flesh, Augustine goes on to say:

> To this is added another form of temptation more manifoldly dangerous. For besides the concupiscence of the flesh which consists in the delight of all senses and pleasures . . . the soul has through the same senses of the body, a certain vain and curious desire, veiled under the title of knowledge and learning. . . . The seat whereof being in the appetite of knowledge, and sight being the sense chiefly used for attaining knowledge, it is in Divine language called the lust of the eyes.

If the quest for knowledge is a "lust," then it would be hard to name an era in history as chaste as that during which Augustine's precepts held sway. There was little sight to pollute it, or reason or mind or science or progress. Once again, as in the pre-Grecian centuries, human beings crawled from generation to generation making tortuously minute improvements in their store of knowledge—while the alleged philosophers were debating such topics as whether a mouse that slips into a church and happens to eat the eucharistic bread does or does not achieve communion with God, and while the masses of the people were existing in a state now recognized as mass neurosis, mass hysteria.

What was the battle cry of the Renaissance? *The right to see.* The right to that "lust of the eyes" denounced by Augustine. In philosophy, the right to study the universe. In science, the right to study physical nature, with the rebirth of such forbidden sciences as anatomy and astronomy. In art, the right to study *this earth* and to depict the full reality of the human body, of nature, of perspective, of three-dimensionality, as perceived by our senses.

And throughout the world today, the most punishable crime in any dictatorship is self-assertion—that is, the exercise of independent judgment, independent sight, in defiance of authority.

It is an act of self-assertion to challenge any dogma, whether that dogma originates in religion, science, government, or the teachings of our parents. It is an act of self-assertion to ask, "Why?"—and to refuse to accept a club, a gun, or a frown of condemnation as an answer.

Remembering once again the Milgram experiments, we can appreciate the act of self-assertion on the part of those few who retained a sufficient moral autonomy to refuse to push the electric shock buttons.[53]

Every new invention, every true work of art, every genuinely creative act—any commitment taken by anyone, anywhere, to his or her own evolution—is an act of self-assertion.

On the simple level of everyday life, one of the most important ways in which we support our self-esteem is through the courage and integrity to say no when we want to say no and yes when we want to say yes. Sometimes such self-assertion is difficult. Doubtless all of us can remember occasions in life when, out of fear of one kind or another, we said yes when we wanted to say no or vice versa, and we know the marks such defaults leave on the soul. I am not referring here to the normal process of compromise and accommodation that all of us practice when motivated by courtesy, kindness, or love; I am talking about violations to the self in which we cooperate when cooperation is neither necessary nor desirable. Sacrificing our judgment, values, needs, self-respect. Giving up a deeply felt ambition because others are not sympathetic to it. Sleeping with someone to break a "siege." Remaining silent and unprotesting when our political convictions are being ridiculed, to avoid being challenged. Relinquishing a personal and passionate vision in order to belong. Declining a career opportunity we long for in order to placate a disapproving family. Running from the possibility of love because we are afraid of hurt and rejection. Fearing to reach out to life because success is not guaranteed.

Sentence completion can help put people in touch with this issue.

> *If I could say no when I want to say no and yes when I want*
> *to say yes—*
> I would be afraid.
> I would like myself more.
> I'd have to risk people's anger
> I think I would like people more.
> I wouldn't so often feel cowardly.
> I might lose some friends.

I'd have more self-respect.
I would probably be kinder.
I could be more relaxed.
I wouldn't be so afraid of other people's expectations.
I would live more adventurously.
I'd feel more.
I'd accomplish more.
I wouldn't get so angry when other people didn't do what
    I wanted.
I might lose my parents.
I'd be a grown-up.
I'd have more dignity.
I wouldn't feel so weak.
I'd trust myself.
I wouldn't hate other people for my own cowardice.
I'd be more alive.
I'd wonder what had ever stopped me.
I'd see that other people are just . . . other people; why
    did I have to take their reactions all that seriously?

Every act of self-assertion is an implicit affirmation of my right to exist. It implies that I am not the property of others and that I am not bound to live my life in accordance with their expectations—neither my parents nor my teachers nor my friends nor my colleagues nor the government nor the salesperson trying to browbeat me into a purchase I have no wish to make. Self-assertion can be frightening—it connects me to my aloneness.

Sometimes I will ask a lecture audience, "Do any of you believe you have a right to exist?" Almost everyone responds affirmatively, but when I ask someone to stand in front of the room facing everyone present and say, "I have a right to exist," take a breath, experience how saying that sentence feels, and say it again five or ten times, the person tends to speak timidly, with hostility, placatingly, defiantly, pleadingly, apologetically, defensively, or resentfully. Even after I point this out and remark that no one is denying the speaker's right to exist, few persons can say the sentence with simple, good-natured serenity. Clearly, the activated anxiety says a good deal about our fear of aloneness and self-responsibility. It also says a good deal about how we were raised and educated, about the values of our culture.

And yet there is a place deep inside us where, I am convinced, we know that we *do* have a right to exist, *do* have a right to the space we occupy. But we need courage to know it and to admit it.

We sometimes seek to conceal from ourselves our fear of self-assertion. "I don't like to be pushy" is a sentence we often hear when a person is reluctant to assert a perfectly ordinary right—such as returning unsatisfactory food in a restaurant, or complaining about unsatisfactory service, or challenging someone's rudeness or disrespect. "I'm a private person" is a favorite rationalization for hiding our feelings when there is no good reason to hide them: concealing our excitement for fear of being thought silly, feeling uncomfortable about holding a lover's hand in a public place, feigning indifference when we are actually hurt or angry or joyful, in order to be thought sophisticated—in other words, misrepresenting the reality of our experience out of preoccupation with our "image."

Obviously there are times when it is not strategic to express our thoughts or emotions. I may not tell a client what I think about some behavior, for instance, because such a communication might not be therapeutic if I am seeking to nurture the client's capacity for independent judgment. I may choose not to express my impatience or anger at someone's incompetent performance of a task because I believe that such a communication will lead to a further deterioration of competence; so I choose to stay focused on the job that needs to be done rather than on my feelings.

The fact remains that our lives are filled with situations where it is appropriate and desirable to express what we think and feel, because such expression can be intrinsically satisfying, can enhance and enliven the moment, can serve our personal integrity. And yet, out of fear, we remain silent. The moment is unlived. For many people, that is the pattern of their entire lives.

Following is the distillation of countless sentence completions that concern themselves with this issue.

If I were more honest about expressing my thoughts and opinions—
  I'd probably lose some of my friends.
  I'd feel cleaner.
  People would know me.

I'd be frightened about other people's reactions.
I wonder if I would be alone.
I think I would find it is all right.
I wouldn't feel like a phony.
I'd at least know that my friends liked the real me.
I'd have to risk being challenged.
I'd have to learn to stick up for myself.
I'd be prouder of myself.
I'd be free.
I'd wonder why I waited so long.
I wouldn't feel like a bystander in my own life.
I'd be in reality.
I'd laugh more.
I'd have a chance to find out if I'm mistaken in my
    thoughts.
I would grow.
I would come out of this fog I'm in.
I'd walk straighter.
I'd understand self-esteem.

If I were willing to be more straightforward about expressing
    my desires and emotions—
I'd be a different person.
I'd have to make some hard choices.
I'd really have to look at my life.
I'd probably have to face some hostility.
I might be rejected.
I might be ridiculed.
I'd have more integrity.
I wouldn't have to resent other people for not being able
    to read my mind.
I'd feel like an adult.
I could have more honest relationships.
I wouldn't worry so much about other people's approval
    or disapproval.
I'd feel stronger.
I'd be more independent.
I'd feel like a person in my own right.
I think my whole life would change.

I think the people who mattered would respect me more.
I'd feel alive.

The next set of stems is especially useful for helping us understand some of the consequences for our life when we fail to recognize our deepest wants and/or to strive for their fulfillment.

If I were to treat my deepest wants with full seriousness—
I'd have to take my life seriously.
I'd think more about how I spend my time.
I'd know that a lot of the ridiculous things I want now are just substitutes.
I wouldn't waste my time pursuing things that don't mean a damn to me.
I'd have to have courage.
I'd have to be willing to take risks.
I'd have to stop kidding myself about most of the goals that occupy me now.
I'd reorganize my priorities.
I'd understand why I've always felt empty.
I'd be true to myself.
I wouldn't just play at life.
I'd question just about everything I'm now doing.
I'd wonder who I gave it all up for.
I'd feel solemn.
I'd feel scared.
I'd wonder if it's too late for me.
I'd have to recognize that what I choose to do is important.
I couldn't pretend I have all the time in the world.
I'd be what people call "selfish."
I'd have more energy.
I think it would be the bravest thing I could do.
I'd tell the woman I care for that I love her, and I'd stop fooling around.
I'd change jobs.
I'd travel.
I wouldn't spend time with people that don't mean anything to me.

I'd play with my children more.
I'd read and study more.
I'd admit how much of my life bores me.
I'd face the frustration in my marriage.
I'd give myself a chance to be young before I grow old.
I wouldn't apologize for loving my work more than my family.
I'd weigh carefully whom I choose to spend time with.
I'd really think about how I want to spend my remaining years.
I wouldn't wonder that other people don't take my wants more seriously than I do.
I think I could have the things I want.
I would have a better sense of who I am.
I wouldn't always be wondering, "Is this all there is?"
I'd feel like more of a human being.
I wouldn't be angry at other people for robbing me of my chances.
I'd feel more self-responsible.
I'd be more aware of my own choices.
I wouldn't be so preoccupied with pleasing other people.
I wouldn't always be worrying if people liked me.
I could create a life that would mean something to me.

Along the path to higher levels of self-expression, self-actualization, and individuation, one of the most formidable obstacles that the self-assertive tendency encounters is the internalized parental message forbidding the individual to evolve beyond a particular point: "You'll never accomplish anything." "You're not to be any happier in your marriage than we were in ours." "It's not what you think that matters, it's what other people think." "Who are you to think you know what's right?" "Dreams are impractical." "Just be happy to get by." "Don't aspire; greatness is not for you." "You're a big disappointment." "Don't be too smart; people won't like you."

Many men and women have too much energy and independence to accept these messages completely—and yet not enough to break entirely free of them. So they live in a chronic state of tension and conflict that they do not understand. The frustration

of their unused capacities—for love, for creativity, for happiness—
may generate an amorphous cloud of rage that permeates their
personalities.

In the course of exploring this problem in therapy, I find
sentence stems such as the following particularly useful: "Mother/
Father was always—"; "Mother/Father always seemed to
expect—"; "With mother/father I felt—"; "One of the things I wanted
from mother/father and didn't get was—"; "Mother/Father gave
me a view of myself as—"; "Mother/Father gave me a view of men
as—"; "Mother/Father gave me a view of women as —"; "Mother/
Father gave me a view of love as—"; "Mother/Father gave me a
view of sex as—"; "Mother/Father gave me a view of life as—"; "If
mother/father thought I was in a happy love relationship—"; "If
mother/father saw me achieving something important with my
life—"; "One of the unspoken messages I got from mother/father
was—"; "When I think of the ways in which mother/father continues to affect my life—."

When an individual has completed approximately ten endings for each of these sentence stems, profound insights have invariably emerged into consciousness, insights that often have the
power to generate change. Now the individual is able to recognize
when the voices within are alien. Now the individual is in a position to question and challenge. But since there are always tacit
rewards for cooperating with mother or father's philosophy and
life scenario, I put the individual in contact with the benefits of
his or her complicity. Thus: "The good thing about sharing my
mother's/father's view of things is—"; "If I were to exercise my
independent judgment against mother/father—"; "If I were to live
by my own vision of life/love/women/men/sex/success—"; "When
I am ready to belong to myself rather than to mother/father—."

At this point it is generally possible to guide the individual
through initial explorations in changing behaviors, in stepping
outside of an unnecessarily limiting model of self-in-the-world.
The ongoing process of individuation and the ongoing act of self-
assertion here become inseparable. We create our self through our
choices, our actions, and the risks we are willing to take.

Breaking free of other people's limiting values, philosophies,
and life scenarios obviously includes a good deal more than breaking free of the influence of mother and father. We may need to

challenge important aspects of the implicit philosophy of the culture in which we live. We may need to check and confront many of the basic premises that almost everyone takes for granted. This is a subtle and difficult task, because we rarely even know where to begin; the premises that need to be questioned are too much a part of our own thinking. The premises involved may pertain to the ultimate meaning of life, the values by which we are to live, the nature of virtue, the meaning of maleness and femaleness, the nature of knowledge, the ultimate nature of existence itself. To think independently and radically about such issues is not an easy undertaking. We shall deal with at least one example of this challenge when we take up the subject of ethics.

But before we turn to the subject of ethics, there is an issue we need to address in more detail—one of the great barriers to individuation, self-esteem, and the art of being.

Fear of death—the other side of fear of life.

11
Death Anxiety

That we are mortal is one of the givens of our existence. Every one of us, one way or another, must confront the issue of death—our own death and that of the people we care about—but it would be difficult to name any other fact of life so fiercely resisted and denied.

We have an immense repertoire of behaviors through which we deny our powerlessness in the face of death; from seeking symbolic immortality through children, flags, causes, fame, to persuading ourselves that we are indestructible by living recklessly and irresponsibly, to consoling ourselves with the belief that death is an illusion.

Thus far in the book our primary focus has been on fear of life: fear of choice, freedom, responsibility, struggle, uncertainty, pain, and failure. Fear of death is the shadow side of the same terror, and it is relatively less well understood. But if both are left unresolved, we can be caught in limbo between them.[67]

While the difficulty of accepting and integrating the fact of mortality is doubtless as old as humankind itself, it has often been observed that ours is a culture in which denial of death is exceptionally pervasive. In the past, when most people died in their homes, surrounded by relatives, it was perhaps easier to accept death as a natural event. Now, with more and more people dying in hospitals, essentially alone, essentially quarantined off from the living, death appears all the more mysterious, all the more frightening, all the more remote from our existence. We are less and less prepared to deal with it or to accept it—just at that moment in history when the entire globe lies under the shadow of death as never before.

One day I was discussing our culture's attitude on death and dying with a physician who specializes in the terminally ill. He remarked, "Doctors and nurses are themselves the worst offenders. Their helplessness when confronted with death is appalling. They become callous, insensitive, even cruel—first, because their own fear of death is mobilized, and second, because they feel like failures. We don't accept death as a natural phenomenon. So very few phsycians know how to deal appropriately with dying patients or their families. The place to begin is with the realization that we ourselves are going to die. If we can handle that, we can handle the death of our patients. But fear of death—and denial of death— is probably what drives a lot of people into the profession of medicine in the first place."

In the course of therapy, clients readily disclose their fear of life. There is no need to go searching for evidence of such a fear; it announces itself constantly. Fear of death is far subtler, less obvious, more indirect in its manifestations. Death anxiety is rarely raised as an explicit problem.

One day, while waiting for the members of a particular group, I found myself wondering about the prevalence of this problem in my own practice. When the group was assembled, I said, "Today we're going to begin a little differently, and I prefer not to explain what this is about. I'll suggest a sentence stem, the person on my immediate left will begin, then we'll rotate around the room, each person repeating my stem and putting on his or her ending. After a while I'll introduce another stem and we'll continue. We'll talk about what it all means later."

As I announced the first stem, "At the thought that I'm going to die someday—," everyone's breathing suddenly seemed to stop. Muscles tensed, eyes shifted nervously; all smiles and relaxation instantly vanished.

> *At the thought that I'm going to die someday—*
>   I am terrified.
>   I don't want to think about it.
>   I wonder what's the point of living.
>   I can't stand it.
>   I wonder how long I've got.
>   What am I doing with my life?
>   I want to crawl into a shell.

I'm upset.
I don't believe it.
I hope I can accomplish something first.
I hope it won't be painful.
Not me, never.
I'm going to live until at least 150.
Maybe medical science will come up with an answer.
I don't care, I believe in reincarnation.
I just won't think about it.
I hate it.
I feel angry.
I feel betrayed.
Why me?
It's not fair.
I wonder who will remember me.
I hope it won't be soon.
This is the worst sentence stem you've ever come up
    with.

By this time, two or three people in the group were crying.
Some were moving about restlessly in their chairs. The atmosphere was filled with anxiety and depression—and anger.

When a child first learns about death—
    She wonders if daddy is going to die, too.
    She's frightened when her parents go out at night.
    He tells himself grandpa is sleeping.
    He runs out to play.
    He wonders if he will be left alone.
    He wonders if it's cold in the ground, and he feels scared.
    He wonders why mummy left him.
    He tries to understand, and he can't.
    He laughs and pretends it's a game.
    She asks a lot of questions that make grown-ups
        uncomfortable.
    He wonders what it feels like.
    He asks his parents when he is going to die.
    He says he's never going to die.
    He decides to stay young forever.

> She tells herself only married people with children die.
> She wants to run and hide.
> He tells himself that if you're in heaven you're not really
>   dead.
> She tells herself if she's really good it won't happen.
> He hides his fear.
> He pretends he doesn't understand.
> He knows it will never happen to him.
> She hangs on to mummy.
> She hopes other people will die in her place.
> He wishes mummy and daddy would live forever so
>   everything would be all right.

This stem had been inspired by some research challenging the conventional wisdom that young children were largely oblivious to the phenomenon of death.[1,95] I chose the impersonal form, rather than "When I first learned about death—," in order to build a measure of safety into the exploration. I hoped that my clients might respond more openly, and they did. It was interesting to observe that the men and women in group were expressing thoughts and feelings they obviously had never put forth before, evidencing considerable agitation and disorientation, while simultaneously, at a deeper level, there was an odd lack of surprise, as if none of this were really new, as if they had always known it.

> *If talking about death weren't such a taboo—*
> Maybe the subject wouldn't be so frightening.
> My parents wouldn't have had to be so dishonest with
>   me when grandpa died.
> I might be able to look at the subject.
> People could talk about dying instead of "sleeping" or
>   "passing away."
> Death wouldn't seem so supernatural.
> We could all make peace with it.
> I think I'd live differently.
> I wouldn't waste so much time.
> I could be more honest.
> Death might not be so terrible, somehow.
> We could find a better way to live.

I wouldn't keep postponing things.
I'd wonder if we could stand it.
I'd live more in the moment.
Just talking this way lets me feel calmer.

If I felt free to talk about my fear of death—
I think I would talk for a long time.
It would be a great relief.
We'd find out we all have the same fears.
I would feel less lonely.
It would feel like a burden lifted off my shoulders.
The lump in my chest might melt.
I wouldn't feel this terror.
I'd appreciate my life today more.
I'd let my children know how much I love them.
I wouldn't keep myself so busy.
I'd read more.
I'd play more.
I'd know no one has all the time in the world.
I wouldn't worry so much about my image.
I'd do what I thought was right, whether others agree
    with me or not.
I'd appreciate all the wonderful things I have.
I could feel how much I love life.
My fear would go away.
I know it would be better than keeping silent.
I could relax into living.
I would wonder why we're all so busy pretending.
I would feel freer.
I would stop thinking about death.
I could forgive my parents for dying.
I would enjoy nature more.
I would feel as if I had been released from prison.

One of the ways I keep myself from dying is—
I refuse to grow up.
I keep busy.
I have a lot of people needing me.
I never fall in love.

I never commit to anything.
I have children.
I take a lot of crazy chances to prove I'm indestructible.
I tell myself that if I refuse to accept death, I won't die.
I make money.
I postpone my most important goals.
I hang out with young people.
I chase women.
I got a facelift.
I surround myself with things.
I never decide on a career.
I don't enjoy anything.
I read books on life extension.
I fantasize that medical science will find a way to keep
    us alive forever.
I keep looking for new vitamins to take.
I tell myself death is only a state of mind and can't
    happen without your consent.
I refuse to live.
I don't participate.
I keep telling myself my life hasn't really begun yet.
I try to be helpful to everyone.
I pray.
I keep putting things off.
I don't have orgasms during sex—only grown-ups can
    have orgasms.
I let people hurt me in little ways, so nothing really bad
    can happen to me.
I study Buddhism.
I'm always in the middle of something very important
    that isn't finished yet.
I keep a lot of people indebted to me.
I numb myself.
I just don't think about it.

Subsequently, I was to repeat exercises of this kind with other therapy groups and with students in my seminars across the country. The results were always essentially the same; the completions listed above were the ones that kept recurring, in one form or another.

Glancing back over these completions, we can isolate some especially significant themes. First, it seems readily apparent that many human beings experience an underlying terror of death that they hardly ever discuss or even apprehend at a conscious level. Second, the problem of death is already a reality for children, and the process of building defenses against it begins very early. Third, the denial of death is deeply entrenched and is sustained by a wide variety of maneuvers aimed at symbolic immortality. Fourth, many of these maneuvers clearly obstruct the normal process of development and individuation. Some harmful maneuvers include clinging to a child's state of consciousness ("I refuse to grow up"), avoiding commitment either to a person or to an occupation ("So long as I do not enter the game, the clock has not begun to tick"), compulsive sexuality ("See how alive I am?"), keeping frenetically busy ("If I run fast enough, death can't catch me"), leaving major tasks undone ("I cannot possibly be taken away before my work is completed"), excessive preoccupation with material acquisitions ("Surrounded as I am by the insignia of power, death would not dare enter"), placing relationships with others above personal development ("If enough people need and are dependent on me, how can I possibly die?"), and taking irresponsible and dangerous risks ("See how invulnerable I am?").

I want to comment on one other theme reflected in the above sentence completions. Sometimes, when parents die, a child (of any age) feels rage. Often this is interpreted as anger at being abandoned, or as resentment over the fact that unfinished business with parents must now remain unfinished forever. Doubtless such explanations are generally true. But another factor is sometimes operative. So long as my parents are alive, I cannot die, since children do not die before their parents. My parents are thus the guarantors of my immortality. *How dare they betray me by dying?*

And there is another side to this betrayal. Parents may resist their children's growing up, because they are then pushed closer to the end of their own life. Death anxiety in parents can be transmitted to a child. The child picks up the message: To grow up is to kill my mother/father. I keep my parents alive by remaining forever a child. And I keep myself alive by the same means, since my parents must die before I do.

We can better appreciate the relationship of death anxiety to the challenges of individuation if we realize that implicit in everything I have been saying thus far is the ultimate defense against death: the refusal to live. If I do not come into existence, I cannot go out of existence. If I do not emerge as a separate entity, there is no one for death to touch. If I remain forever undeveloped and unactualized, if I keep life always ahead of me, then death recedes into the infinite distance.

To exist has its etymological roots in a Greek word meaning "to stand out" or "to stand forth." All growth, biological and psychological, entails a process of differentiation—from the womb, from my body, from my family, from my most recent stage of development. In differentiation there is already death—the death of my previous stage of development. So it is differentiation that makes me vulnerable to annihilation. If I refuse to emerge, I am safe.[95]

Thus I can refuse to individuate, refuse to evolve—and wait. I lose myself in my children, my work, my religion, my cause, my homes and automobiles, my guru, while I wait for a miracle, wait for a rescuer, wait for the universe to take pity on me, wait for some unimaginable solution that will confirm my uniqueness and guarantee my immortality.

I tell myself I do not believe in death—that what we call "death" is merely the process by which a caterpillar is transformed into a butterfly—and I learn to call this strategy "gaining a spiritual perspective."

Meanwhile, the precious days of my life go by, unlived or incompletely lived, while I am telling myself, "What does the moment matter when I am here for eternity? I will tell my children I love them tomorrow; I will correct the problems between myself and my spouse some time in the future; I will begin my most important work next month or next year. Why hurry? Have I not all the time in the world?" And when I finally do approach the end, when I can no longer evade the fact of my mortality, I cry out, "Wait! It's not fair! I'm not ready! I haven't lived yet! *When my life was happening, I wasn't there!*"

An important implication of these observations is that problems that people present in therapy or complain about to others whether or not they enter therapy are often several steps removed from the core difficulty, and if this is not recognized, a good deal of time can be wasted. If, for example, a client fails to grow up emotionally and intellectually, attacking the problem at the level of self-responsibility may yield limited success at best, if the client's deepest secret belief is that to grow up is to die. While obviously there are any number of problems from which people suffer that do not relate to death anxiety, I often find it useful to check out the possibility of such a connection, and when I discover that a connection exists, I find that working at the level of death anxiety is the most rapid way to generate growth.

Strange as it may sound, a good deal of effort is sometimes needed for a client to accept the fact that he or she really *is* going to die, so powerful is the mechanism of denial. But the consequence of doing so is a change in the client's values and priorities in life, a greater willingness to *participate* in life.

If someone had tried to persuade me, when I was younger, that I had never adequately confronted and integrated the fact of human mortality, I doubt that I would have believed it. I am sure I would have said all the appropriate and realistic things. Did I not teach people that one should always live with an acute appreciation of one's own mortality as well as the mortality of those one loves? But when I began exploring these issues in the context of therapy, then conducting seminars and workshops on the subject of our attitudes toward time and death, I began to realize how subtle and insidious the denial of death can be, and my own life began to change in the direction of increased thoughtfulness about my priorities.

I began to see how often I had been reckless about time and how I had permitted myself to defer important goals. I revised my will. My wife and I made funeral arrangements so that no one else would ever have the burden of having to handle such matters. When considering any work or activity, I asked myself, "Am I confident that this is the way I want to invest my time and life?" Not that I do not slip on occasions or that I am not subject to the same fits of blindness as most other people, but I do my best to stay connected with my mortality and that of those I love, and I find that it is not a morbid thought but an enriching one. It is an awareness that increases my appreciation of the preciousness of life.

If we are to live fully in the present, we need the context of our mortality. We need to remember that we do not have unlimited time. The ticking of the clock is not a tragedy. It is essential to the meaning and excitement of life, to the intensity of love—indeed, to the intensity of *any* joy. The glory of life is inseparable from the fact that it is finite.

Our fear of death is intimately tied to our fear of the loss of individuality, that very individuality whose emergence we may have dreaded and resisted. Evidence for this may be found in the small comfort we derive from being told, "Your body never really dies. It merely decomposes into its various elements and becomes reintegrated with nature. In this sense, the body is immortal." The complete irrelevance of such a viewpoint lies in the fact that when my body decomposes and becomes reintegrated with nature, it will no longer be *my body*. My body will cease to exist.

It is no greater comfort to be told: "Your consciousness never really dies. It merely becomes reintegrated into the great cosmic pool of consciousness from which it came. Consciousness is actually immortal." When (and if) my consciousness becomes reintegrated into the great cosmic pool of consciousness—even assuming that such a concept has validity—it will no longer be *my consciousness*. Everything that made it mine will have ceased to exist.

If I choose to draw comfort from such explanations, it can only be because they help me avoid the fact that I, as a unique biological entity with a unique history and a unique set of experiences and a unique perspective on the world, am alive for only a limited time.

Paradoxically, it is those least able to live in and enjoy the moment who seem most preoccupied with longing for eternity.

These are people in whom death anxiety appears to be conscious; they are obsessed with thoughts of death. But on the basis of my own experience, I am inclined to think that this is an illusion—that a morbid and highly verbal preoccupation with death is more often than not a reflection of fear of life (although some fear of death is obviously also present). These people transform the secret knowledge that they are not living now into concern for the brevity of their existence. They become extreme examples of procrastinators who endlessly complain about the swift passage of time.

But these speculations are somewhat academic. The fact of the matter is, a fear of life and a fear of death co-conspire against growth, individuation, love, creativity, and evolution. An unresolved fear of life or of death equally obstructs the emergence of healthy self-esteem.

In this context it is actually irrelevant whether or not there is any sense whatsoever in which individual consciousness might prove to be eternal. If we do not know how to live in the moment, we will not know how to live in eternity.

To accept the reality of death and to love life is one of the meanings of heroism as I understand it.

Indeed, it is precisely the givens of existence, such as this book has been concerned with, that call on the heroic potentialities of our nature. We have seen that one such given is the fact that we are beings of volitional consciousness. Another is that our life depends on our thought and our effort. Another is that success is never guaranteed. Another is that some measure of suffering is virtually inevitable for every human being. We have no choice about the existence of such challenges; our only choice lies in how we will respond.

To be heroic is to persevere. To love the process and the struggle. To laugh without restraint and to weep without restraint. To remain open and vulnerable, which means to remain feeling. To allow the life-force to lift us as high as we can rise.

And to be able to say, at the end, "I loved the adventure of the journey."

But if we are to make that journey successfully, we need a code of values to guide our actions. Which brings us finally to the ethical dimension: the morality of honoring the self.

PART THREE

EGOISM

12
Rational Selfishness

"You mean it's not immoral to be selfish?"

I have repeatedly encountered this question in one form or another throughout all of my professional life, whether I was engaged in psychotherapy, lecturing, or teaching at colleges and universities. The question does not mean, "Do I have permission to violate the rights of others?" Or "Is it appropriate to be indifferent to human suffering?" Or "Are kindness and generosity not virtues?" It means, "Do I have a right to honor my own needs and wants, to act on my own judgment, to strive for my own happiness?"

Ultimately it means, *"Do I have a right to exist for my own sake?"*

Strictly speaking, this question is tautologous. If my right to exist is contingent on services I render to others, I exist only by permission or favor. My life does not belong to me.

Respect for a human being's right to exist for his or her own sake—the ethics of rational self-interest or enlightened selfishness—has been implicit throughout this entire book. It is implicit in the advocacy of autonomy, self-responsibility, a concern with the unfolding of our positive potentialities, and in my emphasis on the centrality of self-esteem to psychological well-being. But it is now time to deal explicitly with the ethics of honoring the self.

It is not my purpose here to provide a comprehensive treatise on ethics, which would properly deserve and require a book in itself, but to provide an explicit ethical framework for the psychological vision I have been developing.

205

First, let us pause on the question, If my life does not belong to me, to whom does it belong?

Traditionally, human beings have received two answers to this query. The first, the religious answer, is God. The second, the social or tribal answer, is others—Pharaoh, Emperor, King, Country, Family, the Race, the State, the Proletariat, or Society.

This wider context is part of the world in which we live. It operates in our educational institutions no less than in our political institutions. It is present in the life of the family, where obedience to elders is the child's first introduction to the meaning of the word *good*. The teaching that we belong to our parents, or to the family, is preparation for the belief that we belong to the company, to the community, to the nation-state, or to the globe.

Almost all ethical systems that have achieved any degree of world influence have been, at root, variations on the theme of self-surrender and self-sacrifice. Unselfishness is equated with virtue; selfishness is made a synonym of evil. In such systems, the individual has always been the victim, twisted against him or her self and commanded to be "unselfish" in service to some allegedly higher value. The simplest name for that allegedly higher value is "Others."

Auguste Comte, the nineteenth-century advocate of collectivism and totalitarianism, coined a term for the modern-day version of this morality: *altruism*. So prevalent has this concept become that it is no longer regarded by most people as the name of a particular view of morality but rather as *a synonym for morality*. Furthermore, the average person takes *altruism* to mean simply benevolence, charity, kindness, or respect for the rights of others. But that is not the meaning Comte intended, and that is not the term's actual philosophical meaning. Altruism, as an ethical principle, holds that a human being must make the welfare of others his or her primary moral concern, placing their interests above those of self; it holds that an individual has no right to exist for his or her own sake, that service to others is the moral justification of one's existence, and that self-sacrifice is one's foremost duty and highest virtue.

It is a curious paradox of human history that a doctrine that tells human beings to regard themselves as sacrificial animals has been accepted as a doctrine representing benevolence and love for humankind. One need only consider the consequences to which this doctrine has led to estimate the nature of its so-called benevolence. From the first individual who was sacrificed on an altar for the good of the tribe thousands of years ago, to the heretics and dissenters burned at the stake for the good of the populace and the glory of God, to the millions exterminated in gas chambers and slave-labor camps for the good of the race or of the proletariat, this morality has served as justification for every dictatorship and every atrocity, past or present, that we have known in the world. People have fought only over particular applications of this morality, over who should be sacrificed to whom and for whose benefit. They have expressed horror and indignation when they did not approve of someone's particular choice of victims and beneficiaries. They have criticized "excesses." Rarely have they questioned the basic underlying principle: that a human being is an object of sacrifice.

In the course of everyday life we are bombarded in a thousand ways with messages to the effect that "service" is the highest mark of virtue, that morality consists of living for others. We are told that personal happiness, self-interest, and the profit motive are ignoble. We are told that the enlightened, the able, the competent, the strong must exist for those who lack precisely those traits, that those who suffer or are in need have first claim on the lives and energy of the rest of the human race, that theirs is the right superseding all other rights. We are told that the individual's mind and effort are the property of the community, of the nation, of the globe.

Most people do not, of course, attempt to practice the doctrine of altruism consistently in their everyday lives. It is not a code to live by—only to die by. But because they have accepted it as *right*, they are left in a moral vacuum: they have no moral principles to guide their choices and actions in practical reality. In their human relationships, they do not know what demands they can permit themselves and what demands they must grant to others; they do not know what is theirs by right, what is theirs by favor, what is theirs by someone's sacrifice. Under the guidance of conflicting social pressures and conflicting personal longings, they fluctuate between sacrificing themselves to others and sacrificing others to themselves, and in no case do they feel in rational control of their lives.* They are forced into the position of being *a*moralists, not by desire but by default.

The doctrine that a human being has no right to exist for his or her own sake cannot be defended in reason, and few of its advocates have attempted a defense, knowing that reason and their morality are incompatible. But they have declared that faith is superior to reason, thereby submerging ethics in irrationalism. The pronouncement that morality is beyond intellect, the demands that human beings throttle their judgment in obedience to authority, the attacks on the efficacy of mind and senses, the claims to an "Aryan logic" or a "proletarian logic" that represents a special, higher form of knowledge above criticism from those outside its system—all have been used as substitutes for rational argument. "To those who understand, no explanation is necessary; to those who do not, none is possible."

From the time we are children, our parents, our teachers, our employers—those in authority—assert that it is easy to be selfish and that it takes courage to practice self-sacrifice. But, as anyone who is engaged in psychotherapy knows, it takes courage to do the opposite: to cherish our own desires, to formulate independent values and remain true to them, to fight for our goals whether or not family or friends approve. To honor the self is anything but easy.

Most people begin practicing self-sacrifice almost from the day they are born. With each year they give away more and more of their desires and ambitions in order to "belong." Predictably, the result of this self-sacrifice is that, in a kind of perverted rebellion, they often end up being petty, narrow-minded, and "selfish" over trivia. Trivia are all they have left to fight for, after they have surrendered their souls.

"Do you mean it's *not* immoral to be selfish?" is a way of asking, "Do you mean I don't belong to others? Do you mean my first obligation is *not* to live up to someone else's expectations?"

Such a thought is both exhilarating and frightening. It promises liberation—but only if we are prepared to challenge the teach-

---

*One of my goals in *The Romantic Love Question & Answer Book* was to show, specifically and concretely, how a proper regard for rational self-interest is combined with concern for the needs and wants of another in the context of a love relationship.

ings of a lifetime and step forth into autonomy and self-responsibility.

If altruism holds that service to the welfare of others is the essence of the moral life, egoism, in contrast, holds that the pursuit of our own well-being and happiness is our proper moral purpose. If altruism maintains that we belong to others, egoism maintains that we have a right to exist for our own sake. As a moral principle, egoism regards every individual as an end in him- or herself, not as a means to the ends of others.

To rethink the whole issue of egoism versus altruism, of selfishness versus selflessness—to challenge the fundamental assumptions of our culture and of most of human history—we need to go back to the question of why human beings *need* a code of ethics or morality. We thus begin, not with ethics, but with *meta-ethics*—with the question of why we *need* a code of values and how we derive an ethical standard of value.

I do not know of any other philosopher who has addressed this issue with the skill, insight, and profundity of Ayn Rand. While I differ with her on a number of philosophical points and do not share her ethical theory in all details, I think the foundation of her ethics is an unassailable contribution.

Indeed, there is no way I can discuss my own views of egoism, selfishness, and ethics in general without reference to Rand's work. We were associated for many years, and I taught her philosophy to many thousands of students. Let me recapitulate, therefore, the essence of her argument concerning the foundation of values and the derivation of an ethical standard.*

We shall not begin by merely observing that human beings pursue various values and by assuming that the first question of ethics is, What values ought human beings to pursue? As I have indicated above, we shall proceed instead to a far deeper question: What are values, and why do human beings need them?

---

*The philosophical differences that I have with Rand do not pertain to what I shall cover in this sequence. At this level of abstraction or generality, the viewpoint I am summarizing is my own. Some of my key differences with Rand are outlined in an article I wrote for the *Journal of the Association for Humanistic Psychology* entitled "The Benefits and Hazards of the Philosophy of Ayn Rand: A Personal Statement."

"A 'value' is that which one acts to gain and/or keep," writes Rand.[64] A value is the object of an action. Since human beings must act in order to live, and since reality confronts them with many possible goals and many alternative courses of actions, they cannot escape the necessity of selecting values and making value-judgments.

And: "'Value' presupposes an answer to the question: of value to whom and for what? 'Value' presupposes a standard, a purpose, and the necessity of action in the face of an alternative. Where there are no alternatives, no values are possible."[63]

An entity incapable of initiating action, or for whom the consequences would always be the same *regardless* of its actions—an entity, in other words, not confronted with alternatives—could have no purposes, no goals, and hence no values. Only the existence of alternatives can make purpose, and therefore values, possible and necessary.

> There is only one fundamental alternative in the universe: existence or nonexistence—and it pertains to a single class of entities: to living organisms. The existence of inanimate matter is unconditional, the existence of life is not: it depends on a specific course of action. Matter is indestructible, it changes its form, but it cannot cease to exist. It is only living organisms that face a constant alternative: the issue of life or death. Life is a process of self-sustaining and self-generated action. If an organism fails in that action, it dies; its chemical elements remain, but its life goes out of existence. It is only the concept of "Life" that makes the concept of "Value" possible. It is only to a living entity that things can be good or evil.[63]

Given the appropriate conditions, the appropriate physical environment, all living organisms—with one exception—are set by their nature to originate automatically the actions required to sustain their survival. The exception is human beings.

Human beings, like plants or animals, must act in order to live; like plants or animals, they must gain the values their life requires. But a human being does not act and function solely by automatic chemical reactions or by automatic sensory reactions; there is no physical environment on earth in which a person could survive by the guidance of nothing but involuntary sensations.

And being born with no innate knowledge of what is true or false, we can have no innate knowledge of what is good for us or evil. *We have no automatic means of survival.*

Our basic means of survival is our mind, our capacity to reason—and the exercise of that capacity is volitional. We must *discover* what will further our life and what will destroy it. If we act against the facts of reality, we place our life in jeopardy. We must discover the principles of action required to guide us in dealing with nature and with other human beings.* Our need for these principles is our need for a code of values.

We need a moral code in order to live, but in order to know what are the values and virtues that will permit us to achieve that purpose, we require a standard. We properly choose our values by the standard of that which is required for the life of a human being, which means we hold "man's/woman's life" as our standard. Since reason is our basic tool of survival, "man's/woman's life" means the life appropriate to a rational being.

To live, we must think, we must act, we must *produce* the concrete values our life requires. This, metaphysically, is the *human* mode of existence.

Just as we are alive, physically, to the extent that the organs within our body function in the constant service of our life, so we are alive, as a total entity, to the extent that our mind functions in the constant service of our life. A person encased in an iron lung, whose own lungs are paralyzed, is not dead; but that person is not living the life proper to a human being. Neither is the person whose mind is volitionally paralyzed.

We are free to act against the requirements of our nature, to reject our means of survival—our mind—but we cannot escape the consequences: misery, anxiety, destruction. Our life depends on achievement, not on destruction. Mindlessness, passivity, parasitism, or brutality are not and cannot be principles of survival; they are merely the policy of those who, not wishing to face the issue of survival, live off the thinking and achievements of others.

To hold life as a standard of value means a good deal more

---

*Not all the principles we need pertain to ethics, of course—some pertain to an understanding of the physical universe—but that in no way alters the point I am making.

than survival for the next moment of time or what is sometimes called "mere physical survival." It means recognition of and respect for the life principle, the ongoing process by which life sustains itself and advances.

The physician who lets a patient die because she, the physician, has chosen to remain ignorant of any scientific discoveries made since she left medical school; the businessman who goes bankrupt because he believed that once he had established himself, no further development was necessary and he could safely rest on yesterday's effort; the laborer who holds the same job for twenty years because he felt that once he had learned the motions of his task it was unfair to expect anything more of him—these are persons who implicitly resent the *human* mode of existence and who ultimately depend for their survival on those who do not resent it. Life, for a human being, is a constant process of thought, of motion, of purpose, of achievement; it is *not* the state of merely not being dead.

The criminal who attempts to survive by violence specifically seeks to escape life as his standard of value. He wants to reverse the nature of reality and to survive, not by producing, but by destroying. He expects to exist by means of those who will practice a code opposite to his own—those who produce that which he seeks to expropriate. The terror that is his chronic state is not primarily fear of retaliation at the hands of the police; it is terror at the dimly sensed and frantically evaded knowledge that he is attempting to survive by means of a contradiction, that he has betrayed his status as a human being, betrayed his self-esteem, made himself into something inappropriate to life.

The person who makes terms with the rulers of a dictatorship, who willingly delivers spouse, parents, family, or closest friends to destruction in exchange for being allowed to survive, does not hold life as the standard of value. Such a person's motive is terror of dying, not passion for living. This person is willing to live without values.

In contrast, the person who consciously and willingly risks his or her life in the attempt to escape a dictatorship, the person who dies in the effort to achieve freedom, knowing that freedom is the only condition proper to human beings, *is* acting on the premise of life as the standard. Such a person knows what human existence is and is unwilling to accept anything less, unwilling to endure and to regard as normal a state in which proper human life is impossible.

The life appropriate to a human being—the life appropriate to a rational being—is not a luxury above the basic requirements of survival. It is the basic requirement of survival. On the individual level, the person who refuses to think, to act, to pursue values, either perishes outright or exists as a parasite on the efforts of persons more rational than him- or herself. In this state, the person is neither living fully nor dying immediately, is incapable of healthy self-esteem and incapable, therefore, of enjoying life. On the social level, when the men and women of an entire nation are forbidden to think and to translate their thought into action, when they are denied freedom to pursue their values, to take chances, to explore, and to create, the result is stagnation, disintegration, and paralyzing terror.

Traditional religionists have declared that if God did not exist, morality would be unnecessary—everything would be "permissible." Secular moralists have declared that if Society did not exist, morality would be unnecessary—any course of action would be as valid as any other. *Would it?* It is not for the purpose of satisfying the wishes of a supernatural being that we need a code of moral values, nor for the purpose of satisfying the wishes of our neighbors. Morality is a practical, *selfish* necessity. Alone on a desert island, an individual would face constant alternatives requiring moral choice: to think or not to think; to perceive reality, identify facts, and act accordingly, or to sulk and pray; to work and produce, or to demand a miracle that would spare the effort; to act on independent judgment, or to surrender to terror. The fact that we live among other human beings should not obscure the intimately personal nature of our need for a code of ethics. Our self-esteem requires it, our happiness requires it, our life requires it.

Life as the standard has been the underlying premise of every word I have written in this book. What we are concerned with here is the justification of that standard. By identifying the context in which values arise existentially, we can perceive the fallacy of the claim that the ultimate standard of any ethical judgment is arbitrary, that normative propositions cannot be derived from factual propositions. By identifying the roots of the concept of "value" epistemologically, we can see that *not* to hold life as one's standard of moral judgment is to be guilty of a contradiction in logic. It is only to a living entity that things can be good or evil. Life is the basic value that makes all other values possible; the value of life is not to be justified by a value beyond itself. To demand such justification—to ask, "Why should a person choose to live?"—is to have dropped the meaning, context, and source of one's concepts. "Should" is a concept that can have no intelligible meaning if divorced from the concept and *value* of life.

Contrary to the prevalent belief that morality is needed to curb the natural human inclination toward self-interest, *it is self-interest that generates the need for a moral code.*

If life on earth is the standard, then it is not the person who sacrifices values who is moral, but the person who achieves them; not the person who renounces, but the person who creates; not the person who forsakes life, but the person who makes life possible.

If man's/woman's life is the standard, a person properly exists for his or her own sake, *neither sacrificing self to others nor sacrificing others to self.*

Life is the standard of morality; our own happiness is the purpose. Happiness is an achievement that demands an understanding of, a respect for, and a nurturing of the life process. Life and happiness are two aspects of the same attainment.

No belief is more prevalent—or more misguided—than that we can achieve our happiness by the pursuit of any random desires we experience. To live for our own happiness, we must learn what that happiness objectively requires.

Rational egoism does not consist of doing whatever we feel like doing, a policy that can clearly lead to self-destruction. Morality exists for the individual, the individual does not exist for morality; but without reason, thought, and knowledge, egoism is meaningless. The purpose of ethics is not to transcend egoism, but to identify the means by which egoism is optimally fulfilled.

In approaching ethics from this perspective, we can see that it would be as reasonable to declare that the purpose of morality is to liberate a human being from the self as it would be to declare that the purpose of medicine is to liberate a human being from the body.

This analogy is singularly apt, since medicine, too, holds life as its standard of value. Rational medicine can never consist of asking an individual to act against the well-being of his or her body. Rational ethics can never consist of asking an individual to act against the well-being of his or her person.

Such is the underlying ethical orientation that, early in my own intellectual development, provided the doorway through which I first began to approach the theme that has occupied me as a psychologist for more than a quarter of a century: self-esteem as the ultimate ground of consciousness and therefore the ultimate ground of our being.

Given the fact that self-esteem pertains to our experience of being appropriate to life, it is not surprising to find many parallelisms between the virtues espoused throughout this book and those we find entailed by the standard "the life appropriate to a human being." I want to comment briefly on some of these parallelisms.

Neither a wish nor a hope nor a prayer will grow food or build a shelter or maintain a business or invent an airplane or discover a cure for a disease or devise a proper political system or preserve and protect a marriage. All of the values on which our life, well-being, and happiness depend require a process of thought and effort. A morality that holds life as the highest value also holds rationality as the highest virtue.[63]

And all the other values of human existence—career, love, art, friendship, philosophy, recreation—are values only because they serve and are the expression of the ultimate value: the life appropriate to a human being. And all such other virtues as independence, integrity, honesty, justice, productiveness, and pride are virtues only because they are expressions and consequences of the basic virtue of rationality.[63]

Rationality is our unreserved commitment to perceive reality to the best of our ability, a commitment to being conscious—an acceptance of reason as the ultimate arbiter and guide in matters of knowledge, values, and action.

Independence is reliance upon our own mind and judgment, the acceptance of intellectual responsibility for our own existence.

Honesty is refusal to seek values by faking reality, by evading the distinction between the real and the unreal.

Integrity is loyalty *in action* to the judgment of our consciousness.

Justice is the practice of identifying persons for what they are and treating them accordingly—rewarding the actions and character traits that are prolife and withholding rewards and/or condemning those that are antilife.

Productiveness is the act of supporting our existence by translating our thought into reality, of setting our goals and working for their achievement, of bringing knowledge, goods, or services into existence.

Pride (as a virtue rather than as an emotion) is moral ambitiousness, a dedication to achieving our highest potential, in our character and in our life—and a refusal to be sacrificial fodder for the goals of others.

All of these virtues are required for the realization of rational egoism or enlightened selfishness. They are principles of action that support and honor life. They are also, as we have seen, the foundation of healthy self-esteem.

Indeed, with the possible exception of justice, every one of these virtues was implicitly or explicitly anticipated in our discussion of the roots and dynamics of self-esteem, so much so that only a few words of further elaboration are needed here. I want to touch on one or two points regarding rationality and productiveness, then take a closer look at the virtue of justice.

Rationality is an attitude of responsibility toward that which exists, acceptance of the facts of reality. At a time when he was world famous, Albert Einstein, it is said, was asked by a reporter, "How do you feel, knowing that so many people are trying to prove you are not right?" Einstein replied, "I have no interest in being right. I am only concerned with discovering whether I am or not."

A scientist may *want* his new serum to be a cure for cancer, because if it is, this will make him famous; a wife may *want* it to be the case that her husband has not been unfaithful, because her whole happiness depends on his love and fidelity; an individual may *want* a supernatural being to exist, because he or she is afraid to stand alone and needs the sense of an omnipotent power as protector; a woman may *want* her partner to be a good business-person, because the success of her project depends on it—but rationality requires of us that we consider all such desires irrelevant in assessing the facts of the situation, just as a mother would dismiss the clamoring of her child to drink from the bottle marked "Poison" in the medicine cabinet.

Sometimes, however, the appropriate application of rationality is far from obvious. It is imperative to remember that reason or rationality on the one hand and what people may regard as "the reasonable" on the other hand do not mean the same thing. Only a few centuries ago, the consensus was that it was reasonable to believe that the sun revolves around the earth and unreasonable to think otherwise.

The consequence of failing to make a distinction between reason and what people may regard as "the reasonable" is that if someone disagrees with our notion of "the reasonable," we can think it appropriate to accuse that person of being "irrational" or "against reason." The temptation to equate our particular model of reality with "reason" is so powerful that we are very prone to dismiss as "irrational" or "antiscientific" any line of thought, any speculation, or *even any data* that our model cannot accommodate.

Another area of confusion concerns the relationship between reason and emotion. Rationality tells us we must not follow our emotions blindly, that to do so is undesirable and dangerous. Who can dispute that? But such counsel does not adequately deal with the possibility that in a particular situation our emotions might reflect the more correct assessment of reality. A clash between mind and emotions is a clash between two judgments, one of which is conscious, the other of which might not be. We do not follow the voice of emotion or feeling unthinkingly; rather, we try to understand what it may be telling us.

The solution for people who seem overpreoccupied with feelings is not the renunciation of feelings but rather greater respect for reason, thinking, and the intellect. What is needed is not a renunciation of emotion but a better balance between emotion and thinking.

This, I might mention, is an example of where my approach differs from Rand's. She was far quicker to assume that in any conflict between the mind and the heart, it was the heart that had

217

to be mistaken. Not necessarily—although ultimately only reason can decide.

Admittedly, there are occasions when we have to act on the best of our conscious knowledge and convictions—even when it is hard, even when it does violence to some of our feelings—because there is not time to work the problem out. But those are, in effect, emergency situations, not a way of life. Our concept of rationality, well grounded in psychological realism, has to contain this understanding; we must respect the complexities of what rationality can mean in practice.

Productiveness is the basic expression of rationality in our relationship to nature—and it is obvious why a morality of survival would attach central importance to this virtue. Productive work is the supremely *human* act; animals must adjust themselves to their physical environment; human beings adjust the physical environment to themselves. We have the capacity of giving psychological and existential unity to our life by integrating our actions with goals projected across a life span.

Morally and psychologically, it is not the degree of a person's productive ability that matters, but the person's choice to exercise such ability as he or she does possess. It is not the kind of work selected that determines moral stature and psychological well-being (provided, of course, the work is not inimical to human life), but whether or not a person seeks work that requires and expresses the fullest, most conscientious use of mind, assuming that the opportunity to do so exists.

The concept of ability, in its prevalent and popular usage, specifically denotes the achievements of human intelligence and ingenuity in the direct service of our practical needs. And it is to this that we are often morally indifferent, and are encouraged to be so by codes of ethics unconcerned with the happiness of individual men and women here on earth. An ethical code that holds life as the standard will value human ability, will prize and appreciate it, will even exalt it—not in a vacuum, not when it is employed to serve antihuman ends, as is often the case in a dictatorship, but when, in a free society, it advances human well-being.

Many people reserve the concepts of genius and spiritual greatness for the philosopher, the sage, the theoretical scientist, and the artist; however, these concepts may equally apply to an entrepreneur, an industrialist, an inventor, a trader—that is, those engaged in the production and exchange of material goods and services. For the failure to understand this, we may thank the religionists who, with their soul-body dichotomy, damn this earth as an inferior realm, condemn production, trade, and profit seeking as ignoble and vulgar, and long for a "higher dimension" where human beings will be unencumbered by such unworthy, material concerns.

The contempt for business and trade used to be a typically European phenomenon; it has become an American one, with painful psychological consequences for millions of hardworking, undervalued human beings. An ethical code that holds life as the standard of value will teach us how to appreciate productive men and women and not leave them feeling psychologically invisible, as they too often feel today, even to their own families.

Just as productiveness is the primary expression of rationality in relationship to nature, so justice is the primary expression of rationality in the relationship of human beings to one another. If we are to live together in a civilized, benevolent way, then justice, not sacrifice, must be the ruling principle among us.

The subject of justice is an enormous one, and all I can do here is indicate a direction, an intention. To be just is to deal with human beings as ends in themselves, not as means to the ends of others; to recognize each person's right to exist for his or her own sake and never to ask that person to exist for yours; to offer admiration for virtues and disapproval for vices; to deal with human beings as they objectively deserve, which means, among other things, to respect the distinction between the earned and the unearned (whether the currency be material or spiritual, wealth or admiration) and not to confuse a desire with a right ("I want" does not mean "I am entitled to").

This concept of justice, I am persuaded, provides the best possible foundation for social cooperation, benevolence, and mutual aid. Reflecting a commitment to self-responsibility, it fosters the growth of individualism but not of narcissism. It reminds us that other people do not exist to satisfy our needs and wants; they are not our servants, as we are not theirs.

This view of justice is entirely incompatible with the ethics of altruism. The essence of altruism is the concept of self-surrender and self-sacrifice. It is the self that altruism implicitly regards as evil, since selflessness is its moral ideal; it is an antiself ethics.

Instead of the goodwill and mutual respect engendered by recognition of individual rights, altruism as a moral commandment produces only fear and hostility among human beings. It forces them to accept the role of victim or executioner and leaves them no standard of justice, no way to know what they can demand and what they must surrender.

It is one's view of oneself that determines one's view of human nature and one's way of relating to other human beings. The respect and goodwill that persons of high self-esteem tend to feel toward other persons is profoundly egoistic; they feel, in effect, "Other people are of value because they are of the same species as myself." This is the psychological base of any emotion of sympathy and any feeling of species solidarity.

But this causal relation cannot be reversed. A person must *first* value him- or herself—and only then value others. Contrary to any number of spurious and utterly unfounded claims that the values of individualism encourage alienation, atomistic self-containment, and antisocial attitudes, there is an enormous amount of empirical research to support the judgment that an individualist value orientation facilitates rather than inhibits behaviors that contribute to human life.*

When we come across human suffering, it is natural and appropriate to wish to offer help or relief. And, generally speaking, it is a virtue to do so. But it is far from being the heart and soul of a moral existence. Disaster is not the most important part of life, and helping victims of disaster is not the most important part of morality. If it were, one would wish to see other people suffer just so that one could achieve virtue by offering help. What, then,

---

*For an excellent review of this research see Alan S. Waterman's "Individualism and Interdependence" in *The American Psychologist*.

are we to feel toward people who do not need us? They deprive us of the opportunity to be moral. Among people who are happy, we will have no way to gain self-esteem. Such is the corruption toward which altruism tends.

I am sometimes asked, "Isn't selfishness incompatible with love?" It would be closer to the truth to say that self*less*ness, the absence of self, negates the possibility of love. As I discuss at length in *The Psychology of Romantic Love* and *The Romantic Love Question & Answer Book*, no one is as badly hampered in efforts to build satisfying relationships as the person with a deficient ego.

To suggest that love is selfless is to maintain that it is not in my self-interest to find a person whom I can admire, delight in, find pleasure with. What I love is the embodiment of my values in another person. In love, the self is celebrated, not denied, abandoned, or sacrificed.

To love selfishly does not mean to be indifferent to the needs or interests of my partner. When we love, our concept of self-interest embraces the well-being of our partner. This is the great compliment of love: to declare to another human being that his or her happiness is of *selfish* importance to ourselves. Do we wish to believe that for our partner the relationship is an act of self-denial and self-sacrifice? Do we want to be told that our happiness is *not* of selfish interest to our partner?

To help us understand this, let us ask ourselves whether we want our lover to caress us *un*selfishly, with no personal gratification in the doing, or do we want our lover to caress us because it is a joy and a pleasure for him or her to do so? And let us ask ourselves whether we want our partner to spend time with us, alone together, and to experience the doing as an act of self-sacrifice. Or do we want our partner to experience such time as glory? And if it is glory that we want our partner to feel, if we want our partner to experience joy in our presence, excitement, ardor, passion, fascination, delight, then let us stop talking of "selfless love" as a noble ideal.

To anticipate a common misunderstanding at this point: If a man continually neglects a wife he loves—goes off to a party, leaves her ill at home and unattended—and if she leaves him and he is then devastated and miserable, we might say that he was "selfish." But it would be truer to say that he had a fool's notion of his self-interest. His irrationality did not consist of his being selfish, but of being thoughtless, careless, and irresponsible about his self-interest.

No one denies that compromise and accommodation are necessary in every relationship. Sometimes I do things to please you that I may not especially feel like doing. Sometimes I will place your immediate concerns above my own. To label such behaviors as sacrifices is to poison their meaning as expressions of love. But if, too often, I ignore my own needs and wants in order to please you, I commit a crime against both of us—against myself, because of the treason to my own values, against you, because I allow you to become someone I will resent.

As is obvious in the above example, there are persons so deficient in maturity, so narrow in their vision of their own interests, that they do not understand the sharing and nurturing so essential to love. Enjoining such people to be less "selfish" will accomplish nothing. They need to learn, not to set aside their own interests, but to expand their understanding of where their interests lie.*

In this context I have been discussing romantic or erotic love. But I think it should be obvious that the principle involved applies to every kind of love.

It seems that most people find it extraordinarily difficult to think clearly on this subject. To challenge the ideal of selflessness strikes them as virtually inconceivable. Sometimes they seek what they imagine is a compromise by declaring that in a fully enlightened human being, the distinction between egoism and altruism collapses; or they declare, "Altruism is the egoism of the superior person." Only two things are accomplished by creating confusions of this kind: the corruption of any intelligible concept of justice— and the avoidance of the need to take a stand on the issue of whether the individual has a right to exist. I do not know how those who take refuge in such strategies can, at best, escape the charge of moral cowardice.

---

*About the difference between self-sacrifice and the legitimate compromises necessary in human relationships, I refer the reader to *The Romantic Love Question & Answer Book*.

Since the concept of self-sacrifice and selfless service is the centerpiece of conventional morality, it is necessary to explore it in greater depth and to consider further some of its psychological consequences in the areas of religion, society, and politics.

13
Self-Sacrifice

Let us begin with the symbol of the cross.

Advocates of the Christian vision sometimes claim, with some measure of justification, that the course of Western civilization has moved forward under the shadow of the cross and that that shadow hangs over our history as its most powerful moral inspiration.

In order to understand the meaning of the Crucifixion, we need to recognize that it is an appropriate task of ethics to offer human beings an image of the perfect embodiment of a particular ethical vision. In terms of the Christian morality, Jesus Christ is the supreme moral ideal, a being without sin, in whose perfect image we are told we should strive to refashion our own souls. Let us accept Christian terms, for the moment, and look at the symbol in its own context. On the cross, the ideal man was sacrificed to human depravity. The highest, noblest, most perfect man was willing to sacrifice himself and die in agony for the sake of persons who are low, ignoble, sinful, evil. The morally superior chose to be immolated for the sake of the morally inferior.

The notion that such a sacrifice is in any sense right, that ignoble men and women may accept it, profit by it, and go on living—living at the price of the perfect man's torture, living on the blood of the ideal—is, I submit, as monstrous an injustice, as profound a perversion of morality as the human mind can conceive. Precisely to the extent to which one may feel love and admiration for Christ, one would be driven to hate the world, hate humanity, and find existence unbearable. And yet this is the symbol hanging, as moral inspiration, over our lives in the Western world.

Of course, there is another, non-Christian way the symbol of the cross can be interpreted, but it is hardly more encouraging: as a signifier that humankind has a predilection for crucifying its saviors.

In traditional moral terms, however, the message of the cross is unequivocal: the nobility of the sacrifice of the higher to the lower.

Christianity by no means holds a monopoly in its advocacy of self-sacrifice. In fact, Auguste Comte attacked Christianity for the outrageous "selfishness" of its concern with personal salvation. Nevertheless, the cross remains a superb metaphor for an ethical vision that is worldwide.

The immolation of the higher in favor of the lower is intrinsic to the very concept of sacrifice. *Sacrifice* means the surrender of a higher value in favor of a lower value or of a nonvalue. If we give up that which we do not value in order to obtain that which we do value—or if we give up a lesser value in order to obtain a greater one—this is not a sacrifice but a *gain*.*

It is important to note that we cannot give up or renounce or sacrifice what we do not possess or value. If sacrifice is a virtue, we must first have something to sacrifice. But we are not told, for example, that earning money is necessarily evil; we are merely told that virtue consists of giving it away. We are not taught to see moral significance in the cultivation of intelligence, but we are encouraged to admire the surrender, the sacrifice, of intelligence to "faith." We are not taught to attach moral significance to the nurturing of our own ability, but we are taught that virtue consists of placing our ability at the disposal of those less able than ourselves. We are not taught to find moral significance in the struggle for happiness, but we are taught to applaud the sacrifice of our happiness for "the good of others."

To sacrifice our happiness is to sacrifice our desires; to sacrifice our desires is to sacrifice our values; to sacrifice our values

---

*I shall treat the meaning and implications of the concept of self-sacrifice rather briefly here, because it is treated in such exhaustive detail in Ayn Rand's *Atlas Shrugged*. I am confining myself here to the barest essentials of the issue. I might mention that while I agree with Rand entirely in her analysis of self-sacrifice, one of our differences is that I place far greater emphasis on the virtues of generosity, benevolence, and a spirit of mutual aid, all of which clearly have survival value, and all of which logically proceed from a code of ethics that holds man's/woman's life as its standard.

is to sacrifice our judgment; to sacrifice our judgment is to sacrifice our mind. *Self*-sacrifice means—and can only mean—*mind* sacrifice. If our mind and judgment are to be objects of sacrifice, what sort of efficacy, control, freedom from conflict, serenity of spirit, or self-esteem will be possible to us?

To those who might find *mind sacrifice* an overly theatrical term, I offer the following illustration taken from the untheatrical world of academic psychology.

Earlier in the book I pointed out that evolution toward psychological maturity is evolution toward autonomy, one of the manifestations of which is the ability to engage in principled moral reasoning. In his article "Individualism and Interdependence," Alan Waterman observes, "Some of the sharpest criticisms of the psychological qualities associated with individualism have been directed against Kohlberg's . . . discussion of principled (postconventional) moral reasoning." He then goes on to quote one such critic, E. E. Sampson:

> The cognitive-developmental thesis itself is rooted to a self-contained, individualistic context; as it is applied, therefore, to issues of moral growth and development, it disposes us to view the moral ideal as one who can stand up in defiance of the group and collective rather than as one who can successfully work within the interdependent context of the group.

If compliance with and conformity to the norms, expectations, and values of "the group and collective" are regarded as the cardinal good, the mind of the individual *has to be* an object of sacrifice. Thus, in the above example, the person capable of principled moral reasoning needs to sacrifice his ability and his judgment to those who have not yet attained a "postconventional" level of moral reasoning: the sacrifice of the higher to the lower.

At the age of fourteen I was profoundly impressed by a particular paragraph in Ayn Rand's *The Fountainhead*. It strikes me as no less impressive now, at the age of fifty-three, and singularly relevant to the immediate discussion.

> We have never made an effort to understand what is greatness in man and how to recognize it. . . . We have come to hold . . .

226

that greatness is to be gauged by self-sacrifice. . . . Let's stop and think for a moment. Is sacrifice a virtue? Can a man sacrifice his integrity? His honor? His freedom? His ideal? His convictions? The honesty of his feelings? The independence of his thought? But these are a man's supreme possessions. Anything he gives up for them is not a sacrifice but an easy bargain. They, however, are above sacrificing to any cause or consideration whatsoever. Should we not, then, stop preaching dangerous and vicious nonsense? *Self*-sacrifice? But it is precisely the self that cannot and must not be sacrificed. It is the unsacrificed self that we must respect in man above all.

An irrational antiself morality necessarily forces us to accept the belief that there is an inevitable clash between the moral and the practical—that we must choose either to be virtuous or to be happy, to be idealistic or to be successful, but that we cannot be both. This view establishes a disastrous conflict on the deepest level of our being: it forces us to choose between making ourselves *able* to live and making ourselves *worthy* of living. *Yet self-esteem and psychological well-being require that we achieve both.*

If we hold life on earth as the good, if we judge our values by the standard of that which is appropriate to the existence of a rational being, then there is no clash between the requirements of survival and of morality, no clash between making ourselves able to live and making ourselves worthy of living; we achieve the second by achieving the first. But under an antilife, antiself morality, to the extent that we make ourselves able to live, we make ourselves unworthy of living.

One of the answers given by defenders of traditional morality is, "Oh, but people don't have to go to extremes!"—meaning, "We don't expect people to be *fully* moral. We expect them to smuggle *some* self-interest into their lives. We recognize that people have to live, after all."

A defense, then, of this code of morality is that few people will be suicidal enough to practice it consistently. Hypocrisy is to be our protection against our professed moral convictions. What does *that* do to our self-esteem?

As examples of what the conflict of egoism and altruism means in our daily lives, consider the following dilemmas. Should a woman stay with a husband she no longer loves and respects,

227

merely because he professes to "need" her? Should a hard-pressed employer retain the services of an incompetent employee who is hurting his business merely because the employee "needs" a job? Should a young man fight in a war he regards to be evil, merely because his political leaders profess to "need" his services? The confusion in most people's minds concerning how such questions should be answered is testimony to how thoroughly indoctrinated we are in the ethics of altruism. When we drop the notion of sacrifice from human relationships, the confusion dissolves—and so does the hypocrisy.

In order for human beings to accept self-sacrifice as a moral ideal, they have to remain ignorant of the concept of rational selfishness. Moralists have commonly declared or implied that our basic alternative is to sacrifice others to ourselves (which they call "egoism") or to sacrifice ourselves to others ("altruism"). This is equivalent to declaring that our basic choice is between being a sadist or a masochist. Just as healthy sex consists of the exchange of pleasure, not pain, so healthy relationships of any kind consist of the exchange of values, not sacrifices.

But if one wishes to control the minds and lives of other human beings, it is imperative to maintain a kind of blackout on a nonsacrificial view of human relationships—to herd people into the pen of self-sacrifice under the threat that sacrificing others to themselves is the only alternative. In the perpetuation of this fraud, religious leaders and political leaders have reinforced each other through many centuries.

"In the hunt for their own happiness," wrote Adolf Hitler, "people fall all the more out of heaven into hell."[34]

If the advocates of an anti-individualist morality assert that self-interest is antisocial, that the profit motive is evil, that the competent and able must work and live for the good of society, that intelligence is a "natural resource," so do the rulers of the modern totalitarian state.

Benito Mussolini:

The world seen through Fascism is not this material world which appears on the surface, in which man is an individual separated from all others and standing by himself. . . . The man of Fascism is an individual who is nation and fatherland, who is a moral law, binding together individuals and the generations into a tradition and a mission, suppressing the instinct for a life enclosed within the brief round of pleasure in order to restore within duty a higher life free from the limits of time and space: a life in which the individual, through the denial of himself, through the sacrifice of his own private interests, through death itself, realizes that completely spiritual existence in which his value as a man lies.[54]

Joseph Goebbels, quoted in *Escape from Freedom*, by Erich Fromm:

To be a socialist is to submit the I to the thou; socialism is sacrificing the individual to the whole.

"In the hunt for their own happiness, people fall the more out of heaven into hell." Would Augustine or Calvin or John Kenneth Galbraith or the current leaders of the Soviet Union, China, or sundry other dictatorships throughout the world disagree?

As for communism, its connection to the altruist morality is too obvious and too well known to require lengthy discussion here. The sacrifice of the individual to the collective, the renunciation of all personal interests and motives, the individual's service to society as the sole justification of his or her existence, society's right to sacrifice the individual at any moment, in any manner it pleases, for the sake of any social goal—this is the essence of communism. "From each according to his abilities, to each according to his needs" is the altruist-collectivist slogan picked up from antiquity and introduced into modern culture by Karl Marx. "In a country where the sole employer is the State," wrote Leon Trotsky, with uncharacteristic candor, "opposition means death by slow starvation. The old principle, who does not work shall not eat, has been replaced by a new one: who does not obey shall not eat." When, during his visit to the United States in 1959, Khrushchev declared, in effect, that communism merely puts into practice the precepts of the Bible, he revealed a better grasp of ethical principles than those who listened to him, aghast.

It is obvious that just as the moral values we accept have consequences for our psychology, so they have consequences in terms of the kind of social system we will create. What are the social implications of proself, individualist ethics?

14
Individualism and the Free Society

A political system is the expression of a code of ethics. Just as some form of statism or collectivism is the expression of the ethics of altruism, so individualism—as represented by laissez-faire capitalism—is the expression of the ethics of rational self-interest.

In this chapter I propose to show why this is so, why such a social system follows logically from the preceding discussion, and what such a social system is and means.

Individualism is at once an ethical-psychological concept and an ethical-political one. As an ethical-psychological concept, individualism holds that a human being should think and judge independently, respecting nothing more than the sovereignty of his or her mind; thus, it is intimately connected with the concept of autonomy. As an ethical-political concept, individualism upholds the supremacy of individual rights, the principle that a human being is an end in him- or herself, and that the proper goal of life is self-realization.

There are many persons who might describe themselves as subscribing to a philosophy of individualism in the abstract, as formulated thus far. But let us think through, concretely and specifically, what this means in social-political terms—because, especially among psychologists, there seem to be a great many persons who profess individualism while in their consulting rooms, working with therapy clients, but who become supporters of statism or collectivism when their focus shifts to the political arena.

The essence of the social system entailed by the ethics I have been developing is contained in a single principle: *No person or group of persons may seek to gain values from others by the use of physical force*—in other words, the principle of voluntarism.

When human beings enter into social relationships, when they choose to deal with one another, they face a fundamental alternative: to deal by means of reason, or to deal by means of force. This alternative is inescapable: either a person seeks to gain values from others by their voluntary consent, by persuasion, by appealing to their mind, or a person seeks to gain values *without* the voluntary consent of the owner, which means by coercion or fraud. This, I submit, is the issue at the base of all social relationships and all political systems.

It is also the single most avoided issue in discussions of social philosophy.

I shall be blunt here, because there is a tendency in this arena to dance around the obvious, to discuss everything but the self-evident. It is at the mind that every gun is aimed. Every use of force is the attempt to compel a person to act against his or her judgment; if the person were willing to take the action, force would not be required.

In a free society, force may be used only as retaliation and only against the person or persons who initiate its use; a distinction is made between murder and self-defense. The person who resorts to the initiation of force seeks to gain a value by so doing; the person who retaliates in self-protection seeks not to gain a value, but to *keep* a value that is already rightfully possessed.

The policy of seeking values from human beings by means of force, when practiced by an individual, is called crime. When practiced by a government, it is called statism—or totalitarianism or collectivism or communism or socialism or nazism or fascism or the welfare state.

Force, governmental coercion, is the instrument by which the ethics of altruism—the belief that the individual exists to serve others—is translated into political reality.

Although this issue has not been traditionally discussed in the terms in which I am discussing it here, the moral-political concept that forbids the initiation of force, and stands as the guardian and protector of the individual's life, freedom, and property, is the concept of rights. If life on earth is the standard, an individual has a right to live and pursue values, as survival requires; a right to think and act on his or her judgment—the right of liberty; a right to work for the achievement of his or her values and to keep the results—the right of property; a right to live for his or her sake, to choose and work for personal goals—the right to the pursuit of happiness.

Without property rights, no other rights are possible. We must be free to use that which we have produced, or we do not possess the right of liberty. We must be free to make the products of our work serve our chosen goals, or we do not possess the right to the pursuit of happiness. And—since we are not ghosts who exist in some nonmaterial manner—we must be free to keep and consume the products of our work, or we do not possess the right of life. In a society where human beings are not free to own privately the material means of production, their position is that of slaves whose lives are at the absolute mercy of their rulers. It is relevant here to remember the statement of Trotsky: "Who does not obey shall not eat."

In a political-economic context, freedom means one thing and one thing only: freedom from physical compulsion. There is nothing that can deprive us of our freedom except other persons—and no means by which they can do it except through the use of force. It is only by the initiation of force (or fraud, which is an indirect form of force) that our rights can be violated.

Voluntarism as a moral principle means libertarianism as a political principle. The only proper and justifiable purpose of government is to protect individual rights—to protect us from physical violence. It is the fact that our rights *can* be violated by others that necessitates the institution of government. If we are consistent in our adherence to individualism, we can see that the sole function of a government is to protect us from criminals, to protect us from foreign invaders, to provide a system of courts for the protection of property and contracts against breach or fraud—*and otherwise to leave us alone.*

In a society where our rights are protected by objective law, where the government has no other function or power, we are free to choose the work we desire to do, to trade our effort for the effort of others, to offer ideas, products, and services on a market from which force and fraud are barred, and to rise as high as our ability will take us. Among persons who do not seek the unearned, who do not long for contradictions or wish facts out of existence, who do not regard sacrifice and destruction as a valid means to gain their ends, there is no conflict of interest. Such persons deal with one another by voluntary consent to mutual benefit. They do not reach for a gun—or a legislator—to procure for them that which they cannot obtain through voluntary exchange.

This is not the place for a treatise on political economy. I will simply say that, today, the difficulty in discussing this issue lies in the fact that most people have all but lost the knowledge of what capitalism is, how it functions, and what it has achieved. The truth about its nature and history has been drowned in a wave of misrepresentations, distortions, falsifications, and almost universal ignorance. Only within the past few decades has there been the beginning of a serious movement among historians to expose and correct the gross factual errors in the literature purporting to describe nineteenth-century capitalism. Almost everyone today takes it as axiomatic that capitalism results in the vicious exploitation of the poor; that it leads to monopoly; that it necessitates periodic economic depressions; that it starts wars; that it resisted and opposed the worker's rising standard of living; that that standard of living was the achievement, not of capitalism, but of labor unions and of humanitarian labor legislation. Not one of these claims is true, but they are among the most common bromides of our culture. People do not feel obliged to question such bromides, since they "know" in moral principle that capitalism *must* result in evils: capitalism is based on the profit motive and appeals to the individual's self-interest; that alone is sufficient to damn it.*

---

*While the following books and authors are not all entirely consistent in their advocacy of economic-political freedom, and there are points of philosophical difference among them, they represent an excellent starting point for anyone wishing to study the nature and history of capitalism, as well as its future possibilities: F. Bastiat, *Selected Essays on Political Economy*; M. Friedman and R. Friedman, *Free to Choose*; H. Hazlitt, *Eco-*

It is a widely held belief, inherited from Marx, that government is necessarily an agent of economic interest and that political systems are to be defined in terms of whose economic interests a government serves. Thus, capitalism is commonly regarded as a system in which the government acts predominantly to serve the interests of businesspeople; socialism, as a system in which the government serves the interests of the working class. It is this concept of government that the libertarian principle rejects.

The fundamental issue is not what kind of economic controls a government enforces, nor on whose behalf; the issue is whether one is to have a controlled economy or an *un*controlled economy. Laissez-faire capitalism is *not* government control of economics for the benefit of businesspersons; it is the complete separation of state and economics. This is implicit in the nature of capitalism, but historically it was not identified in such terms nor adhered to consistently.

It was the United States of America, with its system of limited, constitutional government, that implemented the principle of capitalism—a free trade on a free market—to the greatest extent. In America, during the nineteenth century, people's productive activities were *for the most part* left free of governmental regulations, controls, and restrictions; most thinkers considered themselves thoroughly emancipated from the discredited economic policies of medievalism, mercantilism, and precapitalist statism. In the brief period of a century and a half, the United States created a level of freedom, of progress, of achievement, of wealth, of physical comfort—a standard of living—unmatched and unequaled by the total sum of humankind's development up to that time.

With the Enlightenment, the Industrial Revolution, and the rise of capitalism, an extraordinary transformation took place in men's and women's thinking about the possibilities of life on earth, a revolution so radical that it is still far from fully understood.

---

nomics in One Lesson; P. Johnson, *Modern Times*; R. W. Lane, *The Discovery of Freedom*; T. Machan (ed.), *The Libertarian Reader*; R. Nozick, *Anarchy, State, and Utopia*; I. Patterson, *The God of the Machine*; A. Rand, *Atlas Shrugged; Capitalism, the Unknown Ideal*; and *The Virtue of Selfishness*; A. Rustow, *Freedom and Domination*; H. Spencer, *Man Versus the State*; F. von Hayek, *Capitalism and the Historians* and *The Road to Serfdom*; and L. von Mises, *Human Action; Nation, State, and Economy*; and *Socialism*.

With the collapse of the absolute state and the development of the free market society, people saw the sudden release of productive energy that had previously had no outlet. They saw life made possible for countless millions who could have had no chance at survival in precapitalist economies. They saw mortality rates fall and population growth rates explode upward. They saw machines (the machines that many of them had cursed, opposed, and tried to destroy) cut their workday in half while multiplying incalculably the value and reward of their effort. They saw themselves lifted to a standard of living no feudal baron could have conceived. With the rapid development of science, technology, and industry, they saw, for the first time in history, the individual's liberated mind taking control of material existence.

To the extent that various countries adopted capitalism, the rule of brute force vanished from people's lives. Capitalism abolished slavery and serfdom in all of the civilized nations. Trade, not violence, became the ruling principle of human relationships. Intellectual freedom and economic freedom rose and flourished together. Political thinkers had discovered the concept of individual rights. Individualism was the creative power revolutionizing the world.

A system in which wealth and position were inherited or acquired by physical conquest or political favor was replaced by one in which values had to be earned by productive work. In closing the doors to force, capitalism threw them open to achievement. Rewards were tied to production, not to extortion; to ability, not to brutality; to the capacity for furthering life, not to that for inflicting death.

Much has been written about the harsh conditions of life during the early years of capitalism. Yet when one considers the level of material existence from which capitalism raised men and women and the comparatively meager amount of wealth in the world when the Industrial Revolution began, what is startling is not the slowness with which capitalism liberated people from poverty, but the speed with which it did so. Once the individual was free to act, ingenuity and inventiveness proceeded to raise the standard of living to heights that a century earlier would have been judged fantastic. It would be difficult to name an event of history more impressive than this—or less appreciated.

Capitalism was achieving miracles before human beings' eyes. Yet, from its beginning, the majority of nineteenth-century intellectuals were vehemently antagonistic to it. Their writings were filled with denunciations of the free market economy. Broadly speaking, the antagonism came from two camps: the medievalists and the socialists.

The medievalists found the disintegration of feudal aristocracy, the sudden appearance of fortune makers from backgrounds of poverty and obscurity, the emphasis on merit and productive ability, the concern with science and material progress, and, above all, the pursuit of profit spiritually repugnant. Many of them—such as Richard Oastler, William Wordsworth, Samuel Taylor Coleridge, Thomas Carlyle, Robert Southey, William Cobbett, Thomas Hood, and Thomas Love Peacock—unleashed scathing attacks on the factory system. They were avowed enemies of the Age of Reason. They declared individualism vulgar. They longed for a return to a status society. "Commerce or business of any kind," wrote John Ruskin, "may be the invention of the Devil."[71]

The medievalists dreamed of abolishing the Industrial Revolution. The socialists wished to take it over. Both camps dismissed or gave only grudging acknowledgment to the achievements of capitalism. They preferred to eulogize the living conditions of previous ages. Friedrich Engels, along with Carlyle, regarded the domestic industry's system of the preindustrial era as the golden age of the working classes. The criticisms leveled against capitalism by both camps were remarkably similar: the "dehumanizing" effect of the factory system upon the worker, the "alienation" of man and woman from nature, the "cold impersonality" of the market, the "cruelty" of the law of supply and demand—and *the evil of the pursuit of profit.*

In the writings of both medievalists and socialists, one can observe the unmistakable longing for a society in which the individual's existence will be automatically guaranteed—that is, in which no one will have to be responsible for his or her own survival. Both camps project their ideal society as one characterized by what they call "harmony," by freedom from rapid change or challenge or the exacting demands of competition; a society in which each must do his or her prescribed part to contribute to the well-being of the whole, but in which no one will face the necessity of making choices and decisions that will crucially affect his or her life and future; in which the question of what one has or has not earned, and does or does not deserve, will not arise; in which rewards will not be tied to achievements and in which someone's benevolence will guarantee that one need never bear the consequences of one's errors.*

If we consider the writings of some of capitalism's most famous nineteenth-century defenders, it will help us to understand why people are so confused about the nature of capitalism today— and why statism, during this century, has been swallowing up more and more of the world.

John Stuart Mill's essay *On Liberty* is generally regarded as one of the classic defenses of the rights of the individual. But individual rights is precisely the concept that Mill does not support. His ethical standpoint is that of utilitarianism. In *On Liberty*, he argues that society should leave the individual free. But as justification for his position, he projects an essentially collectivist premise, the premise that the group should permit persons to be free because that will best allow them to serve its interests—thus implying that the individual does not in fact have the *right* to freedom, but is, morally, the property of the collective. Not astonishingly, Mill ended his life as a socialist.

Herbert Spencer defended capitalism by means of spurious analogies to animals in a jungle and the survival of the fittest— which implied a complete misrepresentation of the nature of capitalism, one that was thoroughly in accord with the views of its enemies. An animal's method of survival is not a human being's; we do not survive by fighting over a static quantity of meat (or wealth); we survive by *producing* the values, the goods, our life requires. And what was Spencer's ultimate moral justification for a free market economy? Not the rights of the individual, but the purification of the race; the weeding out of the unfit, in alleged accordance with the principle of evolution; that is, the good of the

---

*One will find the same longing among such contemporary psychologists as Erich Fromm. See, for example, *Escape from Freedom*. I discuss Fromm's viewpoint in some detail in *The Disowned Self*.

collective, of the human species. Aside from all other objections, the ludicrous irrelevance of this defense, sometimes labeled social Darwinism, is that capitalism facilitates the survival and well-being of countless more of the "less fit" than any other system since the beginning of time.

It is historically, philosophically, and psychologically significant that not one of the defenders of capitalism chose to attack the position of its opponents at the root, on the level of basic premises; not one of them challenged the altruist-collectivist frame of reference in which all discussions concerning the value of capitalism were held. Economically, the case for capitalism has never been refuted. Capitalism has lost more and more ground because we have lacked a moral philosophy to sustain and support it.*

In the world of the present, most people regard the right of a government to initiate force against its citizens as an absolute not to be debated or challenged. They stipulate only that the force must be used "for a good cause." Precisely because capitalism in its ideal (that is, consistent) form forbids the use of force to gain social ends, or any other kind of ends, intellectuals dismiss the laissez-faire concept as "antisocial" and "unprogressive." Whatever the differences in their specific programs, all the enemies of the free market economy—communists, socialists, fascists, welfare statists—are unanimous in their belief that they have a *right* to dispose of the lives, property, and future of others, that private ownership of the means of production is a selfish evil, that the more a person has achieved, the greater is his or her debt to those who have not achieved it, that men and women can be compelled to go on producing under any terms or conditions their rulers decree, that freedom is a luxury that may have been permissible in a primitive economy, but for the running of giant industries, electronic factories, and complex sciences, nothing less than slave labor will do.

---

*One of Ayn Rand's major goals in *Atlas Shrugged* was to provide just such a moral justification—and, in my estimation, she succeeded brilliantly, notwithstanding our areas of disagreement.

238

Whether they propose to take over the economy outright, in the manner of communists and socialists, or to maintain the pretense of private property while dictating prices, wages, production, and distribution, in the manner of fascists and welfare statists, it is the gun, it is the rule of physical force that they consider "kind," they who consider the free market "cruel."

Since the moral justification offered for the rule of force is humankind's need of the things that persons of ability produce, it follows (in the collectivist's system of thought) that the greater an individual's productive ability, the greater are the penalties he or she must endure, in the form of controls, regulations, expropriations. Consider, for example, the principle of the progressive income tax: those who produce the most are penalized accordingly; those who produce nothing receive a subsidy, in the form of relief payments. Or consider the enthusiastic advocacy of socialized medicine. What is the justification offered for placing the practice of medicine under government control? The importance of the services that physicians perform—the urgency of their patients' need. Physicians are to be penalized precisely because they have so great a contribution to make to human welfare; thus is virtue turned into a liability.

In denying human beings freedom of thought and action, statists and collectivist systems are anti-self-esteem by their very nature. Self-confident, self-respecting men and women are unlikely to accept the premise that they exist for the sake of others.

A free society cannot be maintained without an ethics of rational self-interest. Neither can it be maintained except by men and women who have achieved a healthy level of self-esteem. And a healthy level of self-esteem cannot be maintained without a willingness to assert—and, if necessary, fight for—our right to exist. It is on this point that issues of psychology, ethics, and politics converge.

If I may allow myself a brief aside, one might imagine that psychologists, social scientists, and philosophers who speak enthusiastically and reverently about freedom, self-responsibility, autonomy, the beauty of self-regulating systems, and the power of synergy (the behavior of whole systems unpredicted by the behavior of the parts taken separately) would naturally be champions of noncoercion. More often than not, as I have already indicated, just the opposite is true. They tend to be among the most vociferous in crying for the coercive apparatus of government to further their particular ideals. To quote Waterman once again:

> It should be recognized that a defining feature of a synergistic society is that participation in it is voluntary. If people do not choose to engage in a given cooperative activity, the implication is that they do not perceive that activity to be helpful, either for themselves or for others. Efforts to promote social cooperation within a synergistic society may appropriately include such techniques as education, persuasion, and negotiation. However, the use of political force to compel cooperation represents the abandonment of the synergistic ideal.[90]

A free society cannot automatically guarantee the mental or emotional well-being of all its members. Freedom from external coercion is not a *sufficient* condition of our optimal fulfillment, but it is a *necessary* one. The great virtue of capitalism—laissez-faire capitalism, as contrasted not only with the more extreme forms of statism but also with the mixed economy we have today—is that it is the one system whose defining principle is precisely this barring of physical coercion from human relationships. No other political system pays even lip service to this principle.

If we pause to look back at the road we have traveled since the beginning of this book, we can appreciate, perhaps, that the whole course of human development and evolution is in the direction of increasing freedom, higher and higher actualizations of personal choice.

Every concept we have entailing the idea of progress, higher levels of development, evolution, and the like contains the same core intention: a wider possible range of action, an increasing absence of constraints on our choices. On the evolutionary scale, when we speak of one species as being higher than another, an essential part of what we mean is that the more advanced species has a greater range of options, a wider repertoire of possible responses, in any given situation. When we speak of a person being more psychologically evolved, less encumbered by blocks, repressions, institutionalized areas of unconsciousness, again we think of this greater freedom. And if we speak of scientific or techno-logical progress, once again we are referring to this wider range. Political freedom is the triumph of this same process in the ex-ternal world of human relationships.

These chapters, as I have already indicated, are intended only to sketch out a general ethical-social-political orientation, not to provide a finished, detailed portrait; the latter would be the task of another book. I am aware that I leave many issues and questions undealt with. But no discussion of the meaning of honoring the self could be complete that did not address itself, however briefly, to such issues as the moral justification of egoism, the destruc-tiveness of the creed of self-sacrifice, and the supremacy and in-violability of individual rights in human relationships.

Now we must face one last group of questions: Is this the end of the journey? Is the achievement of an internal condition of self-esteem and the external condition of freedom the final climax of the evolutionary process? When we have learned to honor the self, psychologically, morally, politically, have we reached the final stage of our development?

15
Self-Esteem and Beyond

In this final chapter, I address myself to the notion that the disappearance of ego is a hallmark of the higher stages of human development and that self-transcendence is the ultimate goal of our psychological and spiritual evolution.

While this view of ego and self-transcendence is very familiar in Eastern religious literature and in mystical literature generally, it has become prominent in Western psychology only with the advent of the fairly recent transpersonal psychology movement. For a long time the cutting edge in psychology has been moving farther and farther away from the view of the so-called well-adjusted personality as the ultimate psychological goal. Being able to function with reasonable effectiveness is a laudable goal, but increasing numbers of psychologists are finding themselves challenged by the possibility of exploring the territory of the optimal. Transpersonal psychologists insist, and I would hardly disagree, that what is commonly regarded as normal, everyday consciousness is suboptimal.[89]

In *Beyond Ego*, the best introductory text to this field, editors Roger N. Walsh and Frances Vaughan state: "*Transpersonal psychology* is concerned with expanding the field of psychological inquiry to include the study of optimal psychological health and well-being. It recognizes the potential for experiencing a broad range of states of consciousness, in some of which identity may extend beyond the usual limits of the ego and personality."

In the enthusiasm that transpersonalists exhibit for their field, it is not always easy to separate the serious from the frivolous, the promising from the pretentious. Often, a certain naivete and irresponsibility manifest themselves at the frontiers of new knowl-

242

edge. For example, many transpersonalists exhibit an alarming naivete concerning claims made in the fields of parapsychology and paraphysics.*Nonetheless, their basic premise—that the course of evolution has not stopped, but continues in us and through us, and that the upper limits of our developmental possibilities are almost beyond speculation—appears to be borne out by research in the fields of biofeedback, hypnosis, psychedelic drugs, meditation, and altered states of consciousness of all kinds. All have supported the belief that we have underestimated our potential for growth, well-being, and evolution.[21] It has certainly never been my own view that once we acquire high self-esteem the process of individuation and development is complete. My point has rather been that the level of development with which I have been concerned *cannot be bypassed*—that it is the foundation for wherever the next steps of our evolution may lead us.

It would take me far beyond the subject matter of this book to discuss what I think is rational or irrational in the transpersonal field. But since I *am* concerned here with honoring the self, and since many transpersonalists (especially those heavily influenced by Eastern religions) have launched what amounts to an attack on the ego and the self, I feel the need to say something about those attacks and their psychological and philosophical meaning.

The theme of self-transcendence and the dissolution of ego has begun to appear more and more prominently in Western psychology since the 1960s. The transpersonal movement was anticipated by Abraham Maslow, one of the pioneers in humanistic psychology, itself a rebellion against the overly restrictive view of human nature promulgated by proponents of psychoanalysis and behaviorism. The chief thrust of Maslow's own work was the further development of his vision of the "self-actualized personality." In the last years of his life, however, he predicted a psychology that would be "transpersonal, transhuman, centered in the cosmos rather than in human needs and interests, going beyond humanness, identity, self-actualization, and the like."[51]

Such a formulation raises formidable intellectual difficulties.

---

*Many such persons would doubtless profit from reading such books as Martin Gardner's *Science: Good, Bad, and Bogus* and James Randi's *Flim-Flam!*

First, there is the purely logical problem: a psychology that purports in any sense to be about human beings and yet to be centered, not on human beings, but on the cosmos, is a contradiction in terms. More important, perhaps, is the fact that whatever human beings can rise to or attain is within the province of the human—it is not transhuman. It may be reasonable to speak of an expanded sense of identity, but not of going beyond identity.

Second—and this is the chief point I wish to develop in this chapter—when and if the gates of enlightenment finally open, however enlightenment is conceived, an individual human being (no doubt transformed) will walk through, or no one will walk through. But let us proceed to see why it should even be necessary to make such an observation.

Since the concept of self-transcendence will figure so prominently in this discussion, I want first to make a number of ground-clearing observations about both the experience of transcendence, of any kind, and that of self-forgetfulness or self-obliviousness. There is a healthy and valid aspect to these phenomena that has nothing to do with the disappearance of self or the annihilation of ego.

To transcend is to rise above a limited context or perspective—to a wider field of vision. The wider field of vision does not negate or deny the previous, narrower field, but goes beyond it. Growth itself, as we have already seen in an earlier chapter, can be conceptualized as a series of transcendences, as we move from one stage of development to a higher one, emotionally, cognitively, morally, and so forth. Thus, for example, according to Piaget's theory of stages of cognitive development, we transcend one level of mental operation to reach a higher level.[60] Similarly, with Kohlberg's theory of stages of moral development, we transcend one level of moral perspective to reach a higher one.[41, 46] In a different sense but within the same principle, when we leave family and learn to exist as self-supporting individuals, we are again engaged in a process of transcendence. And ideally, when I cease to identify exclusively with my body, my emotions, my beliefs, or my thoughts, when I realize that my ultimate "I"—my ego—is awareness itself and not the contents of awareness, I am shifting from a lower vision of self-in-the-world to a higher one. And this, in a psychological context, is precisely what transcendence always means.

But *who* is transcending? *I* am. And *what* am I transcending? A lower level of development. Thus, the concept of *self-transcendence* is logically incoherent— a contradiction in terms. The self is that which transcends, not that which is transcended. On any other view we would have to deal with the impossible question, Who is it who will experience the bliss promised to those who transcend their egos? When I "transcend" awareness, the ultimate witness, I am not enlightened—I am either unconscious or dead.

It is reasonable to talk about transcending a limited self-concept, or perhaps any self-concept, but not reasonable to talk about transcending the self. It is reasonable to talk about transcending an overrestricted concept of ego, but not reasonable to talk about transcending ego.

These observations strike me as so obvious and incontrovertible that the question arises as to why the notion of self-transcendence and the annihilation of the ego can be so prevalent throughout the transpersonal community. (For examples, see articles in *The Journal of Humanistic Psychology*, *The Journal of Transpersonal Psychology*, and *ReVision*.) As regards ego, it might be argued that transpersonalists use the term, not, as I do, to mean the unifying center of awareness, but rather, in a narrower, more restricted sense, to mean an individual self-concept, or that part of the self with which the individual chiefly identifies. But I do not think this explanation suffices because, for one thing, sometimes transpersonalists do use *ego* in the sense I mean, and, for another, the disdain and contempt with which many of them often refer to ego (evidenced by a marked tendency to precede *ego* by such adjectives as *narrow*, *little*, *petty*) irresistibly suggest that considerations deeper than semantics are involved. I believe that an anti-individualist, antiself ideology is so deeply ingrained in our thinking, the notion of virtue so mired in associations with selflessness, that many writers in this field see a seductive glamour in notions of self-transcendence and emancipation from the ego that "transcend" logic.

True, their denigration of ego and self is not social or political, certainly not in its primary thrust; rather, reflecting the perspective of Eastern religions and mysticism in general, their viewpoint is that individuality is an illusion to be transcended through the awareness that we (and everything that exists) are all part of

245

One Great Consciousness—much as a drop of water is part of the ocean and with a nature identical with the nature of the ocean.[15, 79, 89, 91, 92, 93, 94] We shall return to this theme.

But now I want to say a few words about self-forgetfulness in its healthy or desirable aspect.

A person who enjoys a high level of self-esteem is not normally preoccupied with thoughts of how wonderful he or she is. A person of high self-esteem may be cheerfully involved in some task or deeply absorbed in study and quite unself-aware. Obviously neither self nor ego have disappeared, but they are background, not foreground.

If a person is deeply engrossed in the writing of a book, he or she is not simultaneously thinking about self. If we are caught up in contemplating the beauty of nature, or experiencing the thrill of skiing down the side of a mountain, or listening to a great piece of music, or looking into the eyes of the person we love, we may indeed be utterly and ecstatically self-oblivious. Everyday boundaries of self may seem to have melted at the level of immediate feeling. But this hardly means that self has been transcended or ego annihilated. It merely means that life consists of more than self-contemplation.

Once again I am tempted to say that these observations strike me as utterly obvious. And yet examples of this kind are often used to familiarize the uninitiated with what might be meant by "loss of self."

Contrary to what transpersonalists seem to suggest, individualism is not solipsism, the belief that the self can know nothing but its own modifications and that in fact nothing but the self exists. And it is narcissism, not individualism, that inclines one to the attitude that nothing external to one's skin is worthy of attention—narcissism (in its negative meaning) being a condition of unhealthy and excessive self-absorption arising from a deep-rooted sense of inner deficiency or deprivation.

Creativity does not entail "loss of self"; neither does love. If we sometimes choose to forego the ordinary pleasures of life because of passion for our work, this is an act of self-expression, not an act of self-surrender. And if we sometimes choose to forego our own convenience or pleasure for the person we love, what deadlier insult could we deliver than to declare that we do so selflessly? Love that is not self-expression and self-assertion is a contradiction in terms.

With these observations providing a context, let us look more closely at the transpersonal vision of self-in-the-cosmos.

Both psychoanalysis and behaviorism reflected the premises of nineteenth-century materialism, the view that ultimately all that exists is matter in motion, and long after philosophy and science had repudiated this metaphysics, twentieth-century psychology remained mired in it. The transpersonal movement, rebelling against this materialism, has tended to adopt, as its alternative metaphysics, the belief that ultimate reality consists of "Consciousness" or "Mind." "According to this universal tradition," writes Ken Wilber, the most scholarly and articulate spokesman for the transpersonal perspective, "Mind is what there is and all there is, spaceless and therefore infinite, timeless and therefore eternal, outside of which nothing exists."[94]

The goal of our evolution, in this view, is to continue knocking down the ego-generated walls that produce the illusion of separateness from other things and beings in the universe until at last we arrive at a state of consciousness devoid of the experience of separateness, devoid of a sense of personal identity apart from identity with all that exists, identity with (again quoting Wilber) "the Godhead" or the "Ultimate Ground of Being" or the "Suchness of Things."[91, 92, 93, 94] We deal here with the esoteric core of the (predominant) mystical vision of reality, according to which all things are One. A belief in individuality is thus held to represent a kind of "optical delusion."*

In a virtuoso effort to integrate Western and Eastern psychologies, Wilber develops a concept that he describes as "the spectrum of consciousness," which interprets different schools of psychology and therapy as being applicable to different levels of the evolutionary development of consciousness, with the Eastern vision not contradicting the Western so much as completing it, with the individual going through many stages "beyond self-

---

*In this phrase Wilber is quoting Einstein.[94]

actualization," toward the last and ultimate state of "unity con-sciousnes" in which all dualisms, including the dualism of self and other, disappear.[91] This viewpoint appears to enjoy considerable support among transpersonal psychologists.[15]

While I am unable to agree with many of Wilber's conclu-sions, especially his views concerning "unity consciousness" as I understand them, I feel admiration for the extraordinary feats of integration he has achieved, and I emphatically agree with one of his key points. Paraphrasing Wilber, I would say that we cannot go "beyond self-actualization" until we have achieved it. Wilber finds it necessary to stress this point in his writing, it seems to me, because of a tendency among transpersonalists to renounce eagerly an ego or self they can hardly be said to possess.

Of course it can be argued—and in personal conversations Wilber himself has agreed with me on this issue—that even on the transpersonal perspective we never truly go "beyond self-actualization"; we merely move up to higher levels of self-actualization than are normally discussed in Western psychology. As consciousness continues to evolve in the direction of optimal functioning, letting go of inappropriate attachments and discov-ering previously unrecognized powers, is it not the self that is evolving and thus actualizing these latent potentialities? Once again, it seems, we encounter the strange glamour associated with the notion of escaping the self.

But let us stay a moment longer with the metaphysical aspect of the transpersonal vision, because ultimately it is metaphysics that underlies their stance on self and ego. Obviously we are not compelled to believe that reality is ultimately constituted by ei-ther matter or by consciousness. We can be dualists and maintain that neither matter nor consciousness is reducible to the other. Further, we can maintain that both matter and consciousness are manifestations of an underlying reality that is neither. Many phi-losophers have pointed out the difficulties in any attempt to reduce matter to mind or mind to matter, and I shall not repeat their arguments here. But if mind and matter are different in *every respect*, the problem of explaining their interaction—the mind-body problem—appears insuperable. Positing an underlying real-ity of which both matter and consciousness are manifestations would offer us a way out of this dilemma and provide a solution to a problem that has troubled philosophers for centuries. We might even hypothesize that the "unity consciousness" of which transpersonal psychologists and mystics sometimes speak, the ultimate enlightenment they celebrate, may be the experience of consciousness somehow accessing its source, that ultimate, underlying reality of which it is a manifestation. And the practice of meditation may indeed be the most powerful vehicle for carrying us toward this awareness, just as is often proposed.

But—and here is the point to which inevitably we must return—as long as there is awareness, even at the highest level imaginable, there is self. As long as there is awareness, there is ego. After all our self-concepts have been transcended and all our attachments relinquished, as long as we exist as conscious beings in any sense whatever, and with any view of the ultimate nature of reality, the "I" who is conscious remains—which does not deny that, as the individual evolves to higher and higher stages, the internal experience of "I" is transformed.

Transpersonal psychology has been influenced by Buddhism more than by any other world religions. And among world religions, none of which I have knowledge has been quite so unequivocal in its statements concerning the ultimate unreality of an individual self, soul, or ego. Not that all psychologists of a transpersonal orientation accept this view, but it is sufficiently widespread to be worth pausing on, especially in view of its relevance to the themes that occupy us here.

To quote Stace in *Mysticism and Philosophy*:

> This doctrine [of anatta, or no-soul] rejects, by means of an argument which is identical with the famous argument of David Hume, the whole concept of a self or soul. It argues that there is nothing in the mind except its empirical contents, and from this premise concludes, as Hume did, that the "I" is nothing but the stream of conscious states.

Stace goes on to observe, a paragraph later, that "to wipe out the pure ego is to wipe out the mystical experience itself" because, once again, we are back to the question of who it is who is having the experience.

The "famous argument" of David Hume appears in his *Treatise of Human Nature*, in which he wrote: "When I enter most intimately into what I call *myself*, I always stumble on some particular perception, i.e., some particular mental content or other, of heat or cold, light or shade, love or hatred, pain or pleasure. I never can catch *myself* at any time without a perception." From this observation Hume concludes that there is no such thing as a self or ego. The Buddhist version is a little different, of course, in that consciousness is not identified with a stream of sensory perceptions. But both arguments share the idea that what exists is the stream of consciousness and that the concept of an ego or self who is conscious is superfluous and in fact fallacious.

By way of answering this argument, let me point out that since by *ego* or *self* in this ultimate sense we mean consciousness as it exists within an individual organism, it would be extraordinary—in fact inconceivable—for consciousness to *be able* to perceive itself. If consciousness is by nature an organ or perception, it is necessarily directed outward, to some extent, much as our eyes are directed outward and cannot, without a mirror, see themselves.

An interesting aside on the Buddhist position is that most Buddhists believe in reincarnation, as do many transpersonal psychologists—in other words, the transmigration of a soul that does not exist in the first place. No one has ever succeeded in explaining how we can reconcile a belief in the unreality of ego or self with a belief in reincarnation.

In chapter one I mentioned soliciting from a wide variety of psychologists the criteria by which they judged self-esteem. A number of transpersonalists reponded by asking, in effect, "Why bother with this issue when the self is only an illusion, anyway? The goal is not self-esteem but self-transcendence." So there is still more to be said about the effort to deny the reality of self.

Since we are all One, the argument goes, individuality is an illusion—necessary, perhaps, in the early stages of our development, but ultimately to be outgrown if we are to reach our optimal potential.[15]

If the belief that I exist as a separate entity is an illusion, surely it is *my* illusion, which means that in some form I exist.

Even if we wanted to argue that I am only an illusion in someone else's consciousness, then that someone else would exist, and we would enter here into an infinite regress. And if it be argued that all that ultimately exists is cosmic consciousness—then we are led to argue that cosmic consciousness (or God or whatever) is confused about its own nature, is not perceiving reality clearly, is beset by illusions. When we are ready to declare that the Suchness of Things is deluded in its perception of reality, surely it is plain that we have collapsed into logical incoherence. This, I submit, is the dead end of every attempt to deny the reality of separate selves.

None of these criticisms denies the value of researching possible higher states of consciousness above those we in the Western world have regarded as normal or even optimal. The fact is, most people do have to emancipate themselves from overly restrictive views of who and what they are; most people do need to learn not to identify self with everyday attachments, belief systems, and so on; most people need to discover and experience their relationship to everything else that exists in the universe—and I do not doubt that transpersonal psychology can contribute to the realization of these ends. But what the field urgently requires is a vast improvement in its level of intellectual precision and clarity.

I must say, in all fairness, that transpersonal psychologists with whom I have discussed these matters tend to agree; indeed, they have tended to be very receptive to the criticisms I am making; they feel themselves groping toward a vision that they readily admit they do not always know how to articulate. But what makes many of their antiself, antiego utterances irresponsible, in my view, is the fact that they are writing during a century when the most appalling atrocities in history have been perpetrated by totalitarian regimes that were and are vociferous in declaring that the individual is nothing, that a good citizen must rise above the petty concerns of ego, and so on and on and on. Politically, the voice of the antiself is the voice of death. This is not a fact they can pass over lightly simply by declaring, "Oh, but that's not what we mean." Every philosophical or psychological statement exists in a context, and in the world of today no one has the right to be oblivious to the context in which he or she speaks. I believe transpersonal psychologists have a moral and intellectual obligation

251

to acknowledge our present-day context and to make their position unequivocally differentiated from those for whom the denunciation of the individual and individualism is clearly tied to a lust for power.

Not only has this not been done, but one of the central tenets of the transpersonal perspective is that a separate sense of self, even though it is only an illusion, is somehow the root of all evil. Ken Wilber eloquently expresses this viewpoint:

> And mankind will never, but never, give up this type of murderous aggression, war, oppression and repression, attachment and exploitation, until men and women give up that property called personality. Until, that is, they awaken to the transpersonal. Until that time, guilt, murder, property, and persons will always remain synonymous.[94]

As soon as we establish a boundary, he argues, we create the possibility of an adversary relationship. The self can go to war only with that which it regards as the not-self. When and if, therefore, our sense of self or our sense of identity expands to include everything that exists, when I finally realize that I and everything else are One, all possibility of cruelty or hostility ceases.[92] This is one of the classic viewpoints in Eastern mystical literature.*

Now I do not believe for a moment that Wilber intends the social implications that *would* be intended by a political totalitarian who made a statement such as his. I do not suspect Wilber was even thinking in political terms. But his statement is indeed ominous when placed against the social and political events of this century. I must add that, on the basis of personal discussions, I have reason to believe Wilber would agree.

---

*In *Mysticism and Philosophy* Stace writes: "Hinduism, but more especially Buddhism, emphasizes that it is the separateness of each individual ego, and the clinging to this separateness, which is at the root of hatred and of moral evil generally. . . . Only if the separate ego of each man is got rid of, if he can feel himself as not merely 'I' but one with the life of all other individuals and with the life of God, only then can he hope for salvation." And also: "The basis of the mystical theory of ethics is that the separateness of individual selves produces egoism which is the source of conflict, grasping, aggressiveness, selfishness, hatred, cruelty, malice, and other forms of evil; and that this separateness is abolished in the mystical consciousness in which all distinctions are annulled."

Perhaps the following quotation from Arthur Koestler in *Janus* will help to clarify my perspective:

> Throughout human history, the ravages caused by excesses of individual self-assertion are quantitatively negligible compared to the number slain *ad majorem gloriam* out of a self-transcending devotion to a flag, a leader, a religious faith or political conviction. Man has always been prepared not only to kill, but also to die for good, bad, or completely hare-brained causes. What can be a more valid proof for the reality of the urge toward self-transcendence?*

Not self, but the absence of self, is closer to being the root of all evil. Self-alienation impoverishes our capacity for empathy; and in dehumanizing ourselves, we inevitably dehumanize others. In failing to develop an independent and strong ego, to evolve to moral sovereignty, we become capable of unspeakable atrocities, since we do not experience ourselves as responsible for our actions. Interestingly enough, Wilber himself writes:

> In fact, at this point in history, the most radical, pervasive, and earth-shaking transformation would occur simply if everybody truly evolved to a mature, rational, and responsible ego, capable of freely participating in the open exchange of mutual self-esteem. *There* is the "edge of history." There would be a *real* New Age.[94]

Wilber is a transpersonalist with a profound respect for individuality and personal dignity. But I believe that he and other transpersonal psychologists will at some point have to address themselves to the foregoing criticisms and observations.

Now let us consider, finally, one last assault on self and ego as it is found in the transpersonalist approach to ethics.

---

*In fairness to his position, since Koestler himself was highly sympathetic to the transpersonal perspective, I should mention that he saw "the urge toward self-transcendence" as having both a positive and a negative aspect. The negative is the one indicated here. The positive is that with which the transpersonalists are concerned in their concept of an expanded sense of identity that reaches beyond the conventional boundaries of the self.

More and more psychologists sympathetic to the transpersonal orientation are raising the banner of "selfless service" as their professed moral ideal and as the natural extension of their psychological and philosophical perspective.[88]

To quote from John Levy's article "Transpersonal and Jungian Psychology":

> Transpersonal psychologists tend to see service in the world as absolutely essential and central to the kinds of living and being they pursue and advocate. . . . As transpersonal awakening begins, motivations inevitably shift from the egocentric toward the desire to serve others. This kind of service is seen as absolutely necessary if the awakening and development are to continue; transpersonal growth requires a life of service.

Why?

The answer is not given in terms with which we are familiar from our discussion concerning altruism. Certainly neither society nor humanity nor the state are in any sense perceived as objects of worship. True, many of this orientation who advocate selfless service see the world as a place of great suffering and see compassion as a virture of supreme importance, but that per se does not make a life of service a requirement. We need not debate the virtue of compassion, since that is not the point. So far as I am able to understand this position, there seem to be two reasons offered in defense of selfless service as a moral ideal.

The first is quite simply the assertion that at a certain level of evolution—some might say mystical insight—it becomes *self-evident* that one should practice selfless service. The second, and in a way the more interesting argument (the first is not really an argument), is the statement that the value of selfless service lies not so much in the help given to the beneficiaries as in *liberation from ego* on the part of the one who serves. In other words, a life of service facilitates self-transcendence. In secular terms, of course, this is dangerously close to an egoistic justification—although not one that will bear careful scrutiny.

Anyone who chooses to express him- or herself through some kind of productive endeavor cannot help but make a contribution to the world. That is very different, however, from the viewpoint that we are here on earth to serve. And transpersonal psychologists are not insensitive to this difference. One of them protested to me, "But in placing your emphasis on creative self-expression and the joy of productive work, you are back with ego again. In putting the emphasis on contribution and on service, we get people away from themselves." Precisely.

Of course, what a life of selfless service means is far from obvious. Does it mean that we simply ask other people what they want us to do and proceed to do it? Does it mean that we decide what is best for other human beings and impose our vision on them?

And then there is another problem: If people accept our self-less service, are they not being selfish?

Alas, in whichever direction we look, from old-fashioned religion to avant-garde psychology, self and ego appear to have few champions. The lone individual remains the most undefended and uncared for minority on earth. For many people it seems far easier to feel care and compassion for "the planet" than for a single human being.

Individuation is an ongoing process whose end, I believe, is not yet in sight. The attainment of self-esteem and autonomy is not the end of the human journey. The potential of our cognitive powers remains to be discovered. When we contemplate "the possible human," to use Jean Houston's apt phrase, we see nothing but frontiers stretching before us. But until we learn to honor the self, the journey cannot successfully begin.

Customarily it is at the beginning of a book that an author explains for whom the book is written. I am choosing to do so at the end, because only now can I hope that my full meaning will be understood.

I could say that this book is addressed to my colleagues, that I might share with them observations that would prove useful in their own work. I could say that the book is addressed to anyone, in any profession, who is interested in the great issues of psychology and ethics. Both these statements are true but limited.

It is to anyone who loves his or her life and has not known that there is no higher virtue that this book is addressed.

To anyone struggling for personal happiness while being told that personal happiness is the concern of the spiritually inferior; to anyone who understands that ego and self are a height to be climbed, not an abyss to be escaped; to anyone who does not see freedom as a burden or choice and responsibility as a tragedy; to anyone who appreciates the courage and integrity that honest selfishness requires; to anyone who grasps that without self-assertion, no dignity is possible; to anyone fighting for self-esteem against an onslaught that begins in the nursery and extends to the Himalayas; to anyone able to see that this earth is the distant star we must find a way to reach—it is for you that this book is written.

In your defense.

In your honor.

Bibliography

1   Anthony, S. *The Discovery of Death in Childhood and After.* New York: Basic Books, 1972.

2   Bandura, A. "The Psychology of Chance Encounters and Life Paths." *The American Psychologist* 37 (1982): 747–755.

3   Bastiat, F. *Selected Essays on Political Economy.* Irvington-on-Hudson, New York: Foundation for Economic Education, 1964.

4   Becker, E. *The Denial of Death.* New York: Free Press, 1973.

5   Beisser, A. *The Paradoxical Theory of Change.* I. J. Fagan and I. Shepherd (eds.), *Gestalt Therapy Now.* New York: Harper and Row, 1970.

6   Branden, N. *The Psychology of Self-Esteem.* New York: Bantam Books, 1971.

7   _____ . *Breaking Free.* New York: Bantam Books, 1972.

8   _____ . *The Disowned Self.* New York: Bantam Books, 1973.

9   _____ . *The Psychology of Romantic Love.* Los Angeles: J. P. Tarcher, 1980.

10 _____ . *If You Could Hear What I Cannot Say.* New York: Bantam Books, 1983.

11 _____ . "The Benefits and Hazards of the Philosophy of Ayn Rand: A Personal Statement." *Journal of Humanistic Psychology* 24 (1984).

12 Branden, N., and Branden, E. D. *The Romantic Love Question & Answer Book.* Los Angeles: J. P. Tarcher, 1982.

13 Carrington, P. *Freedom in Meditation.* Garden City, N.Y.: Anchor Press/Doubleday, 1977.

14 Coopersmith, S. *The Antecedents of Self-Esteem.* San Francisco: W. H. Freeman and Co., 1967.

BIBLIOGRAPHY

15 Deikman, A. J. *The Observing Self*. Boston: Beacon Press, 1982.

16 Elkins, D. P. *Self Concept Sourcebook*. Rochester, New York: Growth Associates, 1979.

17 Erikson, E. H. *Childhood and Society*. 2nd ed. New York: W. W. Norton, 1963.

18 _____ . *Insight and Responsibility*. New York: W. W. Norton, 1964.

19 _____ . *Identity, Youth and Crisis*. New York: W. W. Norton, 1968.

20 Faber, A., and Mazelish, E. *Liberated Parents, Liberated Children*. New York: Grosset and Dunlap, 1974.

21 Ferguson, M. *The Aquarian Conspiracy*. Los Angeles: J. P. Tarcher, 1980.

22 Freud, S. *The Ego and the Id*. Vol. XIX in *Standard Edition*. London: Hogarth Press, 1961 (originally published 1923).

23 _____ . *The Problem of Anxiety*. Translated by Henry Alden Bunker, Albany: Psychoanalytic Quarterly Press, 1936.

24 _____ . *General Introduction to Psychoanalysis*, Translated by Joan Riviera. New York: Garden City Publishing Co., 1938.

25 Friedman, M., and Friedman, R., *Free to Choose*. New York: Avon Books, 1980.

26 Fromm, E. *Escape from Freedom*. New York: Farrar, 1941.

27 Gardner, M. *Science: Good, Bad, and Bogus*. Buffalo: Prometheus Books, 1981.

28 Ginott, H. *Between Parent and Child*. New York: Macmillan, 1965.

29 _____ . *Between Parent and Teenager*. New York: Macmillan, 1969.

30 _____ . *Teacher and Child*. New York: Macmillan, 1972.

31 Hamachek, D. E. *Encounters with Others: Interpersonal Relationships and You*. New York: Holt, Rinehart, and Winston, 1982.

32 Hartmann, H. *Ego Psychology and the Problem of Adaptation*.

Translated by D. Rapaport. New York: International Universities Press, 1958.

33 Hazlitt, H. *Economics in One Lesson.* New York: Arlington House, 1979.

34 Hitler, A. *Mein Kampf.* New York: Reynal and Hitchcock, 1940.

35 Hoffer, E. *The True Believer.* New York: Harper and Brothers, 1951.

36 Horney, K. *Neurosis and Human Growth.* New York: W. W. Norton and Co., 1950.

37 Houston, J. *The Possible Human.* Los Angeles: J. P. Tarcher, 1982.

38 Huxley, A. *The Perennial Philosophy.* New York: Harper Colophon Books, 1970.

39 Johnson, P. *Modern Times.* New York: Harper and Row, 1983.

40 Koestler, A. *Janus.* New York: Random House, 1978.

41 Kohlberg, L. "Moral Development and Identification." *National Society for the Study of Education Yearbook*, 1962, pp. 277–332.

42 Lane, R. W. *The Discovery of Freedom.* New York: Arno Press/ New York Times, 1972.

43 LeBoyer, Frederick. *Birth Without Violence.* New York: Alfred A. Knopf, 1974.

44 Levy, J. "Transpersonal and Jungian Psychology." *Journal of Humanistic Psychology*, vol. 23, no. 2, spring 1983, p. 49.

45 Lidz, T. *The Person.* rev. ed. New York: Basic Books, 1976.

46 Loevinger, J. *Ego Development: Conceptions and Theories.* San Francisco: Jossey-Bass, 1977.

47 Lowen, A. *Bioenergetics.* New York: Coward, McCann and Geoghegan, 1975.

48 Machan, T. (ed.). *The Libertarian Reader.* Totowa, N.J.: Roman and Littlefield, 1982.

49 Mahler, M. S. *On Human Symbiosis and the Vicissitudes of*

Individuation. Vol. 1, *Infantile Psychosis*. New York: International University Press, 1968.

50   Mahler, M. S., Pine, and Bergman. *The Psychological Birth of the Human Infant*. New York: Basic Books, 1975.

51   Maslow, A. H. *Toward a Psychology of Being*. 2nd ed. New York: Van Nostrand Reinhold, 1968.

52   Masters, R., and Houston, J. *Listening to the Body*. New York: Delacorte Press, 1978.

53   Milgrim, S. *Obedience to Authority*. New York: Harper and Row, 1974.

54   Mussolini, B. "The Doctrine of Fascism." Reprinted in W. Ebenstein, Great Political Thinkers. New York: Rinehart, 1951.

55   Nozick, R. *Anarchy, State, and Utopia*. New York: Basic Books, 1974.

56   Patterson, I. *The God of the Machine*. Arno Press reprint, 1972, 1943. Salem, N.H.: Arno Press, 1972.

57   Pearce, J. C. *Magical Child*. New York: E. P. Dutton, 1977.

58   Penfield, W. *The Mystery of the Mind: A Critical Study of Consciousness and the Human Brain*. Princeton: Princeton University Press, 1975.

59   Perls, F., Hefferline, R., and Goodman, P. *Gestalt Therapy*. New York: Dell Publishing Co., 1951.

60   Piaget, J. *The Moral Judgment of the Child*. New York: Free Press, 1932.

61   _____ . *The Essential Piaget*. New York: Basic Books, 1977.

62   Rand, A. *The Fountainhead*. New York: Bobbs-Merrill Co., 1943.

63   _____ . *Atlas Shrugged*. New York: Random House, 1957.

64   _____ . *The Virtue of Selfishness*. New York: NAL/Signet, 1964.

65   _____ . *Capitalism, the Unknown Ideal*. New York: NAL/Signet, 1967.

66   Randi, J. *Flim-Flam!* Buffalo: Prometheus Books, 1982.

67   Rank, O. *Will Therapy and Truth and Reality*. Translated by J. Taft. New York: Alfred A. Knopf, 1945.

68　Reich, W. "The Discovery of the Orgone." In *The Function of the Orgasm*, vol. I. New York: Orgone Institute Press, 1948.

69　_____. *Character Analysis*. New York: Orgone Institute Press, 1949.

70　_____. *Selected Writings*. New York: Farrar, 1969.

71　Robsjohn-Gibbings, T. H. *Mona Lisa's Moustache*. New York: Knopf Publishing, 1947.

72　Rogers, C. R. *On Becoming a Person*. Boston: Houghton Mifflin Co., 1961.

73　Rustow, A. *Freedom and Domination*. Princeton: Princeton University Press, 1980.

74　St. Augustine. *Confessions*. Translated by T. E. Pilkington. New York: Liveright, 1943.

75　Sanford, J. A. *The Invisible Partners*. New York: Paulist Press, 1980.

76　Satir, V. *Conjoint Family Therapy*. Rev. ed. Palo Alto, Calif.: Science and Behavior Books, 1967.

77　_____. *Peoplemaking*. Palo Alto, Calif.: Science and Behavior Books, 1972.

78　Spencer, H. *Man Versus the State*. Baltimore: Penguin Books, 1969.

79　Stace, W. T. *Mysticism and Philosophy*. London: Macmillan Press Ltd., 1980.

80　Stevens, J. O. *Awareness: Exploring, Experimenting, Experiencing*. New York: Bantam Books, 1973.

81　Tolstoy, L. *The Death of Ivan Ilych and Other Stories*. New York: Signet Classics, 1960.

82　Valliant, G. E. *Adaptation to Life*. Boston: Little, Brown and Co., 1977.

83　Von Hayek, F. *Capitalism and the Historians*. Chicago: University of Chicago Press, 1963.

84　_____. *The Road to Serfdom*. Chicago: University of Chicago Press, 1972.

85 Von Mises, L. *Human Action*. Chicago: Contemporary Books, 1966.

86 _____ . *Socialism*. Indianapolis, Indiana: Liberty Classics, 1981.

87 _____ . *Nation, State, and Economy*. New York: New York University Press, 1983.

88 Walsh, R., and Shapiro, D. (eds.). *Beyond Health and Normality: Explorations of Extreme Psychological Well-being*. New York: Van Nostrand Reinhold, 1984.

89 Walsh, R., and Vaughan, F. (eds.). *Beyond Ego*. Los Angeles: J. P. Tarcher, 1980.

90 Waterman, A. S. "Individualism and Interdependence." *The American Psychologist*, vol. 36, no. 7, July 1981, pp. 762–773.

91 Wilber, K. *The Spectrum of Consciousness*. Wheaton, Ill.: Theosophical Publishing House, 1977.

92 _____ . *No Boundary*. Los Angeles: Center Publications, 1979.

93 _____ . *The Atman Project*. Wheaton, Ill.: Theosophical Publishing House, 1980.

94 _____ . *Up from Eden: A Transpersonal View of Human Evolution*. Garden City, N.Y.: Anchor Press/Doubleday, 1981.

95 Yalom, I. D. *Existential Psychotherapy*. New York: Basic Books, 1980.

Index

About the Author

Also author of *The Psychology of Self-Esteem*, *The Disowned Self*, *The Psychology of Romantic Love*, *The Romantic Love Question & Answer Book* (with E. Devers Branden), and *If You Could Hear What I Cannot Say*, Nathaniel Branden is a pioneer in his studies of self-esteem, personal transformation, and man/woman relationships. Dr. Branden is in private practice in Los Angeles and lives in Lake Arrowhead, California.

As director of The Biocentric Institute in Los Angeles, he offers Intensive Workshops throughout the United States in self-esteem and man/woman relationships. He also conducts professional training workshops for mental health professionals in his approach to personal growth and development.

Communications to Dr. Branden or requests for information about his various lectures, seminars, and Intensive Workshops should be addressed to The Biocentric Institute, P.O. Box 4009, Beverly Hills, CA 90213.